"This is an important book that should be read by theologians, historians and philosophers of religion concerned with the practice and conceptualization of Christian theology. It retrieves a primary sense of theology as embodied practice which is closer to the idea of spiritual exercises than to a merely academic, disembodied theorizing. Through understanding theology as Christian ascesis, the book challenges some abstract understandings of theology and shows how theology is integral to Christian life. Through privileging ascetic practice and therefore the body, the book recontextualises an ancient understanding of theology in contemporary terms. This book articulates a fresh theological vision that points in a new direction, true to Christian roots yet open to contemporary intellectual developments. Anyone concerned with these issues should read this book."

Gavin Flood, Professor of Hindu Studies
and Comparative Religion, University of Oxford

"At a time when Christian theology is increasingly becoming a part of the public domain, when the broken fragments of this once-whole art appear to be popping up in the strangest of places, Nathan G. Jennings does theology an invaluable service by recalling it to the ancient source of its unity, intelligibility, and power to free souls: practices of self-denial. Whilst the latter have not enjoyed great publicity in recent centuries, except among the denizens of a vague 'spirituality,' Jennings re-inhabits the treasuries of Christian wisdom to enrich and enflesh the great gift that such ascesis is, in orienting us to the true source of ourselves in Christ. Drawing upon the native resources of the Christian dogmatic tradition (as well as a vast array of non-Christian literature) this rich and provocative book shows that good theology cannot be done rightly, if at all, apart from the right kind of life, and that the right kind of life cannot be lived without good theology."

Peter M. Candler, Jr., Associate Professor
of Theology, Baylor University

Theology as Ascetic Act

AMERICAN UNIVERSITY STUDIES

SERIES VII
THEOLOGY AND RELIGION

VOL. 307

PETER LANG
New York • Washington, D.C./Baltimore • Bern
Frankfurt • Berlin • Brussels • Vienna • Oxford

Nathan G. Jennings

Theology as Ascetic Act

Disciplining Christian Discourse

PETER LANG
New York • Washington, D.C./Baltimore • Bern
Frankfurt • Berlin • Brussels • Vienna • Oxford

Library of Congress Cataloging-in-Publication Data

Jennings, Nathan G.
Theology as ascetic act: disciplining Christian discourse / Nathan G. Jennings.
p. cm. — (American University studies VII. Theology and religion; v. 307)
Includes bibliographical references and index.
1. Asceticism. 2. Theology. I. Title.
II. Title: Disciplining Christian discourse.
BV5031.3.J46   248.4'7—dc22   2010032710
ISBN 978-1-4331-0990-4
ISSN 0740-0446

Bibliographic information published by **Die Deutsche Nationalbibliothek**.
Die Deutsche Nationalbibliothek lists this publication in the "Deutsche
Nationalbibliografie"; detailed bibliographic data is available
on the Internet at http://dnb.d-nb.de/.

Cover illustration: Photograph of a mural, painted on the interior
of the John the Baptist Church at the Jordan River, by David Bjorgen
Licensing notice: http://creativecommons.org/licenses/by-sa/3.0/

Unless otherwise noted, all scripture quotations are from
The *Revised Standard Version* of the Bible (RSV),
Copyright (c) 1946, 1952 & 1971, National Council of the Churches
of Christ in the United States of America. Used by permission.
All rights reserved. When the RSV is not followed and there is no other note,
the quotation reflects the translation of the author.

The paper in this book meets the guidelines for permanence and durability
of the Committee on Production Guidelines for Book Longevity
of the Council of Library Resources.

© 2010 Peter Lang Publishing, Inc., New York
29 Broadway, 18th floor, New York, NY 10006
www.peterlang.com

Printed in Germany

To Kelly

Abba Lot went to see Abba Joseph and said to him, 'Abba, as far as I can I say my little office, I fast a little, I pray and meditate, I live in peace and as far as I can, I purify my thoughts. What else can I do?' Then the old man stood up and stretched his hands towards heaven. His fingers became like ten lamps of fire and he said to him, 'If you will, you can become all flame.'

Joseph of Panephysis, The Sayings of the Desert Fathers

Table of Contents

Part II. Theology as Ascesis: From Divine Discourse to the Discipline of Christian Discourse

Preface

"Thanks be to God for his inexpressible gift!"

2 Cor. 9.15

THIS BOOK represents a light revision of my dissertation, *Concerning the Relationship of the Task of Christian Theology to Christian Asceticism,* defended in November of 2005 at the University of Virginia. My intention was to work on a theology of Christian sacred text and its interpretation in order to find a ground for Christian theology in general. I found that, as I pursued that line of research, I was continually confronted with the issue of what provided the ground and possibility of meaningful interpretation of sacred text for the Christian theologian in the first place. In the process of working out that issue, I discovered the ancient Christian commitment to ascetical practice assumed by all of the early theologians and critically retrieved in recent scholarship.

I still intend to write a Christian theology of the nature of sacred text. In publishing this book, however, I hope to share my discovery of *ascesis* as foundational to Christian theology. And by foundational I mean not only that ascetic practice, understood theoretically, provides an interesting and helpful theoretical account of theology but rather, more importantly, that ascetic practice itself provides the necessary and inherent structuring practice that grounds theology in the reality its seeks to participate and express, above and beyond mere human ideas. There is a saying: "you cannot think yourself into right action, but you can act yourself into right thinking." In this book I set out to demonstrate that this saying expresses a fundamental truth about the nature of Christian theology.

Thanks again to all those who helped me with the research that led to the dissertation that preceded this book. Thanks to The Rev. Dr. Augustine Thompson, O.P., for directing my dissertation. Thanks to

Alasdair John Milbank for his informal directing of my dissertation alongside its formal advisor. Thanks to Eugene Rogers who advised my dissertation before leaving the University of Virginia, Charlottesville, for the University of North Carolina, Greensboro. Thanks to Gavin Flood who served on the committee during his Sabbatical year at the University of Virginia, Charlottesville, and continued to give constructive criticism and encouragement long after his return from sabbatical. Thanks to graduate student colleagues, especially Tony Baker, Creston Davis and Keith Starkenburg.

Thanks to the Episcopal Theological Seminary of the Southwest for providing the means for research assistants and proof readers. Thanks to Nancy Mourette Bose and Lisa Stolley Hines for their proof reading of the dissertation that preceded this work. Thanks to Kevin A. Dellaria for his work as research assistant to the dissertation. Thanks to Beryl Kenney, Katherine Renee Rodriguez, and Tarah Van de Wiele for their work proof reading this book. Thanks to Laura Waters Jackson for her work in formatting and indexing this book.

Ascesis As Theology

WHAT IS THE RELATIONSHIP between scholarship concerning Christian thought, the unfolding of Christian teaching within Christianity itself, and that practice that Christians call "theology"? Recent scholarship makes it clear that the practice of ascesis[1] is an embodied means of performing a theology. This book explores the indigenous[2] ascetical logic of the various practices that Christians call "theology" to argue that theology participates in and provides an example of Christian "spiritual"[3] exercises, or disciplines, that have traditionally been called "ascesis." First, this introduction gives a brief overview of the issue at hand, namely, how one might understand Christian theology indigenous to Christian practice. It then provides some preliminary definitions for important terms used throughout such as "ascesis," "body," "discourse," and "theology." Finally, the introduction explains the general approach of the project of this book and concludes with the structure of the argument and a sketch of the various chapters that follow.

The Issue at Hand

THIS BOOK CONSTRUES THEOLOGY as an example and part of the concrete Christian practice of asceticism that lies side by side with other approaches that construe theology as an example and part of Christian practice. In his work *Doxology*, for example, Geoffrey

---

[1] Although "ascesis" is a foreign word transliterated into English (see discussion below, under the section "Ascesis"), one will not find it italicized in this book because of its frequent use throughout.

[2] So, in social scientific terminology, the overall approach of this project is *emic* rather than *etic*.

[3] The section "Approach" below, qualifies the use of the term "spirituality," in this document.

Wainwright argues that theology is doxological, and therefore a form of worship.[4] Ellen Charry, in *By The Renewing of Their Minds*, asserts that theology has a pastoral end.[5] Stanley Hauerwas has famously (or perhaps notoriously, depending upon one's persuasion) argued that Christian "ethics" ought to be collapsed into Christian theology; that there is no Christian "ethics" in the modern sense, only theology with a branch within it called "moral."[6] One could even construe Barth's entire *Church Dogmatics* as a dogmatic theology that provides both an aid to and example of proclamation (thus, homiletics).[7]

With asceticism as its starting point, this project approaches theology from the point of view of Christian discipleship as a whole. Ascesis is a word for Christian discipleship as a body-affirming and body-involving discipline. Any of the Christian practical disciplines mentioned above, i.e., liturgics (Wainwright), pastoral care (Charry), moral theology (Hauerwas), and homiletics (Barth), together with ascetical theology, comprehend and are comprehended by one another. Their mutual comprehension represents, at the practical level, the mutual intelligibility of the various *loci communi* of Christian dogmatic thought. Each angle of approach provides a new facet of Christianity—either in terms of practice or thought.

The point of Christian asceticism and ascetical theology is that both Christian practice and Christian intellectual thought (here construed as a practice) exist only to serve one ultimate goal which they may not of themselves *put into practice*, but only *receive as a gift*—the contemplation of God. Christian discipleship, and therefore the Christian religion in general, chiefly concerns itself with the contemplation

---

[4] Geoffrey Wainwright, *Doxology* (New York: Oxford Univ. Press, 1980).

[5] Ellen Charry, *By The Renewing of Your Minds* (New York: Oxford Univ. Press, 1997).

[6] See particularly the introduction to Stanley Hauerwas, *A Community of Character: Toward a Constructive Christian Social Ethic* (Notre Dame, IN: Univ. of Notre Dame, 1981), 1-6.

[7] Note Karl Barth's concluding volume to his *Church Dogmatics*, vol. 5, "Index With Aids for the Preacher" (New York: T & T Clark, 2004). His turn to "Church Dogmatics," as opposed to "Christian Dogmatics," came after writing on Anselm's understanding of the task of theology within the church's practice of reflecting on scripture in prayer.

of and participation in God.[8] Concomitantly, all Christian practices—including the intellectual one known as theology—find their definition in this one goal that Christians must simply receive as a gift.

Ascesis

WHAT, THEN, is ascesis? Preliminarily, it is an exercise or set of bodily exercises that one undergoes in order to reach a religious or transcendent goal.[9] Words such as "ascetic," "ascetical," "asceticism," and its own Anglicization, "ascesis," derive from the Greek word *ascesis*. Ascesis is theology. That is to say, ascesis places theology into existential practice as an expression of fundamental world-views. Ascesis is an attempt to embody the core beliefs of the practitioner, and those of his or her community, concerning God,[10] and is, simultaneously, a means of adding that disciplined body to human discourse about theology—a kind of "body language." Furthermore, those who engage in ascesis do so, at least in part, because they hold that such practices entail contact with the reality that their theology purports to describe.

Ascesis in recent thought

THIS BOOK CONTRIBUTES to the field of Christian dogmatic theology[11] by engaging literature that critically retrieves asceticism. One clear claim that this literature makes possible is that ascetical practice is the attempt to perform theology in and through "bodies," both individual and corporate. So, the central point of this introduction constitutes an

---

[8] For a discussion concerning how suspicion of contemplation in contemporary theology contributes to a misunderstanding of the development of the doctrine of the Trinity and its current theological viability, see Lewis Ayres, *Nicaea and its Legacy* (New York: Oxford Univ. Press, 2004), 388 ff.

[9] J. Giles Milhaven, "Asceticism and the Moral Good: A Tale of Two Pleasures," in *Asceticism*, eds. Vincent L. Wimbush and Richard Valantasis (New York: Oxford Univ. Press, 1995), 376, describes what is common among the many various things named "asceticism" as "a consistent rigorous renunciation of certain pleasure," so that other, transcendent kinds of pleasure may be embraced and promoted.

[10] This could be described, more broadly, as the ultimate nature of reality. That would include, for example, Buddhist asceticism as "theology."

[11] One may find a working definition of "Christian dogmatic theology" below in the section "Christian theology."

overarching interpretative claim concerning this body of literature that has developed within the past twenty years or so. It in no way, however, attempts to make a reductive claim concerning so rich, varied, and even conflicting a body of literature.

Pre-modern literature concerning asceticism was not so much about asceticism in some scholarly sense as it was an example of ascetic literature, that is to say, literature promoting or advocating ascetic practices.[12] These works are found in pre-modern histories, expositions, theologies, and pre-scientific psychological treatises.[13] Over the course of the development of modernity, asceticism suffered a cold reception. Modern literature on asceticism, in its general disdain for tradition and traditional cosmological religion,[14] characterizes asceticism negatively. The first English use of the word "ascetic" in 1646, according to the *Oxford English Dictionary*, was found in a pejorative context.[15] The negative appraisal of ascetic practice in modern thought can be traced from Bentham, through Freud and Nietzsche (although the latter represents an interesting twist in such negative appraisals).

The recent body of literature that has developed in several different fields of scholarship since the 1980's and, it may be argued, as a response to the turn towards ascesis in the thought of Foucault[16] in

---

[12] Vincent L. Wimbush and Richard Valantasis, eds., *Asceticism* (New York: Oxford Univ. Press, 1995), xxi.

[13] *Ibid.*

[14] Gavin Flood, *The Ascetic Self* (New York: Cambridge University Press, 2004), makes the link between ascetical traditions and cosmology. Examples of modern disdain for asceticism still surface when scholars assume—counter to most contemporary scholarship—that ascetics hate the body or identify it with evil. See, for example, Ephraim Isaac, "The Significance of Food in Hebraic-African Thought and the Role of Fasting in the Ethiopian Church," in *Asceticism*, eds. Vincent L. Wimbush and Richard Valantasis (New York: Oxford Univ. Press, 1995).

[15] Oxford English Dictionary, 1970 ed., s.v. "ascetic."

[16] Richard Valantasis, "A Theory of the Social Function of Asceticism," in *Asceticism*, eds. Vincent L. Wimbush and Richard Valantasis (New York: Oxford Univ. Press, 1995), 544—545, identifies three main theorists of the twentieth century that have contributed the most to asceticism scholarship: Max Weber, Michel Foucault, and Geoffrey Harpham. Furthermore, Max Weber's link between the elements of religion and economic implementation is still at the heart of social

the 1970's, represents a kind of "postmodern" rejection of the modern proclivity to dismiss asceticism as at best outmoded and, at worst, simply a neurotic or deranged compulsion in the superstitious and "extremely" religious. Again, what characterizes this recent literature is its discovery or rediscovery of the social and political ramifications of embodying theology through ascetic practice.

The work of Peter Brown in general, and his magnum opus *The Body and Society*,[17] represents this moment of turning in recent scholarship. Brown's contribution, in his own self-qualification, is simply to the field of the history of Christian antiquity.[18] The ramifications of his work have had a much more far ranging influence in religious studies in general. In *The Body and Society*, Brown traces the history of the development and changing perception of ascetic practice, particularly in the form of voluntary celibacy, in Christian antiquity up to the beginning of the cultural and religious divergences between the Latin west and Greek east. Brown has awakened academia to the way ancient Christians understand their own practices of asceticism. The body is a "problem" for ancient Christians exactly because it is to be loved and saved, not because it is "evil."[19]

But Brown's key and most important point is that "Christian attitudes to sex delivered the death-blow to the ancient notion of the city as the arbiter of the body."[20] The body is no longer a simple part of the natural world, subject to human systems of civic duty. The body under Christian practice becomes the gift of God to be returned to God in love. Thus, Brown has begun the process that this recent literature on asceticism has taken upon itself to make clear: that ascetic practice is the performed embodiment of theology as the practice of a (new) political stance within the world that itself makes claims about ultimate reality.

A year earlier than Brown's *Body and Society*, Geoffrey Harpham, in his seminal work, *The Ascetical Imperative in Culture and Criticism*,

---

scientific ascetical theory. There is more on Foucault below, in the section on "Body and Christian Body."

[17] Peter Brown, *The Body and Society* (New York: Columbia Univ. Press, 1988).
[18] *Ibid.*, xiv—xv.
[19] *Ibid.*, 425.
[20] *Ibid.*, 437.

takes up the tradition of Nietzsche and Foucault and interprets it in the direction of literary theory and criticism.[21] Harpham's key goal in this work is to develop "ascesis" as a trope for cultural criticism—and that as a part of culture in general.[22] Playing on Kant's "categorical imperative,"[23] Harpham asserts an "ascetical imperative" in human nature, arguing that asceticism paradoxically both criticizes and constructs human culture. In fact, ascesis is that universal human practice that serves as the elementary background upon which human beings construct culture in its pluriform manifestations.[24]

Harpham also observes that one of the chief ends of the ancient Christian ascetic was that of rendering the body an intelligible sign of the gospel the ascetic sought to practice.[25] Harpham claims that ascesis is closely related to textuality,[26] and that ascetics seek to render their own bodies as signs pointing to the narrative of Christian faith. The transformation of the body through asceticism is simultaneously the rendering of the body as a narrative of Christian faith—an imitable narrative. And this brings the fallen, unintelligible body—and the meaningless life it entails—into an intelligible realm of signs that the body itself enacts in and through its ascetic regimen—ultimately bringing meaning to an otherwise meaningless life. The body is thereby made an intelligible sign expressing a narrative theology of human meaning—an embodied performance of Christian theology with literary, social and political ramifications.

---

[21] Geoffrey Galt Harpham, *The Ascetical Imperative in Culture and Criticism* (Chicago: Univ. of Chicago Press, 1987).

[22] Averil Cameron, "Ascetic Closure and the End of Antiquity," in *Asceticism*, eds. Vincent L. Wimbush and Richard Valantasis (New York: Oxford Univ. Press, 1995), 153, describes Harpham's work as extending the "ascetic" into literary and iconographic realms by arguing that the practice of hermeneutics and criticism is essentially a modern form of ascetic behavior.

[23] Harpham, 241. Harpham explicitly describes ascesis as "the most comprehensive name of the ways in which we understand and refashion ourselves," in "Asceticism and the Compensations of Art," in *Asceticism*, eds. Vincent L. Wimbush and Richard Valantasis (New York: Oxford Univ. Press, 1995), 368.

[24] Harpham develops a now well-known analogy between ascesis as a kind of "MSDOS," or computer operating system upon which culture, as a kind of computer software application, is "written."

[25] Harpham, 277ff.

[26] *Ibid.*, 14.

Other key contributions to this literature would be *Asceticism*, the compilation of essays edited by Vincent Wimbush and Richard Valantasis, and a collection of essays edited by Wimbush and Leif Vaage entitled *Asceticism and the New Testament.*[27] These volumes represent, in both cases, a wide diversity of scholarly perspectives, and, with regards to the first one in particular, many different religions. Their combined contribution supports the assertion that much of the recent literature on asceticism recognizes ascetic practice as a performance and embodiment of particular theologies in such ways as to give social and political relevance to ascetic practitioners—if not always as individuals, then at least as ascetic communities and traditions contributing to cultural discourse about God and reality.

Further afield from the project of this book, Ilana Silbur[28] deals with asceticism from a sociological perspective. Ariel Glucklich looks at asceticism from a physiological perspective.[29] Finally, William C. Bushell, both in his dissertation[30] and in an article in Wimbush's *Asceticism,*[31] offers an interesting medical and biological analysis of the effects of ascetic practice with regards to altered states of consciousness, more efficient use of food, increased energy and immune system function, and even the retardation and reversal of aging.[32]

---

[27]   Leif E. Vaage and Vincent L. Wimbush, eds., *Asceticism and the New Testament* (New York: Routledge, 1999).

[28]   Ilana Frederich Silber, *Virtuosity, Charisma and Social Order: A Comparative Sociological Study of Monasticism in Theravada Buddhism and Medieval Catholicism* (Cambridge Cultural Social Studies), (New York: Cambridge Univ.Press, 1995).

[29]   Ariel Glucklich, *Sacred Pain: Hurting the Body for the Sake of the Soul* (New York: Oxford Univ. Press, 2003).

[30]   William C. Bushell, "Psychophysiological and Cross Cultural Dimensions of Ascetico-Meditational Practices: Special Reference to the Christian Hermits of Ethiopia and Application to Theory in Anthropology and Religious Studies (vols. I and II)," (Ph.D. diss., Columbia Univ., 1994).

[31]   William C. Bushell, "Psychophysiological and Comparative Analysis of Ascetic-Meditational Discipline: Towards a New Theory of Asceticism," in *Asceticism,* eds. Vincent L. Wimbush and Richard Valantasis (New York: Oxford Univ. Press, 1995), 553—567.

[32]   Bushell asserts, contrary to both popular belief and some physicians, that research demonstrates that radical reduction of caloric intake results in a broad range of "psychophysical enhancements." Bushell's conclusion is that the "Desert Fathers" discovered phenomenologically what may now be empirically af-

Virginia Burrus, Caroline Walker Bynum, Mary Carruthers, Elizabeth Clark, Susan Harvey, Amy Hollywood, Lutz Kaelber, and Leif Vaage also contribute to scholarship concerning the history and development of Christian asceticism. Along with their own respective monographs, many of these scholars contribute throughout the entire run of the *Journal of Early Christian Studies*,[33] which began in 1993. In each case, whatever the perspective, asceticism has now gained a new level of respectability as an embodied performance of political empowerment and self-transformation for the sake of, and as a statement of, the theological perspective of ascetic practitioners and their respective traditions.

More recently, Gavin Flood offers his own work, *The Ascetic Self*,[34] as a contribution to this body of literature within the field of comparative religion. In his introduction, Flood offers an interesting suggestion. Theology, he asserts, should ask itself the question: can discipline itself be described as a (divine) gift?[35] In describing the coherence of ascetic practice within the context of Christian teaching, and especially the Christian teaching of the gift of the divine economy of salvation, this book, at least in part, responds to that question.[36]

Flood's work makes great strides towards synthesizing much of the work on asceticism before him, and, importantly in terms of this project, in postcritical directions. So Flood asserts, with Harpham, that asceticism is the internalization of a given tradition by shaping the narrative of the life of the ascetic in accordance with the central narrative of his or her ascetic tradition. For Flood, this means that the most profound ascetic traditions are those that engage a certain "canonical" scripture—be it Hindu, Buddhist or Christian. In doing so, he integrates some of the work of Caruthers by claiming that this performance of narrative in the body of the ascetic is actually a kind of

---

firmed: the body is indeed an autarkic system needing only enough energy to keep its "heat" alive (*Ibid.*, 554—556).

[33] *Journal of Early Christian Studies*, multiple volumes (Baltimore: John Hopkins Univ. Press, 1993—2006).

[34] Gavin Flood, *The Ascetic Self: Subjectivity, Memory, and Tradition* (New York: Cambridge Univ. Press, 2004).

[35] *Ibid.*, xi.

[36] This issue in general, and Flood's work in particular, are taken up in chapter four, below.

performance of "remembering" the narrative of the ascetic's tradition.[37]

Flood's postcritical claim is that any serious intellectual and even academic engagement with indigenous practices of asceticism ought to entail, on the scholar's part, taking seriously the claims of these practitioners that either new or different realms of reality, or the truth about a previously misconstrued reality, is made available to the practitioner as a result of ascetic practice. All ascetic traditions assert that their practices open out access to reality in ways that are unavailable to the non-practitioner.[38] Thus, the embodiment of theology that asceticism entails also means contact with the realities or Reality, which that theology claims to describe.

Many definitions of asceticism throughout this body of literature focus on their physical practices. They often do so in order to make connections between the ascetic practices of traditional religions and the physical exercises of modern culture. In order to make this connection, they sometimes reduce asceticism to the point that anything that even remotely looks like a physically strenuous activity is interpreted as ascetic. Along with Flood, this project disagrees with this use of the term "ascetic," while nevertheless agreeing that making cultural parallels is a useful activity.[39] Again, with Flood, this project takes the position that what makes asceticism ascetic, and what distinguishes it from other forms of dieting, physical exercise and athleticism is the difference between their understood goals or ends. The various ascetic traditions understand and justify themselves insofar as their practices entail the attainment of a transcendent goal. Ascetic traditions claim to open out the body and soul of the practitioner to an ultimate reality that transcends everyday human reality, so those traditions eschew justifying their physical practices in terms of the

---

[37]   See Mary Carruthers, *The Book of Memory: A Study of Memory in Medieval Culture*, vol. 10, Cambridge Studies in Medieval Literature, (Cambridge, U.K.: Cambridge Univ. Press, 1992). See also Mary Carruthers, *The Craft of Thought: Meditation, Rhetoric, and the Making of Images, 400-1200*, vol. 34, Cambridge Studies in Medieval Literature, (Cambridge, U.K.: Cambridge Univ. Press, 1998).

[38]   Flood, 249.

[39]   *Ibid.*, 216—217.

immediately positive and immanent physical effects of exercise or their possible human social and sexual benefits.[40]

A further point developed by Flood that will prove important to this project is his recognition that asceticism entails discourse as well. "Ascetic traditions are forms of collective memory enacted in the body through *praxis* and enacted in language through discourse."[41] In his engagement with ascesis, Flood supports the overall point that ascesis is an embodiment of the theology of a given ascetic tradition; in fact, it "writes" the scriptures of that tradition on the body of its practitioners.[42] But Flood also helps to support the claim that, within indigenous Christian practice, discourse itself undergoes an ascesis in relationship to the central narrative and scriptures of its tradition in order that it may "embody" the narrative of the Christian tradition, and the Reality it intends to engage, in the continued discourse of the Christian tradition.

Although not explicitly writing on the nature of asceticism in antiquity, the figure of Pierre Hadot ought also to be mentioned before the close of this section. Hadot takes up Paul Rabbow's insight that the ancient philosophical schools practiced "spiritual disciplines" not unlike those disciplines practiced among the followers of the exercises of Ignatius of Loyola.[43] Hadot argues that, in light of the fact that the various ancient philosophical schools practiced "spiritual exercises,"[44] it is more accurate to understand ancient philosophy *as a way of life* rather than a mere discursive practice alone.[45] Hadot contributes the significant insight that philosophical discourse must be understood to be secondary to, derivative of, and in the service to, the various an-

---

[40]   That is to say, such social and sexual benefits as, say, "sex appeal."

[41]   *Ibid.*, 9.

[42]   Flood, 218—222.

[43]   Paul Rabbow, *Seelenführung: Methodik der Exerzitien in der Antike* (Munich: Kîsel-Verlag, 1954). Hadot was also influenced by the work of the woman whom he would later marry. See Ilsetraut Hadot, *Seneca und die griechisch-römische Tradition der Seelenleitung* (Berlin: de Gruyter, 1969). Two other philosophers are also influential upon Hadot's thought, André -Jean Voelke and J. Dománski.

[44]   Pierre Hadot, *Exercices spirituels et philosophie antique*, Second Ed. (Paris: Études augustiniennes*, 1981).

[45]   Pierre Hadot, *La philosophie comme manière de vivre* (Paris: Albin Michel, 2001).

cient forms of philosophical life in general.[46] Implicit in his historical philosophical explorations, of course, is a desire to see such a relationship retrieved among modern philosophers. In this respect, this current project in the field of Christian theology is not unlike Hadot's in the field of philosophy.

In response to this recent surge in scholarly literature on asceticism in general, and in response to Flood's more postcritical work in this area in particular, several possibilities emerge with respect to Christian theology as an indigenous Christian practice. If transcendent realities actually open out through traditionary disciplines, then contact with these transcendent realities should dictate the direction that Christian teaching unfolds. This means that theology ought to entail contemplation of the transcendent realities to which any given religion—especially Christianity—promises contact.

Ascesis in Christian tradition

WITHIN THE particular context of Christian asceticism, the assertion of this introduction takes a new shape. Christian ascesis is a theological performance that embodies Christian teaching and involves the Christian body in discourse about Christian reality. This embodiment is possible because Christian ascesis "opens out" for the practitioner the realities or Reality that Christianity teaches.[47]

Practices that may be described as ascetic appear throughout both the Old and New Testaments. Some have argued that these should not be construed as ascetic because they are not formulated within a Greco-Roman context.[48] Nevertheless the verb *askeo*, "to exercise," and the verbal root of the noun *askesis*, appears once in the New Testament in the voice of Paul the Apostle: "I always take pains *(askeo)* to have a clear conscience toward God and toward men" (Acts 24.16).

---

[46] Pierre Hadot, *Qu'est-ce que la philosophie antique?* (Paris: Gallimard, 1995). This theme of Hadot's is further explored in chapter six.

[47] This sketch of a history relies upon the excellent synthesis of the history of the development of asceticism in Christianity found in the sixth and seventh chapters of Gavin Flood's *The Ascetic Self*.

[48] For a presentation of these views together with an excellent argument against them, see J. Duncan M. Derrett, "Primitive Christianity as an Ascetic Movement," in *Asceticism*, eds. Vincent L. Wimbush and Richard Valantasis (New York: Oxford Univ. Press, 1995), 88—107.

Why a clear conscience? It is because of an impending judgment. In this same chapter, Luke has Paul describe the essence of Christianity as "faith in Christ Jesus and . . . [the virtues of] justice and self-control and future judgment" (Acts 24.24b-25). The center of Christianity in this short set of verses revolves around the development of a set of virtues—the development of which always involves the discipline of self-denial[49]—in light of an eschatological promise fulfilled by the coming of the Messiah.

Turning to the cultural context of early Christianity, asceticism is a nearly universal religious phenomenon found throughout pre-Christian, Greco-Roman antiquity. Plato, as the prototypical Greek philosopher, is certainly "religious" in the broad sense, and could also be called an ascetic.[50] According to Plato, virtue is *ou didakton all' asketikon*,[51] not a (didactic) teaching, but a practice or exercise. The word *asketikon* in this context would have conjured up the sense of the word "practice" as an art, craft or profession, e.g., "the practice of medicine." But it would also have meant the process of improving one's art, craft or profession through continued exercise, e.g., "to practice the piano."[52] It is in this sense that the virtues were practiced. Virtue, for Plato, develops independence from the body, where the body is construed as an obstruction to the contemplative grasp of the forms.[53] Not only Plato, but also most every school of Greek philosophy, especially those of Epicureanism and Stoicism,[54] involves their philosophical practitioners in ascetical and virtue forming "spiritual exercises."[55]

---

49 *Ibid.*, 88.

50 John Pinsent, "Ascetic Moods in Greek and Latin Literature," in *Asceticism*, eds. Vincent L. Wimbush and Richard Valantasis (New York: Oxford Univ. Press, 1995), 211.

51 Plato, *Gorgias* 487c, 507d.

52 Pinsent, 211.

53 Another excellent article on asceticism in Plato is John M. Dillon, "Rejecting the Body, Refining the Body: Some Remarks on the Development of Platonist Asceticism," in *Asceticism*, eds. Vincent L. Wimbush and Richard Valantasis (New York: Oxford Univ. Press, 1995), 80-87.

54 Pinsent, 216-217.

55 This is the major thrust of Pierre Hadot's argument in his key works *What is Ancient Philosophy?*, trans. Michael Chase (Cambridge, MA: Belknap Press of Har-

In this context, early Christianity struggles as one philosophy among others.[56] Over the course of the cultural and finally official acceptance of Christianity throughout the Roman Empire there is a movement internal to Christianity from a focus on martyrdom as the chief Christian act of devotion to its virtual replacement by what comes to be called the "white martyrdom." This white martyrdom is *ascesis* as the living practice of self-denial. Monasticism begins in Christianity roughly when martyrdom ceases to be such a live option.[57] Asceticism, although more ancient than and certainly not confined to monasticism, is nevertheless closely tied to monasticism in the development of Christianity as a world religion.[58] The most significant contribution of monasticism in the development of the Christian practice of asceticism is, however, the realization that Christianity requires radical separation of the Christian from worldliness. Monasticism interprets this as the founding of a new, autonomous "city,"[59] first in the desert among the early monastic desert fathers, and, finally, behind the walls of monasteries throughout Christendom.

Over the long course of the development of Christianity into Christendom, another important contribution of monasticism is the absorption and eventual replacement of the earlier and one time contemporaneous Hellenic ascetic traditions.[60] As eastern and western forms of Christianity begin to diverge culturally and theologically, so too eastern and western forms of monasticism and ascetic practice begin to diverge from one another. Brown, and after him, Flood, traces both traditions back to the influence of Evagrius of Pontus.[61] The east

---

vard Univ. Press, 2002) and *Philosophy as a Way of Life: Spiritual Exercises from Socrates to Foucault*, trans. Michael Chase, (UK: Wiley / Blackwell, 1995).

[56] Samuel Rubenson, "Christian Asceticism and the Emergence of the Monastic Tradition," in *Asceticism*, eds. Vincent L. Wimbush and Richard Valantasis (New York: Oxford Univ. Press, 1995), 52. Chapter six, below, engages with this notion of Christianity as one philosophy struggling among others.

[57] Edward E. Malone, *The Monk and the Martyr* (Washington: Catholic Univ. of America Press, 1950), presents this now almost universally accepted argument.

[58] Rubenson, 49.

[59] *Ibid.*, 55.

[60] *Ibid.*; Pierre Hadot in *What is Ancient Philosophy?* also loosely argues this point.

[61] Flood, 148—149; Chapter six of Flood's *The Ascetic Self* traces the eastern trajectory, while chapter seven traces the western.

receives and revises this contribution through the Cappadocian fathers, John of the Ladder, and Maximus the Confessor, whereas the west receives the Evagrian tradition through the works of John Cassian especially as mediated through Augustine, Benedict of Nursia and Gregory the Great.

The east never loses its cosmological focus where human being[62] is a microcosm of creation—each point of anthropology and psychology corresponding to some structure of the universe.[63] Within this context, ascetic transformation is seen as part and parcel of the cosmic salvation offered in Christ. The west, although not totally losing this vision, concentrates more upon ascesis as a tool for positive moral development.[64] Both the east and the west, however, recognize that the ultimate goal of ascesis is contemplation of and participation in God.

The Christian east retains this mediated Evagrian tradition more fully intact to this day. For the west, however, the Reformation meant not only a crisis in doctrine and ecclesial polity, but also in practice and therefore asceticism. The legacy of the Reformation traditions is a systematic doubting of organized asceticism.[65] Protestantism almost universally abandons the monastic tradition. This seriously, though not entirely, curtails the passing down of the ascetic Christian tradition in Protestant churches. Ascetic practices continue to be encouraged in the form of personal piety.[66] Protestant monarchs continued to proclaim days of fasting. Not until the advent of modernity does as-

---

[62]   Throughout, this book uses the term "human being" as a substitute for the abstract noun "man" in order to employ gender inclusive language while enjoying the benefits of abstraction (compare "humankind," a collective noun).

[63]   Flood, 153—166.

[64]   *Ibid.*, 182—189.

[65]   Rowan Williams, *Anglican Identities* (Cambridge, MA: Cowley, 2003), 2, argues that Anglicanism "is committed to a radical criticism of any theology that sanctions the hope that human activity can contribute to the winning of God's favour, and so is suspicious of organized asceticism." In so far as this is part of the Protestant impulse within the Anglican tradition, such a description counts for all Protestant traditions.

[66]   So, for example, Rowan Williams continues the passage quoted in the previous footnote with the parenthetical note that the Protestant Anglican tradition is only suspicious of *organized* asceticism "as opposed to the free expression of devotion to God which may indeed be profoundly ascetic in its form." (2)

ceticism come under real attack in the west—both Protestant and Roman Catholic—as the form that Christian discipleship traditionally
takes.

Nevertheless, in both eastern and western Christianity, where ascetic practices have been retained, under whatever name they may be
called, ascesis remains the performance of theology that embodies
Christian teaching, involves the body itself as discourse about God,
and "opens out" for the practitioner the realities or Reality that Christianity teaches. For in all these cases the goal remains the same—the
contemplation of God through participation in divine being. Whether
as the performance of a cosmic salvation in the microcosm of the human body, or as a simple tool for moral development—or both—
Christian asceticism, ultimately, is a means of contact with the triune
God through imitation of and participation in the life of Christ.

Ascesis in Christian thought   Definition of Ascesis

SO FAR, the introduction has described ascesis as the performance and
embodiment of the theology of a given ascetic community or
tradition. The definition here now focuses on its use as a term
defining practices indigenous to Christianity. The entire first part of
this project constitutes a dogmatic exploration of Christian ascesis,
but this project adopts preliminarily a definition of Christian ascesis
as 1) those traditionary disciplines of self-denial[67] that 2) Christians
recognize as divine gifts in themselves, and which 3) always include
(but sometimes transcend) bodily practices, in order to 4) perform an
imitation of Jesus Christ, thereby 5) "opening out" the ascetic to
receive the gift of communion with and contemplation of (the triune)

---

[67]   In personal correspondence Eugene Rogers objects to the use of the term "self-
denial" in describing Christian ascesis, rightly pointing out that it makes no
sense to call something the "denial" of the self when it actually entails the development of true personhood in relationship to God. Rogers would prefer the term
"self-abandonment" in an ecstatic sense. That objection not withstanding, this
project will continue to use the term "self-denial" with respect to asceticism because of the two-fold sense of the self entailed in the Christian tradition, going
back at least to Paul, between the "flesh" and the "spirit." The true, spiritual self
is not denied, but the fleshy self is "crucified with Christ." This book therefore
takes as essential to the Christian definition of ascetic discipleship the practice
named, almost universally within the Christian tradition, *mortification*, that is, dying to one's (fleshy) self.

God, and, in turn 6) rendering the ascetically disciplined Christian body an intelligible contribution to discourse about God.[68]

A less controversial Christian term, "discipleship," signifies almost exactly what this project denotes in its use of the word "ascesis." One finds the Christian definition of discipleship in Christ's own call, "if any man would come after me, let him deny himself and take up his cross and follow me" (Matt. 16.24). Christian discipleship, as with any discipleship, requires at least two things: 1) submission to a set of disciplines 2) under the authority of a certain teacher. That teacher in Christianity is, of course, Christ. And the disciplines are those that shape the life and character of the believer after the narrative structure of the life and character of Jesus Christ—"take up your cross and follow me." The disciplines involved are those that prepare the Christian practitioner, or, disciple, to be able to accept such a calling, that is, the Christian disciple must "deny himself."

Self-denial in preparation for and imitation of martyrdom is the key to an indigenous understanding of Christian asceticism. Although the word ascesis is not in the New Testament scriptures,[69] as a competing philosophy among others in the Greco-Roman world, it did not take long for Christians to recognize their discipleship as the Christian (and therefore more "true") parallel to pagan philosophical spiritual disciplines. In adopting the term ascesis, Christianity sets itself in deliberate competition with the other philosophical schools of discipline as the only true and real choice. The term ascesis, therefore, means Christian discipleship, but only when such discipleship includes the physical disciplines of self-denial.

It is now fitting to describe a few of the concrete practices that have, by and large, stood up as the core of traditional Christian discipleship, or ascesis. This brief description includes major categories such as prayer, fasting, "alms-giving," repentance and "spiritual" di-

---

[68]   Valantasis, 550, asserts that the four major social functions of ascesis are that it: 1) enables individuals to function within the new world projected by such practices, it 2) provides a means of translating theoretical concepts into patterns of behavior, it 3) retrains perception, and 4) serves as a means through which other domains of knowledge can be incorporated into this "new world."

[69]   That is to say, the form of the word askesis, as a noun. In its verbal form, askeo, it appears, as discussed above, in the mouth of the Apostle Paul in Acts 24.16.

rection—all within the assumed context of the church and her worship.[70] Each of these practices intends to free the practitioner from enslavement to certain falsehoods. Likewise, each of these practices develops a certain virtue or virtues. Finally, indigenous Christian thought assumes that each of these practices open out Christian realities, a certain Christian reality, or simply to union with God.

Prayer is the broadest category of Christian discipline. It includes, of course, the context of Christian corporate worship that individual Christian discipleship assumes. It includes regular worship on the "Day of the Lord," or Sunday, as a *mimesis* of the day Christ rose.[71] It also includes what is traditionally called the daily office—the pattern of daily prayer for Christians, either monastic or lay. The corporate worship of the church quickly developed a liturgical year that shapes the believing community within the narrative of the life of Christ. So too, the pattern of the daily office within a week follows a similar narrative pattern. Although some churches have dropped these structures, regular (Sunday)[72] corporate worship and regular daily prayer are the norm throughout all forms of Christianity today.

Prayer is a corporeal act of self-denial on several levels. Regular corporate worship is a form of denying where one's body might otherwise be on a given Sunday morning—reading the *Times* in bed, sailing on the lake—as opposed to meeting in a local church building. In many Christian traditions it also involves certain bodily motions such as the signing of the cross, genuflecting and bowing, and more rigor-

---

[70] This list represents the culling of various key disciplines from classical manuals of ascetical theology such as: Vernon Staley, *The Catholic Religion, A Manual of Instruction for Members of the Anglican Communion*, rev. Brian Goodchild (Wilton, CT: Morehouse-Barlow, 1983) and F. P. Harton, *The Elements of the Spiritual Life: A Study in Ascetical Theology* (New York: Macmillan Company, 1932), and more contemporary devotional guides that ground themselves in such classical works, such as: Richard J. Foster, *Celebration of Discipline: The Path to Spiritual Growth* (San Francisco: Harper and Row, 1988) and Marjorie J. Thompson, *Soul Feast: An Invitation to the Christian Spiritual Life* (Louisville: Westminster John Knox, 1995).

[71] Furthermore, from the earliest times this seems to have entailed a celebration of the Christian rite of "Thanksgiving," or Eucharist. This continues to be the chief form of worship on Sundays and major feasts in many Christian bodies today.

[72] The parentheses around the word "Sunday" prove necessary in order to include Seventh Day Adventists and other such Sabbatarians.

ous activities such as prostrations.[73] Christian thought has always considered that corporate worship and regular prayer free the Christian from the idolatry of false-hope in finite ends by a perpetual refocusing on the actual center, goal, and end of reality—God. In so doing, prayer develops the virtue of love: recognizing God's love, and returning that love to God and neighbor. Prayer, both corporate and private, opens the Christian to the triune life of God. The Christian prays to God the Father as a member of the Body of God's Son, Jesus Christ, by the inspiration of the Holy Spirit.

Fasting constitutes a broad category of corporeal disciplines of self-denial such as sexual abstinence—either for a committed period of time or for life in celibacy—keeping vigil, taking vows of silence, and retreat (physical solitude)—either for a period of time or for life in cloistered seclusion or as a hermit. Each of these practices entails some form of corporeal self-denial. The most common use of the term "fasting" however, refers to denying a certain quality or quantity of food for a set period of time.[74] Corporately, the Christian body expresses this in the observance of Lent and most Fridays throughout the year. In fasting, the Christian hopes to reject physical dependencies and addictions, and hopes to gain the virtues of dependence upon and trust in God for physical needs and personal satisfaction. Christians understand this category of corporeal self-denial as a kind of participation in martyrdom in the form of an imitation of Christ—both in his desert temptation and, ultimately, in his death on the

---

[73] The breath and posture prayer exercises of eastern Hesychasts would, of course, qualify as another important example. On the relative strenuousness and difficulty of the practice of prostrations as a strength building and aerobic exercise, see William C. Bushell "Psychophysiological and Comparative Analysis of Ascetic-Meditational Discipline" in *Asceticism*, eds. Vincent L. Wimbush and Richard Valantasis (New York: Oxford Univ. Press, 1995).

[74] So, for example, one may fast by abstaining for a given period of time (e.g., a day) from luxurious or superfluous foods (e.g., meat, alcohol, sweets), or by actually reducing food in-take. Ancient ascetics would often go days with no food at all. Classical Anglo-Catholic and Roman Catholic practice defines fasting as one light meal and one small "respite" (at about three o'clock) for one day. (Again, see, for example, Vernon Staley, *The Catholic Religion*, [General Books, 1894] and F. P. Harton, *The Elements of the Spiritual Life*, [Londond, S. P. C. K, 1947).

cross—that opens out the reality of the divine "self-denial" of God in the incarnation.

"Alms-giving" is a more ancient Christian term that means what many traditions today call "stewardship." This includes practices such as "tithing" to the local church, giving money to charities or directly to those in need, spending time on "service projects," Christian service to the poor and ill in charitable institutions and hospitals, and even monastic vows of poverty. In each case, such disciplines reject the falsehood that the material universe "belongs" to human being or beings—either corporately or individually. It also rejects the falsehood of "scarcity"—that God does not provide "enough" for his creatures. These disciplines develop the virtues of simplicity and hospitality. The Christian practitioner of such disciplines may expect concrete and existential knowledge of the Christian teaching of creation *ex nihilo*—that God creates all things, out of nothing, and that one may therefore trust God as abundant source.

The Christian practice of repentance is Christianity's most ancient and most heavily biblically documented spiritual discipline.[75] This includes confession before the community or a trusted member of the community,[76] the "ministry of reconciliation" (II Cor. 5.18), making amends to those whom one has wronged (Matt. 5.23—24), and such Ignatian practices as daily and "particular" examination of conscience.[77] Repentance is the entry into the Christian life and the first step to developing all other forms of ascesis. In confessing, making amends, and changing life patterns, Christians deny the falsehood that they are "at the center of the world," that they are incapable of

---

[75] Jesus' entire gospel message begins with the proclamation of repentance in the face of the in-breaking kingdom of God. The book of Hebrews provides one telling passage where the author, attempting to delve into more "solid food" for the sake of the believers, admonishes the readers to "leave the elementary doctrine of Christ and go on to maturity, not laying again a foundation of repentance from dead works and of faith toward God (Heb. 6.1)." Repentance may not be an "advanced" Christian teaching, but it is clearly central to its foundation.

[76] James 5.16: Therefore confess your sins to one another, and pray for one another, that you may be healed.

[77] Ignatius of Loyola, *Spiritual Exercises*. See especially the edition translated by George E. Ganss: *Ignatius of Loyola: The Spiritual Exercises and Selected Works*, Classics of Western Spirituality (Mahwah, NJ: Paulist Press, 1991).

change or transformation. It develops the virtues of humility and love of neighbor. In doing so, the Christian is opened to concrete and existential knowledge of the Christian teaching of original sin and salvation from sin through the work and forgiveness of God in Jesus Christ.

Finally, what many would now call spiritual direction or "advising,"[78] was once the role of the pastor or "bishop" in the fledgling and persecuted early Christian community, and what would become the role of the "abba" in the desert or the "abbot" or "abbess" of a monastic community. Evangelical Christians today might call such a relationship—coming from a more egalitarian perspective—an "accountability partnership."[79] Whatever the name, this discipline involves a kind of master and pupil relationship that assumes that no one is an accurate judge of his or her own spiritual progress. This may sometimes also take the form of a written or traditional "rule" to which the master holds the pupil accountable—or to which the abbot holds the monastery accountable. Such practices reject the notion of absolute autonomy and develop the Christian virtue of obedience and submission, offering the practitioner concrete and existential knowledge of Christ as the "master" of all Christians.

In summary, ascesis is an exercise or set of exercises, having to do with the body, that one undergoes in order to reach a religious or transcendent end. Ascesis embodies the core beliefs of the practitioner and his or her community concerning the ultimate nature of reality. Simultaneously, ascesis adds the disciplined body to human discourse about the nature of reality. Indigenous ascetic traditions understand such practices as divine gifts that open up and entail contact with that reality or set of realities that theology purports to describe. In the specific context of Christianity, the goal of ascesis is the contemplation of God through participation in divine being; its means are those of somatic self-denial in imitation of Christ. Christian asceticism gives a

---

[78] Christopher Bryant, "The Nature of Spiritual Direction: Sacramental Confession," in *The Study of Spirituality*, eds. Cheslyn Jones, Geoffrey Wainwright, Edward Yarnold (New York: Oxford Univ. Press, 1986), 568—570.

[79] For example, see Tom L. Eisenman, *The Accountability Man* (Downers Grove, IL: InterVarsity, 2004).

means of contact with the triune God in this imitation of and participation in the life of Christ.

Definitions of Other Key Terms

Body and Christian body

THE WORD "BODY" gained significant new use due to an explosion in
its semantic content in the social sciences and continental philosophy[80]
beginning as far back as the 1970's. The contribution of this literature
to social scientific and philosophical thought, and its consequent
influence upon current scholarship on Christian thought, has quickly
become so influential and pervasive that this project assumes its
impact as part of its background. The literature expanding this use
and meaning of the word "body" is immense, and a full discussion of
it is beyond the scope of this work.

The following represents a few of the key works that have contributed to this semantic expansion. J. Blacking's *The Anthropology of
the Body* (1977), C. Shilling's *The Body and Social Theory* (2003), and the
volume edited by Maurice Godelier and Michel Panoff, *La production
du corps: approches anthropologiques et historiques* (1998) contribute to
the social sciences.[81] All of these social scientific approaches assume
that the body in human culture should be taken as socially constructed, rather than some kind of pre-cultural and biological "fact."

In continental philosophy the single most important contribution
to the expansion of the use of the word "body" must be traced back to
Michel Foucault. His two works that relate most closely to this project

---

[80] Similar to the divide between analytic and continental philosophy, Elizabeth A.
Clark, in"The Ascetic Impulse in Religious Life: A General Response" in *Asceticism*, eds. Vincent L. Wimbush and Richard Valantasis, (New York: Oxford Univ.
Press, 1995), 510, observes how the divide between postmodern theory and traditional historiography affects asceticism scholarship. This project identifies more
with the continental and postmodern side of this divide without stressing this
difference or refusing to benefit from other approaches.

[81] This list derives from the work of Gavin Flood: John Blacking, *The Anthropology of
the Body* (New York: Academic Press, 1977); Chris Schilling, *The Body and Social
Theory* (London: Safe Publications, 2003); Maurice Godelier and Michel Panoff, *La
production du corps: approches anthropologiques et historiques* (Amsterdam: Archives
contemporaines, 1998).

would be *The Order of Things: An Archaeology of the Human Sciences* (1970), and *The History of Sexuality*, especially its second volume: *The Use of Pleasure* (1984).[82] What is so significant about Foucault's contribution is his synthesis of two important but often irreconcilable streams of continental theory—phenomenological hermeneutics and structuralism—in a way that also creatively transforms them.

Inheriting Nietzsche's "genealogy," Foucault combines in his "archaeology" the critical distancing of structuralism with the inescapability of subjective appropriation described by continental hermeneutics.[83] Paradoxically, Foucault's work participates (in) what it criticizes. The "idiosyncrasy"[84] of his writing is itself a performance of the will-to-power that he simultaneously exposes in the history and philosophy he engages. The key use of these approaches to "bodies" is the way that this combination of phenomenology, hermeneutics and structuralism allows for polyvalence in the term "body" without mere equivocation.

The use of the word "body" and "Christian body" throughout this text will reflect the way that these various continental approaches enrich "body" as a signifier. A hermeneutics of the body inscribes human discourse and knowing in embodiment *qua* human. A phenomenology of the body recognizes it as an encounter that is both corporeal and corporate. Finally, structuralism contributes the insights of the social sciences through the mediation of a critical philosophy. Ideology, religion, and culture shape and are shaped by the socially constructed body as both "individual" and as "body politic."[85] The combined effect of such approaches recognizes that "body" intends a double entendre between body as corporeal and body as corporate. And this is because these two aspects of "body" are indices

---

82 Michel Foucault, *Les mots et les choses — une archéologie des sciences humaines* (Paris: Gallimard, 1966); and *Histoire de la sexualité*, vol. 2, *L'Usage des plaisirs* (Paris: Gallimard, 1984).

83 This account of Foucault's contribution closely follows Harpham's account in *The Ascetic Imperative* (see nt. 21.)

84 Harpham, 223.

85 For example, Patrick Olivelle, "Deconstruction of the Body in Indian Asceticism," in *Asceticism*, eds. Vincent L. Wimbush and Richard Valantasis (New York: Oxford Univ. Press, 1995), 188, assumes the human body, as itself culturally structured, is the primary symbol of the social body, the body politic.

or signifiers of one another within both cultural systems and subjective encounters. Much of the sociological and philosophical speculation on the body has already come to influence Christian discourse and scholarship on Christianity.[86]

Henri de Lubac, in his book *Corpus Mysticum*,[87] describes one important source of the use of the term "body" as understood indigenously within the Christian structure that came before such sociological and philosophical expansions of the term. De Lubac effectively argues that the ancient church understood itself to be the "real body," or "true presence" of Christ, re-membered through corporate unity. The "mystical body," on the other hand, was used to refer to the *eschatic*[88] manner in which Christ was made fully present to the church in the eucharistic elements in the ritual mystery of the sacrament of communion. During the middle ages a semantic shift occurred in the use of these two terms and they were reversed. The church slowly became a "mystical body" in a loose and unrealizable sense—at least in terms of actual corporate institution. The "real presence" then transferred to the ritual mystery, and, as a result, Christ's ritual presence was transformed into an atomistic presence in the eucharistic elements of bread and wine themselves.

This project aligns with de Lubac's observations and critiques of this semantic shift and with those who have pursued this same problem such as Michel de Certeau[89] and, more recently, William Cavanaugh.[90] With them this project emphasizes the ritual mystery of the presence of Christ as performed by the church in its eschatologically oriented performances, together with the real or true presence of Christ in the corporate institution of the "Christian body."

---

[86] See, for example, Benedict M. Ashley, *Theologies of the Body: Humanist and Christian* (St. Louis: Pope John Center, 1985).

[87] Henri de Lubac, *Corpus Mysticum: L'Eucharistie et L'église au Moyen Âge* (Paris: Aubier, 1944).

[88] "Eschatic" here meaning of or having to do with the *eschaton*, or the last day.

[89] Michel de Certeau, *La Fable Mystique, XVIe-XVIIe Siècle* (Paris: Éditions Gallimard, 1982).

[90] William Cavanaugh, *Torture and Eucharist: Theology, Politics, and the Body of Christ* (Malden, MA: Blackwell, 1998), and *Theopolitical Imagination: Discovering the Liturgy as a Political Act in an Age of Global Consumerism* (Edinburgh: T. & T. Clark, 2002).

Throughout this text, the term "Christian body" denotes the particular *corporeal* body of one integrated within the Christian structure, insofar as one attempts an imitation, *mimesis*, or iteration of Jesus Christ by and in the somatic and performative interpretation of the *corpus* of Christian literature—the holy scriptures. But the Christian body is also the particular, local, *corporate* body of Christians that, again, integrates within the Christian structure through communal *mimesis* in and through the somatic interpretation of scripture by means of ritual performance. Moreover, the Christian body, from a point of view indigenous to the Christian "structure," is also the entire corporate and universal "Body of Christ" insofar as the Christian religion structurally entails an ecumenical openness to the "Other" among the various local and particular corporate Christian bodies. This project employs the term "Christian body" with respect to these corporate meanings, as synonymous with the more traditional terms "church" and "Church."

As a rough sketch of the use of the term "church" as the most encompassing sense of "corporate Christian body," four things characterize most Christian organizations that could be identified as "ecumenically oriented and liturgically grounded."[91] These are: 1) a commitment to Christian scripture;[92] 2) a commitment to official or traditional teachings that guide the interpretation of those scriptures, such as a creed, confession, etc.; 3) a commitment to regular worship that involves the ritual "sacraments" of Baptism and Eucharist; and 4) a commitment to an ordered life of worship based upon a recognizable set of officers who have authority. These four things provide a minimal definition of the church as an ecumenical and liturgical corporate Christian body: scripture, tradition of interpretation, liturgical ritual, and ministry.

---

[91]   The generalizations and descriptions that follow are primarily derived from: World Council of Churches, *Baptism, Eucharist, and Ministry*, Faith and Order Paper No. 11 (Geneva: World Council of Churches, 1982), and from *The Chicago-Lambeth Quadrilateral 1886, 1888*, in *The Book of Common Prayer and Administration of the Sacraments and Other Rites and Ceremonies of the Church* (New York: The Church Hymnal Corporation, 1979), 876-878.

[92]   Needless to say, the canon of scripture is a point of dispute among various churches.

Discourse

DISCOURSE MEANS intelligible communion or communication with another. At its highest level, it means the intelligible communion or communication of some kind of shared reality, be it noetic content on the part of human beings, or God's own intelligible being on God's part. On a more mundane level, it connotes simple conversation of various lengths, degrees of formality, histories, etc., where concrete intelligible content is shared by means of signs. This includes "academic" discourse and discourses. Finally, and related to the preceding sense, "discourse" sometimes simply means "a discourse" that is, an extended and usually written essay on a particular subject.

Discourse, for human beings is necessarily embodied; that is to say, it must involve tongues, lips, vocal cords, hands, eyes, ears, etc. But this embodiment may also include the use of human artifacts (i.e., writing) as the *products* of the human mind and body, and not simply the body alone. Thus, this meaning of the word "discourse" as a written work fits within the somatic context of human communication.

Christian theology

THEOLOGY IS an ancient word, first coined by the Greeks. In its broadest possible construal, "theology" simply designates "god-talk."[93] This broadest sense of "god-talk" even atheists could engage—their theologies would be "a-theologies." For the Pre-Socratics, Plato, and Aristotle, theology was the name of that science which discussed the nature of the gods or of divinity. Theology when conceived as Christian teaching usually refers most properly to the Christian teaching of the Trinity.[94] Denys the Pseudo-Areopagite called the writers of the scriptures "divine theologians."[95] Augustine assumed that Christian teaching was nothing more nor less than the teaching of scripture.[96] This view regards Christian exegesis as the

---

[93] "Theology" comes from the Greek word *theologia*, etymologically from *theos*, which means "god," and *logos*, which means word, discourse, or "talk."

[94] That is to say, "God-talk" as talk about the Christian and therefore triune God. The Christian east most prominently holds this position.

[95] Pseudo-Dionysius, *On Divine Names* 1.1

[96] Augustine fundamentally assumes that Christian teaching is scriptural exegesis in *De doctrina christiana* as is evident simply from the relationship of the content of the work to its title. Although this work primarily addresses issues in scrip-

true task of theology. So from a very early time in Christianity, theology has been associated with its chief doctrine, the Trinity, and its primary texts, the scriptures.

Nevertheless the word "theology" is often used in equivocating ways in Christian discourse. The word "theology" is now used almost coterminously with what one would have once named "Christian teaching." Thus, people often use the term to identify that which distinguishes the various confessional bodies within the Christian church today, e.g., "Methodist theology," "Baptist theology," "Catholic theology," etc., when the words "dogma," "doctrine," or "teaching" would probably be far more appropriate. On the other hand, the word "theology" is often used to designate academic and scholarly rumination upon, or attempted exploration and extension of, Christian teaching, thought, or thinkers, according to the canons of secular logic and modern academic scholarship. "Scholarship" or "criticism" might be more appropriate here.

This distinction between theology as concrete Christian teaching and reflective discourse concerning these teachings proves not entirely unhelpful. One gains some clarity by distinguishing "theology" understood as dogma, doctrine, or the "teachings" of Christianity from "theology" as reflection upon those teachings. "Theology" as Christian teaching is often conceived of didactically or propositionally. And in this sense Christian "teaching" may be understood, logically, by anyone capable, without need of faith in the reality of the things taught.[97] But in one important sense, "Christian teaching" may be better understood in an existential and performative way.

In this case the word "teaching" serves both to indicate a concrete reality, event, or person, and those practices that allow the subjective appropriation or encounter of that reality. So, "teaching," as a gerund, indicates the practice that opens out Christian reality to the practitioner; as an abstract noun, "teaching," becomes the actual concrete real-

---

tural exegesis and hermeneutics, its title is not "On Biblical Interpretation," but "On Christian Doctrine" or "On Teaching Christianity."

[97] This explanation follows Thomas Aquinas' position that anyone—believer or unbeliever—may intellectually grasp *sacra doctrina* as a kind of human knowledge, regardless of the fact that sacred teaching itself is a gift from God. See Thomas Aquinas, *Summa Theologica* 1.1.1-10.

ity taught, e.g., God as triune, Jesus as God-incarnate, etc. Still, these concrete realities are not abstractions—it is the triune God who is encountered, not "the doctrine of the Trinity;" it is Jesus as God being made flesh that is encountered, not "the doctrine of the incarnation." This existential and subjective appropriation allows the practitioner actual ontological contact with what Christianity teaches—in Christian terms, with the reality of God and God's works.

Such existential and performative teaching of Christianity may be called the "unfolding" of Christian teaching into and as the life of the Christian body. This unfolding holds both at corporate and corporeal levels of the Christian body. Teaching unfolds into the corporate Christian body as the life of a Christian community. Likewise, teaching unfolds into the corporeal Christian body as the life of an individual Christian. The first part of this book explores the sub-thesis that the Christian practice of discipleship, or, ascesis, teaches Christianity. Christian teachings that are sometimes treated abstractly thereby prove to be concrete in and as ascesis. Theology as Christian *teaching* is ascesis, therefore, insofar as ascesis teaches Christianity. And this corresponds to the recent scholarly description explored throughout this introduction of ascesis as the performance of (a) theology.

Turning now to the second part of this distinction in the use of the term "theology" when used to indicate reflective discourse concerning Christian teaching, "theology" best describes what is specifically called *dogmatic theology*, or, simply, *dogmatics*.[98] Popular imagination may sometimes perceive the logical, intellectual project of dogmatics as inherently academic, scholarly and therefore especially *abstract*. Combined with the first sense of "teaching" above, as abstract dogma *describing* what Christianity teaches (rather than the dynamic realities themselves or the living disciplines that allow their appropriation), "dogmatics" becomes an abstract academic study of already obtuse religious obfuscation. Because of this, the popular imagination may justifiably approach Christian teaching itself as needless abstraction.

Regardless of whether or not, or the degree to which, these perceptions are justifiable, this book uses "theology" in the sense of

---

[98] Therefore other "branches" of Christian theology (e.g., historical, moral, exegetical, etc.) are not the main topic of this discussion and beyond the scope of inclusion within this project.

"dogmatics" to describe that Christian practice which disciplines (provides an ascesis for) Christian discourse concerning Christian teaching. In this sense, dogmatics is primarily the name of an active practice or discipline that engages in reflection upon and exposition of Christian teachings as performative means of contact with concrete reality or realities. As reflection upon Christian teaching, theology unfolds Christian teaching *into discourse*. But this sense of the unfolding of Christian teaching is secondary to, derivative of, and in service to its first and primary meaning as the performance of Christian teaching in the life of the Christian body.[99]

The sub-thesis of the second part of this book explores the practice of theology itself as also one of these "appropriating performances" that teaches Christianity—in this case, within the realm of human discourse. Because discourse is an embodied human practice, it is appropriate to call theology an ascesis of discourse. Theology (especially as dogmatics), although sometimes treated as mere abstraction, proves to be the concrete practice of disciplining Christian discourse. So, this project takes its chief interest in the nature of Christian teaching and concomitantly, theological reflection upon it.

Approach

THE PROJECT of this book performs a paradoxical statement within dogmatic theology because it defines the field of dogmatic theology by pointing out that its foundation (the manifestation of God) and goal (participation in God) lie beyond itself and granted only as a (divine) gift. In terms of approach, therefore, this book does not further historical and philosophical scholarship on asceticism. It does not provide a history of Christian asceticism; nor does it give an historical theology. All of these disciplines come into play, but because the thesis statement is dogmatic, the method is dogmatic. The various texts explored throughout contribute towards this dogmatic statement and are read accordingly. These texts are not approached primarily historically, philosophically, or historical-theologically—

---

[99] This understanding of the relationship of *dogmatics to Christian teaching* is quite similar to, and, indeed, indebted to, Hadot's work on the relationship of philosophy as discourse to philosophy as a way of life (see the section on "Ascesis in recent scholarship," above; Hadot is discussed in more detail, below, in chapter six).

although all of those approaches must come into play to certain degrees in order accurately to make dogmatic claims.

The approach of this project to its task, conditioned as it is by the author's desire as an Anglican Christian to speak to an ecumenically oriented and liturgically informed audience of dogmatic theologians, looks back to major developmental points within the (ecumenical, and largely western) Christian tradition, e.g., the fathers. It depends upon the "fathers"[100] of the church as authoritative. That is to say, "authoritative" as the loci of the first or clearest unfoldings of Christian teachings. This dependence holds because the author and his audience agree to the common relevance and authority of these figures in their shared Christian tradition.

The second part of this project engages patristic texts or events in each chapter: Denys the Pseudo-Areopagite, Gregory Nazianzus, and Augustine, respectively. Chapter eight reflects on the meaning of the Council of Nicea as an event participated in by early church fathers, through the help of Ephraim Radner's recent theological and historical reflection on it. This project, especially in its first part, also engages certain contemporary figures in order to remain in dialogue with current dogmatic scholarship. These contemporary dogmatic theologians are also to some extent or another committed to the ecumenical Christian tradition. Some key examples would be the neo-patristic movement as represented by John Zizioulas and Pavel Florensky, and the *Resourcement* movement, especially Hans Urs von Balthasar. The last chapter engages the contemporary Postliberal thinker, Eugene Rogers.

Because this project is an exercise in dogmatic scholarship, it should not be understood as an attempt to provide a practical guide to Christian ascesis or ascetical practices. In that sense, it is not an example of Christian "ascetical theology." Rather, this thesis is a dogmatic reading of theology as itself an ascesis. This book should therefore be approached as a call for the Christian practice of theology to take its place among and within the church's regular regimen of discipline and training for formation in the faith. This project, there-

---

[100] One may legitimately ask, what about the "mothers" of the church? The answer is complicated and beyond the scope of this present work. An excellent volume attempting to address this problem of misogyny in the Christian textual tradition is Andrew Kadel's *Matrology* (New York: Continuum, 1995).

fore, has especially to do with the shaping of discourse, and, therein and thereby, both prayer on the one hand and worldviews, ecclesial cultures, and conceptual categories on the other.

As a final qualifier within this section, the terms "spirituality" and "spiritual theology" have recently become popular as substitutes for what throughout Christian history would have traditionally been called ascesis and ascetical theology. Gavin Flood argues the point that ascetic traditions make sense only within religions that have cosmological commitments.[101] It is exactly the loss of cosmological commitment in modern Christianity that has contributed to the decline of ascesis and the rise of so-called "spirituality."

This modern idea of "spirituality" may be described as the result of no longer seeing the corporeal and corporate Christian body as the participant at a microcosmic level in a macrocosmic process of salvation. Such "spirituality" is the escape from an unnecessary body for those who no longer see the body of the human person as an index for the body of God's creation as a whole. Insofar as this distinction remains between the terms "spirituality" and "ascesis," the difference between the reflective self-understanding of these two practices must be seen in opposition to one another, even if their outward practices may be quite similar. Only asceticism opens "spirituality" to the psychosomatic unity it really seeks.[102] For this reason, although this project discusses something that might be called "spirituality" in today's popular parlance, this word is deliberately eschewed and replaced with the traditional Christian terms of ascesis, asceticism, etc.

Structure and Outline

THEOLOGY, as discussed above, sometimes means "teaching" or "doctrine." In this sense, ascesis is already theology if teaching is understood in a dynamic, performative, and "lived" sense, rather than a didactic and propositional sense. Part one, therefore, takes this

---

[101] Flood, 2.

[102] In their introduction to *Asceticism* (xxxi), Wimbush and Valantasis point out that many contemporary proponents of "spirituality" perpetuate, in their approach to their task, the body/spirit dichotomy they attempt to transcend. Instead, such "spirituality" ought to engage "postmodern" discourse about asceticism where spirit and body cohere.

relatively uncontroversial ramification of recent scholarship on asceticism and shows how Christian ascesis teaches Christianity, in this existential sense—how it embodies Christian teaching.

The second part then returns to deal with theology, but here construed as it is more often used and understood as a kind of discursive practice or product (e.g., "a book of theology"). Part two shows how theology as an embodied practice is a microcosmic example of what is described at a broader level in part one: just as ascesis extends Christian teaching into and as the Christian body, so too then theology, as an ascetic practice involving discourse, within and among ascetic practice in general, extends Christian teaching into discourse.

Each half of this book consists of four chapters, each with two steps towards its thesis. The first step in each is to clarify and transform some insight provided by recent scholarship in asceticism in light of recent Christian constructive thought, to establish a constructive theological claim. The second step is dogmatic in nature, pushing this theological construction back into the divine life itself and claiming that the human process of ascesis corresponds directly to, and entails participation in, the divine life in some way. The theses of these chapters reflect ways in which ascesis teaches Christianity concretely, as subjective appropriation by placing the ascetic in direct ontological contact with reality itself. These theses support the overall thesis of part one, that *ascesis teaches Christianity*; it *teaches* (Christian) *reality*.

Likewise, the thesis of each chapter in part two presents theology as a microcosmic example of the ascetic Christian world-view described in part one by reflecting some way in which theology itself is an ascetic practice. In part two, the first step of each chapter is to shed some light on Christian theology as a discursive practice through the insights of recent scholarship on asceticism. The second step in each chapter of part two is also, as with the second step in the chapters of part one, dogmatic in nature. It seeks to push the logic of the claim that theology is ascetic back into the divine life itself and show how the practice of theology entails participation in the divine discourse of God. The various theses of each chapter in part two serve to support the claim that *theology is itself an ascetic practice*—it performs an *ascesis of Christian discourse*.

The project demands for its conclusion one final step. It must demonstrate that, to be recognized as such, Christian theology must be pursued within its proper broader context of ascesis as a particular ascetic discipline among others and, furthermore, that it therefore cannot be effectively practiced outside of those general ascetic practices of which it constitutes a mere example. This holds true at the corporate level of the Christian body, in terms of the teaching of the various churches, and at the level of the corporeal Christian body, in terms of the practices of the one who desires to pursue the vocation of what the Christian body recognizes as a *theologian*.

Part I

A Theology of Ascesis: From the Divine Life to the Life of Christian Discipline

Do you not know that in a race all the runners compete, but only one receives the prize? So run that you may obtain it. Every athlete exercises self-control in all things. They do it to receive a perishable wreath, but we an imperishable. Well, I do not run aimlessly, I do not box as one beating the air; but I pummel my body and subdue it, lest after preaching to others I myself should be disqualified.

I Corinthians 9.24-27

CHAPTER ONE

Ascesis and the Ecstasy of *Theosis*

> [God's] divine power has granted to us all things that pertain to life and
> godliness, through the knowledge of him who called us to his own glory
> and excellence, by which he has granted to us his precious and very great
> promises, that through these you may escape from the corruption that is in
> the world because of passion, and become partakers of the divine nature.
>
> II Peter 1.3-4.

CHRISTIAN ASCESIS teaches ecstatic personhood; that is, it unfolds
personhood as existing only in communion with other persons, thus
rendering concrete in the life of the Christian body the Christian
teaching of the Trinity as radical and ecstatic personhood. Christian
ecstasy (in *theosis*) forms an analogue to, and provides a share in, the
Son and Spirit's ecstatic "return" to the Father in the *perichoresis* of the
divine processions. This chapter first focuses on how certain scholars
who contributed to Wimbush and Valantasis' important volume,
Asceticism,[1] define asceticism in terms of the "self" or "personhood" as
a negative category, due to the association of ascesis with "self-
denial." This chapter turns to Bruce J. Malina's article entitled "Pain,
Power, and Personhood: Ascetic Behavior in the Ancient
Mediterranean"[2] as an exemplary model of an insightful, but, for the
purposes of this project, problematic approach to this kind of
definition of Christian asceticism, and places John Zizioulas, as an
eastern Christian theologian, in dialogue with Malina in order to
argue that ascesis is the shape that Christian *ecstasis* takes after the
fall.

---

[1] The volume *Asceticism*, edited by Wimbush and Valantasis, substantially contributed to the development of the retrieval of asceticism in recent scholarship, as
discussed above in the introduction.

[2] Bruce J. Malina, "Pain, Power, and Personhood: Ascetic Behavior in the Ancient
Mediterranean," in *Asceticism*, eds. Vincent L. Wimbush and Richard Valantasis
(New York: Oxford Univ. Press, 1995).

Malina and the Shrinkage of the Self

ONE CAN UNDERSTAND Malina's article as an answer to the question: what is meant by "self-denial" with regards to asceticism in antiquity? Malina's answer, in short, is that ascesis as "self-denial" simply means the attempt on the part of ascetics to deny and to set themselves up in radical opposition to whatever definition of "self" that their current societal context offers. Therefore, ascesis as self-denial entails what Malina calls "shrinking the self:" "[a]sceticism . . . is about what people did and do to get away from the self, whatever type of self existed or exists in a given society."[3]

Malina's applications of both the past and present tenses in the first sentence of the above quotation ("did and do") indicates another of Malina's goals: the comparison of ascesis in ancient Christian and modern secular contexts. Malina seeks out psychological, social psychological, but mainly cultural anthropological "viewpoints" for achieving this goal of ancient and modern comparison in defining the nature of ascetic self-denial.[4]

His key category of "shrinking the self," however, derives directly from its use as a modern psychological term, and he refers to the work of Mitchell (1988) and Harre (1980) in his initial definition of "asceticism as the shrinkage of the self motivated by avoidance or attainment goals."[5] The use of this modern psychological term as a definition of the nature of ascetic self-denial causes Malina to conflate immanent-oriented practices with truly ascetic, transcendence-oriented practices:

> Other behaviors work to this end [of avoidance or attainment goals] as well, for example: alcoholism, suicide, binge eating, sexual masochism, anorexia, drug addiction, hysteria, workaholism, dedicated jogging, world class sports competition, and the like.[6]

Such a definition of ascetic self-denial is a boon to an indigenous Christian exploration of the meaning of Christian asceticism insofar as it helps to link and compare modern and secular practices to both ancient and modern Christian asceticism. Such comparison can

---

3   *Ibid.*, 168.
4   *Ibid.*, 162.
5   *Ibid.*; See Stephen A. Mitchell, *Relational Concepts in Psychoanalysis: An Integration* (Cambridge, MA: Harvard Univ. Press, 1988), and Rome Harre, *Social Being: A Theory for Social Psychology* (Totowa, NJ: Rowman and Littlefield, 1980).
6   Malina, 162.

actually aid Christian reflection in its ascetic goal of cultural critique. The problem with applying Malina's insights to an indigenous Christian understanding of ascesis is its failure to recognize that asceticism always entails a transcendent orientation, unlike those practices listed in the above quotation.[7] This immanent account of ascesis explains Malina's exclusion of the ecstatic, and not merely "shrinking" aspect of Christian ascetic self-denial.

Malina observes that antique culture defined the "self," first in terms of the physical body, and then secondarily (but with growing importance) in terms of the body as social unit with the self as socially "embedded."[8] Here one may discern the deep interrelation between the physical and social body that almost all recent students of asceticism have rediscovered or assumed. Malina deliberately sets such a "self" up in contrast to a modern or secular self. To this ancient definition of the self Malina contrasts the modern secular definition: "in the last century or so, especially in the West, the self began to take precedence over the group."[9]

Malina describes this as a kind of "new" religious-like faith in an "overgrown, overemphasized self:"[10] "each person is different, special and unique, with an obligation to cultivate inner potential in order to achieve his or her specially assigned destiny."[11] This bloated self of the modern secular situation requires a different kind of "shrinkage" than the ancient self, but first a look into Malina's description of the shrinkage of the self in Christian antiquity is in order.

Recall that according to Malina, shrinkage of the self always entails avoidance and attainment goals. But it is also the avoidance and attainment of goals that represent a contrast to the self as currently socially defined. Therefore, in the ancient context of self as physical body within a tight body politic, shrinkage of the self turns out to mean a rejection of these deeply penetrating social bonds and ties.[12] So the self that is "shrunk" is the self as defined by society. Thus, instead of "fitting in," the ascetic self "stands out" as an individual over against communal society. Although one could construe this as an escape from a self that society has already fashioned to an individually

---

[7]   Flood, 2; (see Intro., nt. 34).
[8]   Malina, 164.
[9]   *Ibid.*, 165.
[10] *Ibid.*
[11] *Ibid.*
[12] *Ibid.*, 163.

produced definition of the self, Malina does not pursue that possibility. According to Malina, shrinkage of the self does not produce a new self; it only rejects and "escapes from awareness of the self."[13]

Malina then contrasts this ancient mode of ascetic self-denial with modern secular ascetic-like behavior. The one constant is that ascetic self-denial attempts to dislodge the individual from its current societal definition as a self. Recall that Malina describes the modern secular definition of the self as a kind of "bloated" individualism, that is, one that has, in contrast to an ancient account of the self, already rejected the body politic as its chief defining factor. The modern self takes on its own individual burden to maintain itself in this bloated form over and against the now subordinated social obligations.[14] Self-shrinkage in the modern and secular context would then seem to require a rejection of self-maintenance over against corporate societal institutions. It would seem to imply a return to the communal and to the traditionary. But this is not the direction Malina takes his argument.[15]

Instead, Malina pursues the performance of ascetic activity in the context of what he calls the "free-standing" modern secular social institutions in general, and in the United States in particular. He contrasts these freestanding institutions to the more enmeshed vision of societal structure in antiquity: "[t]he modern individual is socialized into a society in which kinship, politics, religion and economics are

---

[13]   In the same volume, Elizabeth A. Castelli, "Asceticism- Audience and Resistance: Response to the Three Preceding Papers," in *Asceticism*, eds. Vincent L. Wimbush and Richard Valantasis (New York: Oxford Univ. Press, 1995), 185, critiques this part of Malina's argument. "In general," she asserts, "I wonder whether asceticism is better defined, not as an escape from self-awareness, but rather as an intensification of self-awareness." Gavin Flood has similar points to make about asceticism as an "intensification" of the self: "It is almost as though the restriction undergone in asceticism is a necessary condition for the *intensification of subjectivity* that transcends desire and individualism" (Flood, 14; italics mine). This points to the critique and re-contextualization that is the goal of this particular chapter: ascetic self-denial as turning from one kind of self to another, transcendentally defined self.

[14]   Malina, 165.

[15]   Castelli also picks up that Malina does not take what seems to be an almost obvious direction for his argument here. Insofar as religious tradition, and particularly western religious and ascetic tradition, is defined by *textuality*, Castelli objects that "Malina's hermeneutic of asceticism does not engage textuality or discourse, but focuses rather on the social effects of a large range of behaviors . . . Malina's ascetics are not readers and interpreters" (Castelli, 179).

perceived and treated as free-standing social institutions."[16] Malina then construes modern secular ascetic-like behavior involving self-denial in terms of its context within these separate social institutions,[17] focusing on the individual's relationship to the market. Malina argues his thesis of contextual self-denial in terms of the "asceticism" of the "workaholic" businessperson who is today's modern "monk,"[18] placing commitment to economic security and success above all other personal and societal goals.[19]

As observed above, even though Malina conflates practices without transcendent ends with truly ascetic practices, the insight of his comparison has nevertheless the potential of bearing much fruit for Christian reflection on asceticism and Christian cultural criticism.[20] Furthermore, Malina leaves his reader with the insight that self-denial as self-humiliation and the endurance of self-inflicted pain has the potential of gaining power and honor within societal structures and institutions that legitimate such sacrifice on their behalf.[21] But despite these illuminating points, Malina's systematic exclusion of the transcendent from his definition of ascesis and ascetic self-denial, makes his definition ultimately problematic for use within the logic of Christian thought.[22] Christianity seeks transcendent aims, and therefore Christian thought cannot define "self-denial" only in terms of "shrinking" the self. The thought of John Zizioulas provides a Christian context wherein an indigenous Christian account of ascetic self-denial may make use of Malina's insights.

---

[16] Malina, 168.

[17] *Ibid.*, 169.

[18] *Ibid.*

[19] Again, Castelli finds difficulty in accepting Malina's comparison of "workaholism" to ascetic self-denial: "I would probably interpret U.S. capitalism as more gluttonous than ascetic" (Castelli, 187).

[20] For example, a Christian writer could declare contemporary society's "false" ascesis of "business" to be simply another form of greed with a built-in self-justification, and contrast it to "true" ascesis, which has the love of God and love of neighbor as its end.

[21] Malina, 170.

[22] This approach would be problematic to academic post-critical thought as well, whether Christian or not.

Zizioulas and Christian Personhood

IN HIS MAGNUM OPUS, *Being as Communion*, Zizioulas pulls together a Christian anthropology and ecclesiology in relationship to Orthodox Trinitarian teaching. At the heart of this Christian anthropology and ecclesiology is his development of the category of "personhood." According to Zizioulas, the Christian teaching of the Trinity actually teaches the very meaning of *personhood* itself—whether created or uncreate. In fact, Zizioulas makes a bold but dangerously tenuous[23] argument that Christian reflection on God's triune nature actually had direct ramifications upon the development of the concept of "person" in western thought. Whether or not one can determine the veracity of Zizioulas' historical claim, the focus of this project is constructive, and that will be the focus of this exposition of Zizioulas.

Zizioulas approaches Christian reflection from an Eastern Orthodox perspective that assumes the overarching eastern Christian vision of deification or *theosis*:

> [S]oteriology means, as it was the case in the patristic period, not so much a juridical reality by means of which forgiveness is granted for an act of disobedience, but rather a realization of *theosis*, as communion of man—and through him of creation—in the very life of the Trinity . . .[24]

Zizioulas counters a soteriology within the horizon of *theosis* to a caricature of a Western soteriology of substitutionary atonement.[25] More importantly, however, Zizioulas takes up *theosis* as the Eastern Christian understanding of human being's ontological foundation in the ecstatic being of God through its creation as *imago Dei*, together with the Christian and ecclesial practice of restoring and developing union with God after the fall through the work of Jesus Christ, the God-man. One may not identify *theosis*, as the Christian vision of ontological and eventually total personal union with God, with either Hellenic epic *apotheosis* on the one hand, or a panentheistic

---

23   Lewis Ayres, 313, (see Intro., nt. 8), expresses the view of many historians and historical theologians in revealing the difficulties he has with this historical claim on Zizioulas' part.

24   John D. Zizioulas, *Being as Communion* (Crestwood, NY: St. Vladimir's Seminary Press, 2002), 211.

25   This is typical of Eastern Orthodox polemic with the Western Christian tradition. Often Anselm of Canterbury is blamed as the source of the West's "dangerous" and "erroneous" soteriology. For more on this argument, see David Hart, "A Gift Exceeding Every Debt: An Eastern Orthodox Appreciation of Anselm's *Cur Deus Homo*," *Pro Ecclesia* 7 (Summer 1998), 333–49.

"absorption" on the other;[26] and this is chiefly because the practice of this union with God, as Christian and ascetic, works out in terms of "personhood" and communion, and not in philosophical (or mythomorphic) terms of realization of, or absorption within, substances or natures.[27]

Zizioulas elaborates his argument, in part, as a polemic against just such misleading "substantialist" ontologies. So, within this Eastern Christian context of *theosis*, Zizioulas works out his vision of personhood as ecstatic, that is, as having its ground outside itself in the other, in communion. Andrew Louth makes the important point that *theosis* within Orthodox Christianity does not simply serve as an equivalent to a soteriology of sanctification as is found in Western Christianity, but is actually of archetypal structural significance within Orthodox Christianity.[28] It constitutes a counterpart to the teaching of the incarnation and encompasses the teachings of the (economic) Trinity, Christian anthropology, and the nature of creation as a whole.[29] Louth delineates two major contours to *theosis* as an ar-

---

[26]   James Starr, "Does 2 Peter 1:4 Speak of Deification?" (paper delivered at *Partakers of the Divine Nature* lectures at Drew University, Madison, NJ, 21 May 2004). See also James Starr, *Sharers in Divine Nature, 2 Peter 1:4 in Its Hellenistic Context*, Coniectanea Biblica, New Testament Series 33 (Stockholm: Almquist and Wiksell International, 2000).

[27]   Eugene Rogers, *After the Spirit: A Constructive Pneumatology from Resources Outside the Modern West* (Grand Rapids: William B. Eerdmans, 1995), 47-49, explains the danger the Christian theologian confronts in making claims concerning *theosis* as the danger of blurring the very creature and creator distinction that drives and makes the logic of the incarnation and *theosis* possible. In order to avoid these problems, Rogers lays down four traditional ground rules for Christian discourse about *theosis*: 1) *Theosis* crosses but does not erase the ontological divide; 2) Human persons share in the divine nature, but they do not become divine *Persons*; i.e., they do not become further *hypostases* within the Trinity; 3) Whatever the case, there is no human, or for that matter creaturely, participation in the divine act of creation itself; 4) Finally, when this participation is understood as proper to human being itself, it is a share in the divine characteristics promised as what Christians would traditionally call "salvation" or "glorification."

[28]   Andrew Louth, "The Place of Deification in Modern Orthodox Theology," (paper delivered at *Partakers of the Divine Nature* lectures at Drew Univ., Madison, NJ, 21 May 2004).

[29]   Gregory Collins, "Simeon the New Theologian: An Ascetical Theology for Middle-Byzantine Monks," in *Asceticism*, eds. Vincent L. Wimbush and Richard Valantasis (New York: Oxford Univ. Press, 1995), 343, makes the claim that Chalcedonian dyophysite Christology is also a high Christology of redemption

chetypal structuring element within orthodoxy: the role of ascesis as a necessary commitment to the practice of *theosis* as a process, and the role of the apophatic in theology as actually formative of the link between God and human being in the *imago Dei*, rather than merely verbal negation.[30]

In discussing the meaning of personhood, Zizioulas explores what he claims to be the "discovery" of the concept of person on the part of the fathers of the church.[31] Zizioulas claims that, in ancient thought, "personhood does not have any ontological content."[32] In Latin, the very word "person" (*persona*) means merely "mask,"[33] and in the conceptual framework of pre-Christian antiquity, a human being is merely part of a greater cosmic process to which his or her "person" is reducible. Personhood is reducible to other ontological principles because of what Zizioulas refers to as Greek philosophical Monism, "the being of the world and the being of God formed, for the ancient Greeks, an unbreakable unity."[34] Following logically upon this ancient Greek ontological Monism, the principle of "being" is always more fundamental than any particular being, be that God or a human person. The church fathers alone were able to understand and define personhood in such a way as to leave it irreducible to any other "higher," or "deeper" ontological principle:

> The substance of God, "God," has no ontological content, no true being, apart from communion . . . Nothing in existence is conceivable in itself as an individual . . . God exists thanks to an event of communion . . . it is

---

through *theosis*. John Damascene later synthesizes this faith in the east, but given the common inheritance of the Council of Chalcedon, *theosis* is actually something common to both east and west.

[30]   There is more on the connection between ascesis, *theosis* and apophatic theology in chapters five and six.

[31]   Throughout the introduction to *Being as Communion*, Zizioulas makes reference to the "fathers of the church" as a whole, but throughout the rest of the work he tends to refer only to those he calls the "Greek fathers." This reflects Zizioulas' share in the general Eastern Orthodox mistrust of Western Christian traditions, including Western fathers. In order to reflect the more ecumenical orientation of the work as a whole, especially as represented within his introduction, the author simply makes note of Zizioulas' references to "the church fathers," regardless of qualifiers he may later add.(15-26)

[32]   Zizioulas, 34.

[33]   *Ibid.*, 33—35.

[34]   *Ibid.*, 16.

communion which makes being "be": nothing exits without it, not even God.[35]

So Zizioulas constructs an ontology, grounded in the patristic theological tradition, where being itself proves secondary to theological reality, the theological event that is personhood in communion.

How did the fathers discern such an understanding of personhood? Christian reflection on the nature of God that led to the teaching of the Trinity is nothing less than reflection upon the nature of personhood, according to Zizioulas, for the triune God is the ground of all personhood: "The Holy Trinity is a *primordial* ontological concept and not a notion which is added to the divine substance or rather which follows it [logically] . . ."[36] Zizioulas explains, "the concept of the person with its absolute and ontological content was born historically from the endeavor of the Church to give ontological expression to its faith in the Triune God."[37] So, only the personhood of God has "absolute ontological content" because Christianity teaches that God is *personal*, that is to say, God is (at least one) person; God possess personhood. This Christian teaching of the personhood of God opposes an attribution of the same such "absolute ontological content" to "God" as denoting an abstract "substance" or "being:" "It would be unthinkable to speak of the 'one God' [as substance] before speaking of the God who is 'communion,' that is to say, of the Holy Trinity."[38] "The ontological 'principle' of God is traced back, once again, to the person."[39] In other words, the divine being is not grounded upon an abstract ontological principle or upon some kind of generic divine "substance" from which one could make such abstractions. The fathers, according to Zizioulas, radicalized ontology by defining the na-

---

[35]   *Ibid.*, 17.

[36]   *Ibid.*

[37]   *Ibid.*, 36; The claim that the fathers in general, and Athanasius in particular, argued for an ontological expression of the Christian experience of God as triune is further supported by Khaled Anatolios,"The Immediately Triune God: A Patristic Response to Schleiermacher," *Pro Ecclesia* 10 (Spring 2001), 160.: "The formulation of classical Trinitarian doctrine is grounded precisely in the experience of being in an unqualifiedly immediate relation to God and is meant to express and safeguard that experience of immediacy [through ontological discourse]."

[38]   Zizioulas, 17.

[39]   *Ibid.*, 41.

ture of "being" itself as personhood. God is because God is person, and God is person because God is *communion*.

Following the logic of such an ontology, if one is to understand the nature of *being* one must understand the nature of *personhood*. The reality of personhood, Zizioulas explains, mutually grounds communion, and vice versa. Without communion there can be no person; without person there can be no communion. And without this mutual person-communion reality, there is no "being," no ontology:

> (a) There is no true being without communion. Nothing exists as an "individual," conceivable in itself. Communion is an ontological category.
>
> (b) Communion which does not come from a "hypostasis," that is, a concrete and free person, and which does not lead to "hypostases," that is concrete and free persons, is not an "image" of the being of God. The person cannot exist without communion; but every form of communion which denies or suppresses the person, is inadmissible.[40]

But how may one discern either person or communion if both are dependent upon the other? This is a Christian reality, granted by revelation, which only the practice of Christianity makes accessible:

> Philosophy can arrive at the confirmation of the reality of the person, but only theology can treat of the genuine, the authentic person, because the authentic person, as absolute ontological freedom, must be "uncreated," that is, unbounded by any "necessity," including its own existence [and therefore God]. If such a person does not exist in reality, the concept of the person is a presumptuous daydream. If God does not exist, the person does not exist.[41]

The reality of the mutual grounding of being in a communion of persons obtains only in God's self-grounding triune infinitude: the only ultimate and eternal reality.

God grounds all being and reality as an eternal communion of persons who love in freedom. Zizioulas opposes, consistent with his reading of the fathers, any notion of the Trinity that would ground the reality of the divine persons within some abstract "substance" which the three share. God is not God because of some kind of "God-stuff," some kind of divine substance that pre-exists—either temporally or logically—God's reality as a *personal* being. It is because God lives as the "Father" that is, as *person*, that God has being. And the Father is a *person* because he lives in communion with the Son and the

---

[40]　*Ibid.*, 18.
[41]　*Ibid.*, 43.

Spirit by eternally begetting and "spirating" each of these divine persons, respectively:

> The one divine substance is consequently the being of God only because it has the three modes of existence, which it owes *not to the substance but to one person*, the Father. Outside the Trinity there is no God, that is, no divine substance, because the ontological "principle" of God is the Father. The being of God is identified with the person.[42]

The ontological "principle" of God is not to be found in a neat ontological term such as "substance," but in the dangerously vague but living reality of "person," in this case, the person of the Father.[43]

Therefore God is "one" not in virtue of some abstract principle of "substance," but because of the one "Father, who is the '*cause*' both of the generation of the Son and of the procession of the Spirit."[44] The teaching of God in Christianity is the teaching of *Trinity*, not the teaching of a philosophically discernable substance. And the teaching of Trinity teaches God the Father, who begets the Son and breathes the Spirit, generating and living within a communion of infinite, mutual love and freedom:

---

[42] *Ibid.*, 41.

[43] "Dangerously vague" here means that under Zizioulas' and similar theologies, "person" is that category or term that is shared between the sundered sides of the ontological divide, namely, God and creation. The common term "person" provides a means to express the point of contact between creation and its creator. But for the very same reason, as a term, it must be rather "content free" in terms of any substantial definition in order to maintain the strictness of that very divide. Zizioulas achieves this by defining "person" in terms of relationality. His thought here hints at and may be expanded towards a non-substantive definition of "person" *as performance*—a performance that is capable of execution by realities on either side of the ontological divide: God and human persons (human persons by the help of divine persons, of course). This performance is nothing less than the performance of grounding one's personal being in that of someone else—it is a performance of *ecstasy*. Because this is *Christian* ecstasy, that someone, for persons on both sides of the ontological divide, is God.

[44] *Ibid.*, 41; italics mine. The Father as "cause" of the Son and Spirit, and, therefore, of the communion that constitutes deity, is what is actually at the heart of the classical Trinitarian doctrine of the "divine monarchy," where "mono-" is parsed as "single," and "arche" is parsed as "source." Thus *monarchia* simply means "single source," not despot or some other metaphor indicating inequality or subordination *with regards to deity* within the Godhead. See, for example, Thomas Aquinas *Summa Theologica* I.33. Contrast this with the Trinitarian heresy of *Monarchianism*, which is a kind of subordinationism.

> This *ecstatic* character of God, the fact that His being is identical with an act of communion, ensures the transcendence of the ontological necessity which His substance would have demanded—if the substance were the primary ontological predicate of God—and replaces this necessity with the free self-affirmation of divine existence. For this communion is a product of freedom as a result not of the substance of God but of a person, the Father—observe why this doctrinal detail is so important—who is Trinity not because the divine nature is ecstatic but because the Father as a *person* freely wills this communion.[45]

Communion means "standing outside one's" person in relationship to other persons, and this "standing outside" is *ecstasy*. Zizioulas recognizes just such ecstasy as the very ground of being. For God's own being as communion is *ecstatic*—not as an ecstatically existing *substance*, but rather as the concrete ecstasy of a *person*: the Father in a communion of love with other persons, Son and Spirit, who, in turn, share in similar *ecstasis* with and within the Father. Thus, the fundamental unity, the fundamental "oneness" of the God of Christian monotheism is one God, the Father, in a *communion* of persons, Son and Spirit; and therefore, any ontology grounded in such Christian theological reflection defines being as nothing less than communion *in ecstasy*.

In virtue of this theological context of Christian ontology, Zizioulas pursues a Christian anthropology that corresponds, as an image, to this vision of the Trinity as ecstatic being of persons in communion. Human being as *imago Dei*, therefore, is not some kind of abstract "nature" or "substance" any more than is the being of God, "it is precisely this that gives man, in spite of his different nature, his hope of becoming an authentic person."[46] In virtue of her creation in *imago Dei*, being human means to exist as *person(s) in communion*. Zizioulas clearly delineates that human nature ("man") is qualitatively different from that of God. Nevertheless, the hope for genuine personhood is found in the Godhead through *theosis*, through communion with God. God grants authenticity of human personhood in communion, primarily, with the divine persons of the triune God, but also, secondarily, in communion with other human persons—reflecting as an analogue at a finite level the infinite communion of the divine persons. One cannot reduce being human to an abstract ontological category anymore than one could reduce the divine being to such

---

[45]   Zizioulas, 44; italics mine for "ecstatic."
[46]   *Ibid.*, 44.

categories; but, as with God, human personhood must be understood as *ecstatic* personhood *in communion*.

The Christian teaching of the fall subtly nuances this vision of being as ecstasy of personhood in communion. The Christian may understand the fall, according to Zizioulas, as the result of an attempt on the part of the human person to establish human *being* as God establishes God's own divine being—within its own, independent reality. Only God, however, can ground God's own being in God's own self-same but infinite reality of divinity. Human being, as created, can only ground being upon its source—God:

> Between the being of God and that of man remains the gulf of creaturehood, and creaturehood means precisely this: the being of each human person is given to him; consequently, the human person is not able to free himself absolutely from his "nature" or from his "substance," from what biological laws dictate to him, without bringing about his annihilation.[47]

The fall keeps human being from actualizing true humanity as persons in communion by dislodging human being from its ground and source—being as communion of the Godhead—and this dislodging leads only to death.[48]

Another result of the fall, therefore, is that human personhood is taken out of its proper context within the loving and ecstatic communion of God and other human persons within God. This dislodging of human being from the divine being leads inevitably to its dissolution:

> [O]utside the communion of love the person loses its uniqueness and becomes a being like other beings, a "thing" without absolute "identity" and "name," without a face. Death for a person means ceasing to love and to be loved, ceasing to be unique and unrepeatable, whereas life for the person means the survival of the uniqueness of its hypostasis, which is affirmed and maintained by love.[49]

---

[47] *Ibid.*, 18—19.

[48] *Ibid.*, 47, speaks further about the difference between death as biological and death as theological reality: "Death becomes tragic and unacceptable only when man is regarded as *person*, and above all as hypostasis and unique identity. As a biological event death is something natural and welcome, because only in this way is life perpetuated" (italics mine).

[49] *Ibid.*, 49.

God creates human being in *imago Dei*, grounded in the imitation of God.[50] This imitation is twofold. Being human means to imitate God through existing as grounded in God's own infinite being, just as God grounds God's own being in God. Being human also means to imitate God as a communion of love among persons, both divine and human. The Fall, however, entails a false imitation of God: human being attempts to ground its own being in a false and futile imitation of God's self-grounding ecstasy. The immediate result is a fall from both the loving communion of the divine persons and loving communion among human persons.

Zizioulas' discussion of ecclesiology follows on his reflections on the fall, for he understands the church to be God's answer to the problem of the loss of loving communion among divine and human persons. The church is the site of *theosis*, wherein God reestablishes ecstatic being and personhood. It is the church that restores human being to its true humanity by reestablishing full personhood. So human being receives, again, its full, true personhood, its "ecclesial being,"[51] in communion with the divine as disclosed in the frail and haphazard human institution called church:

> The ecclesial existence of man, his hypostisization [sic.] in a eucharistic manner, thus constitutes a pledge, an "earnest," of the final victory of man over death. This victory will be a victory not of nature but of the person, and consequently not a victory of man in his self-sufficiency but of man in his hypostatic union with God, that is a victory of Christ as the man of patristic Christology.[52]

Christ, as the God-man, re-connects the true reality of being human with and within God's triune personhood:

> Jesus Christ does not justify the title of Savior because he brings the world a beautiful revelation, a sublime teaching about the person, but because He realizes in history *the very reality of the person* and makes it the basis and "hypostasis" of the person for every man.[53]

Although it may be more or less clear how Christ re-connects human and divine reality, it is less clear how individual human persons

---

50   The connection between human being created in *imago Dei* and its performative expression in human imitation of God will be further fleshed out below, in chapter two.

51   *Ibid.*, 53.

52   *Ibid.*, 64.

53   *Ibid.*, 54.

benefit from that re-connection. For the answer to that, Zizioulas turns to Pneumatology.

The Spirit gives human persons a share in Christ's reconnection of divine and human being by granting them *incorporation* within the body of Christ. The same Spirit by whom God the Son became incarnate of the Virgin Mary adopts other human persons and grafts them into the living Christ:

> Another important contribution of the Holy Spirit to the Christ event is that, because of the involvement of the Holy Spirit in the economy, Christ is not just an individual, not "one" but "many." This "corporate personality" of Christ is impossible to conceive without Pneumatology.[54]

And further:

> The Spirit is not something that "animates" a Church which already somehow exists. The Spirit makes the Church *be*. Pneumatology does not refer to the well-being but the very being of the Church. It is not about a dynamism which is added to the essence of the Church. It is the very essence of the Church.[55]

The Spirit manifests human incorporation in the Body of Christ chiefly and visibly at the meal of Thanksgiving, that is, the Eucharist, as the concrete reality of *communion* within temporal and physical human existence. Speaking of the early Christian church, Zizioulas writes:

> [T]he eucharist was not the act of a pre-existing Church; it was an event *constitutive* of the being of the Church, enabling the Church to *be*. The eucharist *constituted* the Church's being.[56]

So Zizioulas reflects upon the nature of personhood within the overall Eastern Christian framework of *theosis* and the teaching of God as Trinity. In this way Zizioulas plays out his ontology of communal and ecstatic personhood in terms of Orthodox ecclesiology and liturgical theology.

Theosis and Ecstasy, Missions and Processions

WHEN PERSONHOOD IS DEFINED as ecstatically grounded in communion, self-denial takes on a different set of possible meanings. Christian personhood, which according to Zizioulas simply derives its being in communion, entails within it inherently a kind of "self-

---

[54]   *Ibid.*, 130.
[55]   *Ibid.*, 132.
[56]   *Ibid.*, 21.

denial," insofar as ecstasy implies the "denial" of the person as a self-grounding entity. However, this is a *metaphorical* (and non-analogical) use of the term "self-denial," because, in the ecstasy of communion, "self"[57] is not so much denied as simply mutually and communally granted. In this case, "self-denial" in its robust and proper sense serves as an answer to the fallen condition of being human. The "self" that is denied in this sense is no real self, that is, not the person that God has created, but the false self that the futile attempt to ground one's own being has produced.

Within recent asceticism literature there is a kind of continuum of possible construals of the relationship of ascesis to the "self." Malina says that the self is "shrunk" by ascesis. Most others, such as Peter Brown for example, say that far from shrinking the self, the self is actually asserting itself, politically, through ascesis. Finally, somewhere in the middle, one finds Kallistos Ware,[58] who says that the self is fulfilled in ascesis. Christianity asserts the paradox of finding oneself only by losing oneself in the life of Christian discipleship. Especially in the theology of John Zizioulas, the paradox of "person" in the Christian tradition makes sense in light of the Christian ascetic teaching of the Trinity. The radical continuum in scholarship is a misunderstanding, or simple lack of apprehension, of the paradox inherent in the Christian ascetic practice of the teaching of the Trinity.

The examination of Zizioulas, above, noted that communion means "standing outside one's" person in relationship to other persons, and this "standing outside" is *ecstasy*. Recall that Zizioulas recognizes ecstasy as the very ground of being. For God's own being as communion is *ecstatic*—not as an ecstatically existing substance, but rather as the concrete ecstasy of a *person*: the Father in a communion of love with other persons, Son and Spirit, who, in turn, share in simi-

---

[57] That is, insofar as "self" and "person" are really capable of being used as interchangeable terms. If one pushes this in the direction such that "self" is either a) merely a grammatical illusion, or b) actually a fallen corruption of personhood, then one could actually say that this ecstatic "self-denial" is more than merely metaphorical and is actually analogical, insofar as to affirm personhood is to deny both a) that the person is merely a grammatical illusion or (speaking in an ontologically stronger form) b) the fallen state of current created personhood.

[58] Kallistos Ware, "The Way of the Ascetics: Negative or Affirmative," in *Asceticism*, eds. Vincent L. Wimbush and Richard Valantasis (New York: Oxford Univ. Press, 1995), 4, explains that the ascetic life is that of *anachoresis* or withdrawal from the world. Perhaps such *anachoresis* might be logically coherent with the ecstatic *perichoresis* of the triune life.

lar *ecstasis* with and within the Father. Here the Christian teachings of the divine processions and *perichoresis* unfold. Because the divine missions directly correspond to the divine processions, Christian ecstasy (in *theosis*) forms an analogue to the Son and Spirit's ecstatic "return" to the Father in the *perichoresis* of the divine processions.

Insofar as Christian ascesis involves self-denial, ascesis is the shape that Christian *ecstasis* must take after the fall has robbed human being from her original state of being grounded in the life of God. Ascesis, therefore, *performs* Christian personhood. Ascesis teaches the triune God through the somatic performance of *ecstasis*, of being grounded in a person other than the self. In this process of *theosis* the Christian appropriates knowledge of God through direct ontological contact. Ascesis grants access to the life of God through a share in the ecstatic personhood of the triune life. In the context of such sharing, the human person realizes actual, existential knowledge of God.[59]

This theological context allows an indigenous Christian account of ascetic self-denial to make use of Malina's insights. Malina's scholarship, and others like it, may be useful in a Christian critique of the false asceticisms of modern culture. Ascesis, as radical and political embodiment of Christian teaching, rejects the coercively designated self of modern culture and economy. Christian thought could move in the direction Malina's argument failed to develop, where a "shrinkage of the self," that self that is consigned to human persons by modernity, would mean a rejection of the modern "bloated self" and the return to communal and traditionary modes of self definition. On that basis, one could argue that the church is an alternative body politic and self-forming society of discipline over-against the bloated self of modern individualism and radical autonomy.

Christian ecstasy (in *theosis*) forms an analogue to the Son's and the Spirit's ecstatic "return" to the Father in the *perichoresis* of the divine processions. Ascesis is the shape that this Christian *ecstasis* takes after the fall. Christian ascesis teaches, therefore, ecstatic personhood;

---

[59]   Robert L. Wilken, "Maximus the Confessor on the Affections in Historical Perspective," in *Asceticism*, eds. Vincent L. Wimbush and Richard Valantasis (New York: Oxford Univ. Press, 1995), 417- 418, treats of the connection of love to knowledge. In Maximus' thought, relation is required for knowledge, for love binds knower to thing known. When knowledge is construed as loving participation among persons, then love is a *natural* part of epistemology—love grounds knowledge, and not just virtue.

it renders concrete in the life of the Christian body the teaching of the Trinity as radical and ecstatic personhood.

CHAPTER TWO

Ascesis and the *imago Dei*

Let all bitterness and wrath and anger and clamor and slander be put away from you, with all malice, and be kind to one another, tenderhearted, forgiving one another, as God in Christ forgave you. Therefore be imitators of God, as beloved children. And walk in love, as Christ loved us and gave himself up for us, a fragrant offering and sacrifice to God.

Ephesians 4.31-5.2

THIS CHAPTER first clarifies and transforms Geoffrey Galt Harpham's description of ascesis as *mimetic*, in light of the thought of Pavel Florensky, in order to establish the constructive theological claim that ascesis is the shape that *mimesis*[1] takes after the fall when self-denial

---

[1] Throughout this book, use of the term *mimesis*, although similar to Erich Auerbach's famous use, is not identical to or derivative of that use. See Erich Auerbach's *Mimesis: The Representation of Reality in Western Literature*, trans. William R. Trask (Princeton, N.J.: Princeton Univ. Press, 2003). Auerbach gives a critical description of the role of literature in Western history as that of providing a kind of *mimesis* or imitation of reality. Throughout this book, however, the term is closer to its use as a technical philosophical phrase in ancient Greek philosophy. Platonic philosophy strictly distinguishes between divine (*demiourgia*) and human (*poetikai/techne*) creation. There is, however, one mode of creation that is shared by the gods and human being, and that is *mimesis*. *Mimesis* is the production of a *copy*. So, for example, a man may make a statue of himself, and the Demiurge creates the cosmos as an imitation of himself. In both these cases the Platonist would point out that the copy has a lower ontological status than the original. Plato employs this concept in order to explain that the sensible world is created in *mimesis* of the intelligible world. For a bibliography and commentary see Francis E. Peters, *Greek Philosophical Terms: A Historical Lexicon* (New York: New York Univ. Press, 1967), s.v. "Mimesis." One final note: John Thomas Higgins, "Toward the Good: Levinas, Platonism and Philosophy as Practice," (Ph.D. diss., Univ. of Virginia, 2004), provides a description of the relationship of the ancient philosophical pupil to his philosophical master as that of *somatic mimesis*.

becomes necessary in order to set fallen human *mimesis* right. Second, this chapter pushes this theological construction back into the divine life itself, and claims that the human process of corporate cultural production corresponds directly to the triune processions wherein the Logos proceeds as *image* of the Father. In this case, Christian ascesis performs the *imago Dei* as *mimesis* of God's own internal ecstatic and creative love. The thesis is that ascesis teaches *imago Dei*, as performance, by re-aligning broken human *mimesis*.

Harpham on the Ascetic Foundation of Culture

HARPHAM TAKES AN INTEREST in ascesis as a mimetic source of culture because he invests in the ethical implications of asceticism as a trope for both literary criticism and cultural production itself. Harpham asserts that criticism and cultural production are *ethical* insofar as they attempt imitable models of understanding or producing culture and cultural artifacts:

> Literary theory, especially as it concerns interpretation, is therefore a covertly but constantly ethical activity . . . Criticism exerts an ethical force not by arguing explicitly propositions about values or by challenging some values with others more fundamental, but by offering *imitable models of understanding*, models generalized and systematized by interpretation theory.[2]

Harpham wants to use Christian asceticism as a trope for the way that criticism provides a ground for ethics but cannot itself be considered a part of the field of ethics.[3] So too, asceticism grounds and "resists" culture, providing both the *mimesis* necessary for cultural production and the "self-denial" necessary to perform a critique of the results of such mimetic production.

Harpham generates a metaphor between ascesis as the matrix for cultural production and MS-DOS as an operating system on personal computers:

---

[2]   Harpham, 240; italics mine. (see Intro., nt. 21)

[3]   Here Harpham's reasoning is analogous to Aristotle's "sciences." The first principles of any science define that science but cannot, in turn, be defined in terms of that science. First principles of any given science must be founded by a higher science within the hierarchy of sciences. Likewise, ethics as the science of the "good life" must in turn be grounded upon asceticism as the science of simply being human (and therefore communal and cultural). Therefore criticism, as ascetic, provides ground for ethics; but if it takes sides it loses its ability to serve as a ground for ethics by simply becoming straightforwardly ethical. So, ascesis, for Harpham, is always *ethical,* but never *ethics.*

> As a new computer-literate, I find myself thinking of asceticism as a kind of MS-DOS of cultures, a fundamental operating ground on which the particular culture, the word processing program itself, is overlaid. Where there is culture there is asceticism: cultures structure asceticism, each in its own way, but do not impose it.[4]

Culture structures asceticism, but is itself grounded upon an ascetic "imperative" that culture does not, of itself, impose.

Like MS-DOS, ascesis is a necessary and programmed human activity, but it is "pre-cultural" in the way that MS-DOS is not yet actually any particular computer application or program. Software companies design applications to run on MS-DOS as their overarching operating system—thus rendering multiple applications mutually compatible. So too, then, the many "applications" that are necessary to "run" any given culture are "programmed" on top of ascesis in order to be mutually compatible. But the applications and their variations and combinations are infinite in possibility. According to Harpham, the element or core to the nature of ascesis that makes possible the "running" of culture "on-top" of it is *self-denial*.

All culture demands self-denial, for all culture demands the individual to curtail and structure his or her desires for the sake of the "whole" that both generates and is generated by, that given culture:

> [A]ll cultures are ethical cultures; for the idea of ethics is inescapably ascetical. No matter how hedonistic, materialistic, self-indulgent, wicked, or atomistic they may be, all cultures impose on their members the essential ascetic discipline of "self-denial," formulated by the Christian ascetics as the resistance to what Augustine calls "nature and nature's appetites."[5]

Self-denial is that purely intelligible reality[6] that human beings enact in their bodies and over the narratives of their lives that separate them from the natural world and thereby generate the distinction between nature and culture.[7]

---

4   Harpham, , xi.
5   *Ibid.*, xi—xii.
6   Self-denial in human behavior is the immediate fleshing out of purely intelligible realities, because "negation" is a purely linguistic phenomenon (*Ibid.*, 17). This links ascetic behavior to apophatic Christian thought. More on this follows, below, in part two.
7   Cultural generation and cultural criticism are immediately and structurally related, according to Harpham, insofar as the self-denial inherent in culture-building corresponds to the kind of self, or self-consciousness that is formed by asceticism and which may be described as "self-critical" (*Ibid.*, xii).

Harpham connects ascesis, as both the "ethical" and as cultural production, to *mimesis* through the (ethical) need to provide recognizable, and therefore intelligible, (ethical) models. Ascesis, as self-denial, structures and manages human desire, both communally and individually, and that is its chief power for generating culture.[8] But without the ability to understand and emulate such behavior, asceticism, and the culture it generates and perpetuates, could not be passed down. For Harpham, then, asceticism is that "ideology," or, more accurately, set of traditional practices, that both provides and enables human being to follow models.

Models can only be followed and imitated if they are intelligible to the follower. Harpham plays out the direct and even inherent coherence between intelligibility and imitability found in ascesis, where ascesis "is the way in which a human being can become imitable, how he can meet what are sometimes called the conditions of representation."[9] *Mimesis* is evident in all human arts but ascesis is *mimesis par excellence* because it fleshes out *the self* as a work of art, and "[t]he ascetic body is in this sense an exemplary artifact: what the ascetics displayed to their audience was precisely their form."[10]

This kind of ascetic *mimesis* finds its goal in intelligibility, and that understood as narratival and even linguistic. One can only imitate that which one understands. But, more importantly, one only understands that which is imitable, repeatable, and ascesis renders the otherwise inchoate body "self aware, structured, knowable, and valuable."[11] This is because the body is made a sign in the act of ascesis. It is made a sign for that which it attempts an imitation:

> For by characterizing an entire life as an "imitation of Christ," or as "a pattern for believers," asceticism both denigrates and dignifies the body, casting it at once as a transgressive force always on the side of "the world" and as the scene or stage for discipline, self-denial, ascesis.[12]

Ascesis renders the body intelligible by rendering it imitable, and it renders the body imitable through the repetition or imitation of an authoritative form or narrative. This allows Harpham to assert that,

---

[8]   *Ibid.*, 61.

[9]   *Ibid.*, xiv.

[10]   *Ibid.*, xv.

[11]   *Ibid.*

[12]   *Ibid.*, xiv; This quotation also clearly shows the paradox of the fall within creation in Christian thought, and, perhaps, Harpham's conflation of the two.

"from the ascetical point of view it is self-denial that is eminently imitable."[13]

Now the most obvious Christian candidate for imitation is Christ.[14] But ascesis does not always immediately imitate Christ. There is a means of imitating Christ that is more direct than ascesis, and that is martyrdom. The martyr performs a perfect *mimesis* of Christ in imitation of Christ's ultimate self-denial in his sacrifice on the cross. The ascetic imitates the martyr and thus extends *mimesis* from Christ to the contemporary ascetic:

> In the Pauline tradition, Christ was himself a "repetition" of Adam; *The Life of Anthony* carries repetition into the human community, showing how the origin of the Incarnation, already a repetition, could be extending into the future.[15]

Martyrs imitate their Lord, and martyrdom, then, is that which the ascetics attempt to replicate in their own bodies through simple and self-limiting self-denial.[16] In his explanation of this chain of *mimesis*, Harpham describes how "textuality" holds a central place in this (Christian) *mimesis*.

Harpham points to *The Life of Anthony* as the "master text of Western asceticism."[17] In it, Athanasius not only attempts to persuade others to imitate Anthony in his imitation of Christ, but, Harpham argues, Athanasius actually performs a narrative imitation of the saint through committing his life to the pages of his text. Hagiography itself is Christian *mimesis*:

---

13   *Ibid.*

14   Gregory Collins' article "Simeon the New Theologian," (see ch. 1, nt. 29) connects John Climacus and Maximus Confessor with regards to the imitation of Christ. Climacus defines a Christian as one who imitates Christ—thus tying the very definition of Christianity to *mimesis*! For Maximus, charity and service to others represent the clearest expression of such *imitatio Christi* (344).

15   Harpham, 84.

16   Harpham believes that, unlike ideology, asceticism is, by virtue of its approach, inherently self-limiting and self-critical. There are certain truisms to Christian ascesis, according to Harpham (*Ibid.*, 64—66): The first is that temptation defines the human condition. Second, temptation may be resisted. But the third is the most important, and that is that the greatest temptation is to believe that one is free from temptation due to the depth and success of one's ascesis. "This built-in limit to the perfectibility of the self gives asceticism a certain irreducibility, for it is both dynamic and static; the ascetic is constantly progressing, but never arrives" (43).

17   *Ibid.*, 3.

> The value of the text lies in its capacity to replace and extend the life of Anthony; the poetic function even enables the text to be superior as a "picture for ascetic practice" to Anthony himself. So both Athanasius and his readers strive for the impossible perfect imitation of Anthony.[18]

Hagiography performs, and thereby enables, the further performance of Christian ascetic *mimesis*.[19] Because "[w]e owe to asceticism the notion that the exemplary self is observable, and especially that it is narratable,"[20] therefore, to be ascetic is to be represent-able, and that renders the Christian ascetic the perfect occasion for literary production. The Christian ascetic is therefore "self-as-literature," as opposed to the old Pagan ascesis with its "self-as-work-of-art."[21] And this textual and literary nature of Christian asceticism brings the discussion within orbit of another key Christian reality, scripture.

The very textuality of Christian ascesis points in the direction of Christian scripture. Harpham describes hagiography as a *mimesis* of scripture in much the way that ascesis is a *mimesis* of Christ and the saints. In fact, the "tropological sense" of scripture is not the attempt to use scripture as a trope for the Christian life; rather, this spiritual sense of scripture indicates that it is in fact the saint's life that is a trope for the scriptures.[22] The scriptures are primary and "literal;" the Christian life becomes the trope. The saints, through either martyrdom or ascesis, "write" the scriptures upon their own bodies and the narrative structure of their lives. In doing so, the ascetic becomes not only imitable, not only representable, but *legible*—the saint becomes text:

> Asceticism is dominated by what might be called the ethics of legibility. What *The Life of Anthony* discovered and promoted was that the truest self of a man, his divine essence, was recuperable in his biography, which redeemed a contingent, sequential life on earth by representing it as an imitation, placing it in the line begun in the Gospels.[23]

---

[18] *Ibid.*, 5.

[19] In "Ascetic Closure," (see Intro., nt. 22) Averil Cameron describes, along the lines of Harpham, how ascesis is double linked to both the economy of desire and textual hermeneutics because Christian lives are expected to follow the pattern of the text. Ascetic texts themselves, therefore, are profoundly *mimetic* (154).

[20] Harpham, 27.

[21] *Ibid.*, 42. Harpham seems to generally adopt Foucault's appropriation of Seneca's description of ascesis as a techne of the self. For all its uses this chapter seeks to contrast *mimesis* to *techne* in its explication of the productive side of ascesis.

[22] *Ibid.*, 72. This book explores more on scripture, below, in chapter seven.

[23] *Ibid.*, 73.

The inchoate and contingent life of the unredeemed becomes the meaningful and "logofied" life of the saint when the saint recapitulates the life of Christ in the scriptures of the Gospels. In Harpham's writing, the distinction between culture and nature seems clear because culture is something human being constructs out of non-narratable and chaotic "pure" nature.[24] Christian culture is produced, therefore, by Christian ascesis, which is a textual mimetic chain starting with Adam and continuing through Christ and the saints to any given contemporary ascetic. But this scriptural chain of *mimesis* not only goes forward into the future for the claiming of humanity as lives of saints, it also goes back to the inner life of the God who inspires the scriptures and demands their imitation.

Christian *mimesis* is itself grounded in the second Person of the Trinity; God's own Logos is the "image" of the Father,[25] an imitation at the origin of all and the origin of all imitation.[26] Harpham discusses Augustine's conversion in these terms. Augustine reads about Anthony's imitation of Christ in Athanasius' own narratival *mimesis* of the same in the *Life of Anthony*. In this encounter with Christian textuality, Augustine converts because he is able to recognize that imitation of Christ is possible for him as well, because Christ "stands at the origin of imitation:"[27]

> This origin is itself an imitation, translating divine power into knowledge through what might be called primary repetition, originary imitation. In converting, Augustine is situating himself in the chain of imitation that extends back to and even includes the origin.[28]

The convert thus imitates Christ and, in so doing, becomes imitable.[29] Christ as both origin and *telos* brings the imitation full circle. In this case, Harpham gestures towards Jacques Derrida when he says that, like Derrida, the Christian ascetic actually wants to *perform* the assertion that, "*il n'y a pas de hors-texte*"[30]—the Christian ascetic wants

---

[24] Culture and some kind of "raw" nature may not be so easily separable within human nature, if God has designed human beings to *naturally* produce *culture* as a mimetic act of sub-creation.

[25] Colossians 1:15—19.

[26] In "Ascetic Closure," Cameron asserts that ascesis is essentially aesthetic, that is to say, a work of art and a literary creation as an embodiment of *logos* (153).

[27] Harpham, 96.

[28] *Ibid.*

[29] *Ibid.*, 120.

[30] *Ibid.*, 15; here Harpham quotes Jacques Derrida, *Of Grammatology*, trans. Gayatri Chakravorty Spivak (Baltimore: John Hopkins University Press, 1976), 158.

to be wholly consumed by the scriptural text, and ascesis is the means of purging all that might be "outside the text."[31]

So Harpham pursues his trope of criticism and cultural production as a Kantian-style "ascetic" imperative,[32] garnering insights along the way about the nature of Christian ascesis as mimetic, textual, and therefore scriptural. Especially insightful is his final connection of *mimesis* to the Logos himself. Many of Harpham's insights are generated by his initial identification of Christian ascesis with *mimesis*, and *mimesis* with criticism and cultural production. The only problem for the direct appropriation of Harpham's insights for use in the exposition of Christian ascesis as a practice indigenous to Christianity is his lack of logical distinction between self-denial and *mimesis* (as the source of cultural production) within Christian ascesis, especially insofar as he advances the claim that ascesis both founds and critiques culture. This is because, by virtue of his "critical" rather than indigenous approach, he cannot take the "doctrine" of the fall into account. But before "baptizing" Harpham's account of the ascetic source of human culture, this chapter turns to Florensky's thought for a Christian understanding of ascesis in light of the Christian teaching of creation and the fall.

Florensky on the Return to Creation in Ascesis

IN ORDER TO MAKE USE of Harpham's insights for a Christian theological account of ascesis, it is necessary to resettle some of his thought away from the immanent world-view of modern academic cultural criticism into the Christian and transcendent teaching of creation and fall. Pavel Florensky's magnum opus, *The Pillar and Ground of Truth*, constructs a Christian ascetical theology within the Christian teaching of creation in his pursuit of an Orthodox theodicy and aesthetical theology.[33] To reclaim Harpham's insights after

---

31 Harpham, 120.

32 *Ibid.*, 241.

33 Pavel Florensky's life spanned from the nineteenth through the early twentieth centuries. Although not banished by the communist party after the revolution, he was eventually commanded to silence and finally died in Siberian exile. All that Florensky might have produced is therefore unavailable. His most well known works include *The Pillar and Ground of Truth: An Essay in Orthodox Theodicy in Twelve Letters*, trans. Boris Jakim (Princeton, NJ: Princeton Univ. Press, 1997), originally published in 1914, and an informative and eccentric reflection upon

reflecting upon Florensky's theology of ascesis and creation, this chapter develops an analogy within the logic of Christian thought that ascesis serves as a kind of "fever," that heals the "infected" *mimesis* of the now fallen *imago Dei*.

The subtitle for Florensky's *Pillar and Ground of the Truth* is *An Essay in Orthodox Theodicy in Twelve Letters*. A theodicy is usually an attempt to justify God in terms of human justice, reconciling God's omnipotence with God's goodness.[34] But that is not the sense in which Florensky is using the term. In this case, Florensky seems to be using the term to refer to a kind of justification of the reality of God before the canons of modern, post-Kantian reason. In order to out-do Kant and his transcendental approach to human "pure" reason, Florensky takes one step further back than Kant and "poses an essential question about reason: 'How is rationality possible?'"[35]

Florensky answers this question in a way that assumes *participation*, and therefore, that epistemology and ontology are inseparable:

> The answer to this question went like this: "Rationality is possible not in itself but through the object of its thought . . . Finally, "rationality is possible if Absolute Actual Infinity is given to it." But what is this Infinity? It turns out that such an Object of thought, making thought possible, is the Trihypostatic Unity [of the Trinity].[36]

Florensky, *contra* modern thought, places reason back in the object, and, specifically, in the only infinite "Object:" the triune God. So, instead of developing a "method" for overcoming the problem of knowledge caused by the difference between subject and object, Florensky pursues an Orthodox theodicy through an aesthetical theology, whereby "beholding the form"[37] of *beauty* means

---

icons originally published in 1922, *Iconostasis*, trans. Donald Sheehan and Olga Andrejev (Crestwood, NY: St. Vladimir's Seminary Press, 2000).

[34] "Etymologically the justification of God. The word was coined by F. W. Leibniz . . . and since then it has been applied to that part of natural theology which is concerned to defend the goodness and omnipotence of God against objections arising from the existence of evil in the world . . . Theodicy came to be more and more regarded in connection with the entire complex of Natural Theology, of which it is now sometimes used as a synonym." *Oxford Dictionary of the Christian Church*, 1997 ed., s.v. "Theodicy."

[35] Florensky, *The Pillar and Ground of Truth*, 347.

[36] *Ibid.*

[37] This phrase represents a deliberate use of Hans Urs von Balthasar's phrase used throughout his work, *The Glory of the Lord*, vol. 1, *Seeing the Form* (San Francisco: Ignatius Press, 1982). Both von Balthasar and Florensky are trying to overcome

participation in beauty and, thereby, knowledge of God and reality through that beauty.

Because God is beauty itself, and because rationality is possible only in God as infinite object,[38] participation in beauty is the means of rationality and rational knowing. The form of beauty is God's triune being, and that triune being as ecstatically self-grounding. The ascetic actually participates in this divine self-grounding through the "purifications" of ascesis:

> [Ascesis leads one] to the absolute root of creation, when, washed by the Holy Spirit, separated from his selfhood through self-purification, he has found in himself his own absolute root—that root of creation which is given to him through coparticipation in the depths of Trinitarian [and, therefore, ecstatic] Love.[39]

The ecstatic "*kenosis*-like" self-grounding love of the triune God is the infinite form of beauty itself. Human participation in this infinite form of beauty, in the current, fallen human condition, requires the aid of the Christian ascetic tradition—for human beauty (as *mimesis*) has now been transformed by the life of Christ. Ascesis thus makes existential knowledge of God possible as a kind of mystical experience, but a real experience nonetheless.[40] So Florensky links his Trinitarian theological aesthetics with a theology of ascesis.[41]

---

the kind of epistemological problems that the traditional modern subject and object division generates. Both look to aesthetics and beauty for a solution insofar as they both look to *form* as a category distinct from subjectivity or objectivity. Both are also attempting to solve the problem through a collapsing of this distinction in a participatory gnoseology where knowledge obtains through actual ontic participation in its object. See chapter three, below, on von Balthasar.

38 One way of understanding the epistemological problem that Florensky wishes to overcome is in terms of the "problem" of the principle of identity. Kant's epistemology demands that the human person (subject) take the world into herself (object) in order to gain knowledge. This is, according to Florensky, a kind of epistemological selfishness, solipsism, or narcissism. Florensky's Christian solution to this epistemological selfishness is to look to the Trinity. In the Christian triune God, otherness is possible in the same substance or being. Knowledge of different realities is possible without having to posit an insuperable ontological divide between the knower and the known. Thus, Florensky asserts that knowledge obtains where identity (hypostasis) and "sufficient reason" (infinity as ground of unity within difference) meet (Florensky, 347).

39 *Ibid.*, 230.

40 *Ibid.*, 47.

41 In "The Way of the Ascetics," Kallistos Ware quotes Florensky: "*Asceticism* produces not a good but a beautiful personality." His point is to show that asceti-

As part and parcel of this Christian theological aesthetics, Florensky grounds Christian ascetical theology in the Christian teaching of creation. Florensky dedicates an entire "letter," or chapter, to the Christian teaching of "Creation,"[42] but it focuses on ascesis as the affirmation of created reality in its current sinful state:

> Objectivity does exist. It is God's creation . . . [Objectivity is found] not with the creation that man has corrupted but with the creation that came out of the hands of its Creator; to see in this creation another, higher nature; through the crust of sin, to feel the pure core of God's creation . . . But to say this is to posit the requirement of a restored, i.e., a spiritual person. Once again, the question of asceticism arises.[43]

When one sees creation as its creator intended, as the "Sophia"[44] of God, then one has access to the mind of the Creator. How to discern creation as God intended it remains the main problem. Neither a "scientific" nor a "hermeneutical" method approaches a solution to this problem, only ascesis: "For it is not fasts and other bodily exercises, nor tears and good works that are the goods of an ascetic, but a personality restored in its integrity."[45] For only a person that is restored in his or her integrity can behold the form of God's beauty in creation such that real knowledge of God and reality obtain.

Florensky does not hold asceticism to be necessary as part of God's original will for creation, but rather as a response to and remedy for the current fallen state of God's creation. He quotes a contemporary Russian bishop[46] at length in order to explain this approach:

> [A]sceticism as the collection of certain kinds of limitations and restraints for the achievement of moral perfection was necessary not because Christianity requires this. No, Christianity requires of man only positive, moral development. But sinful man turns out to be wholly incapable of living

---

cism is not only ethical but also aesthetic—and the shape of the gospel narrative has transformed this aesthetic (3).

[42] Florensky, 190—230.

[43] *Ibid.*, 192.

[44] Florensky is one of the earliest of the Russian "Sophiologists." Florensky's "Sophia" is nothing more than the final result of the deification of creation as a single and whole rational hypostasis—God's will for reality made perfectly manifest.

[45] *Ibid.*, 192.

[46] In Florensky's endnote 452, he identifies this bishop as one Feodor Pozdeevsky, Rector of the Moscow Theological Academy. The following quotation is from "Lectures on Pastoral Theology: Asceticism," delivered in Sergiev Posad, Russia, 1911.

directly as this Christian ideal demands, and he is compelled to have recourse to various measures to suppress in himself the accumulated sinful content of life.[47]

This means that, were there never a fall there would never have been a need for ascesis. That is to say, the fall corrupts the human condition such that it no longer fully manifests God's intended human nature. Ascesis, within Christianity, represents those disciplines, which imitate Christ, that enable the ascetic to begin to return to full human nature.

What kind of activity would human beings engage in order to put themselves in contact with God and the rest of reality, were they in an unfallen state? *Mimesis* is the best way to conceive of human action at its natural level, regardless of its condition. Ascesis is therefore the shape that *mimesis* takes when human being finds itself in a fallen condition.[48] Ascesis is *mimesis* together with negating (and not merely ecstatic) self-denial. But, one may ask at this point, *mimesis*, or imitation, of what? Flood makes a good point when he shows that every scriptural and ascetic tradition attempts to remember a primordial and pristine past through corporeal or somatic imitation.[49] As already discovered above in exploring Harpham's thought, imitation returns as far as possible within the logic of Christian thought to a non-temporal but purely logical origin—the triune life of God. In Christian ascesis, it is the inner-life of the triune God that the Christian ultimately seeks to put into action. Another way of saying this is that the Christian teaching of the *imago Dei* is performative and not just static.[50] So, according to Christian teaching, human being performs

---

[47]   Florensky, 192-193.

[48]   Giulia Sfameni Gasparro, "Asceticism and Anthropology: Enkrateia and "Double Creation" in Early Christianity," in *Asceticism*, eds. Vincent L. Wimbush and Richard Valantasis (New York: Oxford Univ. Press, 1995), 127—146, points out that some early Christians saw the fall as a fall from *nature* into *culture*. And this is a valid historical point. But if one understands culture to be natural for human beings, and human being to be saved *qua* human, then culture must actually be both salvageable after the fall and producible on the part of human activity before the fall.

[49]   "Through ascetic performance the ascetic self looks back through tradition to an origin, to a source that also becomes a future goal" (Flood, 11).

[50]   Patristic theology makes a famous distinction between the "image" and "likeness" of God in exegesis of the first chapters of Genesis. The "image" is described as the static part of human nature as "substance" in the ancient sense. But already among the fathers a more dynamic view of the *imago Dei* was developed in

mimesis as the enactment of the *imago Dei*. But in order to find the point that links Harpham's ideas concerning *mimesis* to Florensky's notion of unfallen creation, this chapter looks to Florensky's theology of *Sophia*.

Ascesis is the Spirit's work of redirecting creation towards God in order once again to manifest God and reality within the created order. Sophia is the link between Florensky's aesthetic ascesis and Harpham's mimetic ascesis because "Sophia" is Florensky's hypostatization of divinized creation as a rational whole—creation itself being an image or imitation of the Logos; the Logos himself an image of the Father.

> [A]ll creation was revealed to our pilgrim as an eternal miracle of God, as a living being praying to its Creator and Father. Such a perception is highly typical for our pilgrims, and its individual features are embodied in many works of art.[51]

So both Harpham and Florensky recognize that God's intended pattern of human behavior (whether for the sake of discerning knowledge or producing culture—two sides of the same human reality) is found in imitation of the Logos, who, himself, is an imitation of the Father at the origin of all Being:

> [I have clarified ascesis as] this bridge leading the ascetic to the absolute root of creation . . . that root of creation which is given to him through coparticipation in the depths of Trinitarian Love. A new question necessarily arises now: How is creation thought in itself? This is the question of Sophia.[52]

Creation in itself is not ascetic—nor is human development of culture ascetic in itself. Creation in itself is the pure, mimetic participation of the created whole in its creator. Christian thought must affirm that there would be culture had there been no fall, just as there would have been full human beauty had there been no fall. But that requires the placing of a kind of nuance within Harpham's identification of ascesis with the root of all human culture. There must be a root to

---

terms of the "likeness of God." This "likeness" represents the *imago Dei* in its dynamic, mimetic sense of holiness through active contemplation and imitation. Florensky assumes this Patristic distinction in his own thought. See for example Irenaeus *Adversus Haerses* 5.16.2; Clement of Alexandria *Protrepticus* 12; Origen, *De Principiis* 3.6.1, *Contra Celsus* 4.30; Cyril of Jerusalem *Procatechesis* 14.10.

[51] Florensky, 230.

[52] *Ibid.*

human culture, to human "sub-creation"[53] that is "unfallen," which the self-denial inherent to ascesis attempts to set right.

But *mimesis* itself, without the fall to overcome, need not be ascetic, and Christian thought must assume that imitation of God would not have been ascetic had human being never fallen. Only God creates. Human culture, as human sub-creation, imitates the creativity of the triune God in God's inner-relationality. Christianity teaches that the unified action of the triune God creates, because the works of God that are "outside" of God, with respect to the Trinity *non divisa sunt.* The three divine Persons work in concert to bring about the logoi of creation within and according to the Logos of God.[54] Human being, in *imago Dei*, creates, or rather, sub-creates, in imitation of God—both in imitation of God's creativity, and of God's unity in community—for culture is a communal activity and achievement, *par excellence.*[55]

---

53   J. R. R. Tolkien coins this word in his article "On Fairy-Stories." Originally an Andrew Lang lecture given at the University of St. Andrews on 8 March 1939, it is reprinted in *The Monsters and the Critics and Other Essays* (London: Harper Collins, 1997, 109—161). Tolkien makes use of his neologism in order to describe the kind of literary reality achieved by what may be called "fairy story," "myth," or "fantasy:" "An essential power of Faërie [story] is thus the power of making immediately effective by the will the visions of 'fantasy' . . . This aspect of 'mythology"—*sub-creation*, rather than either representation or symbolic interpretation of the beauties and terrors of the world—is, I think, too little considered" (122; italics mine). His point is that the fantasy writer or "mythographer" is not attempting a *mimesis* of the created world as such, but a *mimesis of the very act of creation itself:* "What really happens is that the story-maker proves a successful 'sub-creator.' He makes a Secondary World which your mind can enter. Inside it, what he relates is 'true:' it accords with the laws of that world" (132). This chapter adopts this word and extends Tolkien's original intention in order to refer to the human act of cultural production and participation in general. Insofar as culture and myth, or literature (following Harpham), entail and participate in one another, it is faithful to Tolkien's intended use of the word. This word is also employed in order to deliberately eschew a more recent neologism "co-creation," used to refer to the relationship of divine and human partnership in the economy of creation. This more recent word fails to sufficiently address the infinitude of divine transcendence and, therefore, the impossibility of anything like a partnership of "equals" (implicit in the "co-" of "co-creation") to obtain between God and human being.

54   Here the term *logoi* is used in the sense employed by Maximus. George C. Berthold, ed., *Maximus the Confessor: Selected Writings*, Classics of Western Spirituality (Mahwah, NJ: Paulist Press, 1985).

55   Throughout *The Ascetic Self*, Harpham describes ascesis as the "resistance" to temptation necessary to make desire, as a human reality, possible. And desire

Ascesis, Mimesis *and the* imago Dei

REFLECTION ON Harpham's insights concerning ascesis in light of Florensky's Christian doctrine of creation provides the discovery that within the logic of Christian thought, *mimesis*, as a significant component of Christian ascesis, begins within the life of the triune God. The procession of the Logos from the Father is one of *mimesis*, for the Logos is the *image* of the Father—the Logos performs the super-rational imitation of the Father in the relationship that obtains between these two divine hypostases within the communion of the Spirit.[56] And, as Harpham discerns, imitation is at the very origin of all things. Imitation plays itself out, therefore, at every level of Christian teaching.

The actions of God outside the inner triune life are always a united act of all three divine Persons. Therefore creation itself is a mimetic act. God the Father creates through the Logos (that is to say, the Father's own eternal, hypostasized and perichoretic *mimesis*), in the Spirit. Creation through the Logos entails multitudinous created but rational *logoi* that both in their own created integrity, and especially in concert, reflect and imitate the infinite Logos through whom they find their being. Thus, in that creature that is created to be and to body forth the image of God, human being, one finds *mimesis* repeated again not only by participating in *theosis*, but by the act of subcreation, the act of human cultural production.[57] This human *mimesis*

---

yields human culture as a kind of "social contract" of compromise between various others and their competing desires. Yet again, however, Harpham confuses what Christianity must distinguish, given the doctrines of the creation and fall. If desire were not fallen, then human being would have no need of "self-denial" proper for the construction of communal and cultural human reality, because human desire is inherently designed for, and directed towards, human community.

[56]   Colossians 1:15—17: He is the image of the invisible God, the first-born of all creation; for in him all things were created, in heaven and on earth, visible and invisible . . . all things were created through him and for him. He is before all things, and in him all things hold together.

[57]   As important as sub-creation is to performing the *imago Dei*, contemplation of God is still higher than cultural production because the God whom Christians imitate has a life logically prior and superior to the act of creation. In order to imitate God's life, Christians must not only imitate what God does in creating, but who God is, logically prior to creation. Human contemplation therefore imitates the divine processions and God's life of perichoretic unity. Theology as contemplation will be explored in chapter five, below.

is the participation of human will in divine freedom and holds a part in the progressive nature of God's economy of human *theosis*.

In humanity's current, fallen condition, however, ascesis serves as *restorative mimesis*, a *mimesis* that both critiques and generates culture because it is the imitation of Christ who *recapitulates* human *mimesis*. The Christian tradition receives the Christological notion of *recapitulation* from Irenaeus' development of Paul's allegory[58] of Christ as the New Adam.[59] For Irenaeus, recapitulation is a description of the entire economy of God's incarnation as Christ. Christ, by both what he does and what he suffers, summarizes both human nature and the human condition. But recapitulation in this Christological vein means more than mere summary; it also entails *reversal*. For through the very act of passive summation, that is to say, Christ's passion, death, and resurrection (as passively received from the Father in the Spirit) Jesus Christ reverses the impurity, guilt and falsehood that the human condition has accumulated. And this reversal that retrieves intended human nature is accomplished in this very act of summation.

Christ's recapitulation, *as* summation and reversal, as reversal *in* summation, is nothing less than *restorative mimesis*. Insofar as the *imago Dei* is performative, it is a *mimesis* of God's life. Christian ascesis both performs and realigns *being* human as the *imago Dei*. So one may call Christian ascesis *restorative mimesis*. The aspect of self-denial must be logically separable from *mimesis* in the practice of ascesis because *mimesis* is imitation of God, and God requires no self-denial, *per se*. Human self-denial responds to the corruption of the *imago Dei* in the fall. Therefore, although human being has lost her ability to imitate God as originally intended, through imitation of Christ, the Spirit enables the Christian to imitate that narrative-shape that restores the human condition and so reestablishes and initiates true imitation of God.

This last assertion requires two notes of clarification about *mimesis* in general and Christ's restorative *mimesis* in particular at this point. First, *mimesis*, although an act of will, ought not to be understood in Nominalist terms of simple one to one correspondence. *Mimesis* does not exhaust the meaning of participation. Human imitation of God actively performs an *analogue* at an infinite level removed from God: a

---

58   1 Cor. 15; See also Irenaeus, *Adv. Haer.*
59   Much of this description relies upon chapter two of Rowan Williams, *The Wound of Knowledge*, 2nd rev. ed. (Cambridge, MA: Cowley Publications, 1991).

finite imitation of an infinite reality. A creature, a finite being, can never achieve imitation of God by his or her own finite autonomy. If imitation occurs it is "by grace"[60] through participation of one finite level of ontological reality (the human) in God's level of ontological reality (infinite). This participation is possible precisely because of the "unbounded" possibility available to God in God's infinitude.

Second, this description of Christ's restorative *mimesis* does not represent a "moral influence" model of the atonement as found in the thought of someone like Peter Abelard.[61] Given the above participatory criteria of *mimesis*, a merely nominalist moral influence model of atonement is logically ruled out. Following the Irenaean model of recapitulation, Christ performs both the only true human *mimesis*— what Adam should have done, but failed to do—and a new *mimesis* that reverses the ill affects of human failure, realigning the human condition to a "pre-fall" status so as to reinstate the possibility of accurate human *mimesis*. As with the above clarification, so too here, human being cannot simply choose to follow this restorative *mimesis* by pure autonomy. Participation is necessary, and participation is a gift. But now that the image imitated is incarnate, the participation must also be incarnate. Only participation in Christ's body renders this restorative *mimesis* accessible to other human beings. The ritual mysteries of "washing" and "thanksgiving" make participation in the body of Christ, the church, possible. Ascesis, as a divine gift that seems to arise inevitably from the fallen human condition, enables the Christian to imitate Christ, through participation in the same, and thereby to restore the Christian body (both corporeal and corporate) to its proper mimetic condition of divine participation.

In the logic of Christian thought, a question may arise at this point: if ascesis, as generator of human culture and life, is the "natural" or inevitable form that *mimesis* takes after the fall, how can it not be seen as a result of the fall? That is to say, if ascesis is inevitably tied

---

[60] Grace, freedom, and their relationship to ascesis in Christian practice are discussed further, below, in chapter four.

[61] Peter Abelard, *Exposition of the Epistle to the Romans* (An Excerpt from the Second Book), trans. Gerald E. Moffatt, ed. Eugene Rathbone Fairweather *A Scholastic Miscellany: Anselm to Ockham* (Philadelphia: Westminster Press, 1956), 280—84. A caricature of Abelard's position is not intended here. However, his nominalism necessarily entails a lack of ontological participation on the part of the imitator in the reality of the imitated.

up with human *mimesis* and culture, how then can ascesis be viewed as anything other than itself a fallen form of *mimesis*? Furthermore, how can the culture that is its product escape the same problem?

Take fever as an analogy. Fever, although painful, is a helpful process that the human body endures in its current condition of susceptibility to infirmity. In its paradisal state, the Christian may assume that the human body would be fully resistant to disease. In its current condition, it may contract disease in general and viruses in particular. The "natural" reaction of the human body to a viral infection is fever—it is an overheating of the body to the end that the invading life form might be "boiled" out. Physicians often encourage fever, and control it, in order to aid in the patient's recovery. Fever can, however, get out of hand. In these cases fever actually winds up "backfiring" on its original purpose to kill the invading infection, and may actually, inadvertently, kill the feverous person. Physicians take an opposite approach in this case and attempt to reduce the fever in order to save the patient's life.

Ascesis, with regards to the corporate human body, that is to say, to human society and culture as a whole, operates in much the same way. In a paradisal state, imitation of God as loving and cultural-creative community (that is to say, human *mimesis* of the divine life) would be unsusceptible to finite corruption. But now humanity's fallen condition has inaugurated the corruption of human relationality and creativity (again, that is to say, human *mimesis*). The "natural," that is to say inevitable, reaction of the corporate human body to this "infection" is a kind of "fever"—ascesis as a human activity of self-denial. This "overheats" the corporate body in its radical critique of the corrupted roots of human culture. Spiritual directors (abbas, pastors, bishops, etc.) encourage this "fever" and control it, in order to aid in the recovery of true corporate human life (*mimesis*). It can, however, "backfire" when it gets out of hand and actually destroy the life of the individual who engages in extreme ascesis, or the life of the community that cannot sustain such criticism. One may creatively extend this analogy in several directions,[62] but the purpose of the analogy is clear: ascesis responds to the fall in a way that is not, itself, a part of the human, fallen, condition.

---

[62]   For example, cultures with too much or too little "fever" may die—either from the fever itself, or from its inability to kill off the "virus."

Christian *mimesis* performs, or enacts, the image of God in the body and life of the Christian ascetic. Thereby, the Christian ascetic somatically performs the Christian teaching of *imago Dei*. This somatic performance allows subjective appropriation and existential knowledge of the Christian tradition and the realities in which it participates. There are therefore two logically distinct, but ontologically inseparable aspects to ascesis: *mimesis* and self-denial. *Mimesis* is that aspect of ascesis that produces culture. Self-denial is that aspect of ascesis that allows *mimesis* to function, after the fall, through radical opposition to and criticism of corrupt culture and cultural production. Contrary to Harpham, it is not ascesis so much as *mimesis* that produces culture. Ascesis is the name of *mimesis* after it develops the "fever" of self-denial in an attempt to correct the "virus" that has infected cultural production.

This human process of corporate cultural production corresponds directly to the triune processions wherein the Logos proceeds as *image* of the Father. Christian ascesis performs *imago Dei*, therefore, as *mimesis* of God's own internal ecstatic and creative love. Ascesis, however, is the shape that *mimesis* takes after the fall, when self-denial becomes necessary in order to set fallen human *mimesis* right. Ascesis therefore teaches *imago Dei* as performance through re-aligning broken human *mimesis*.

CHAPTER THREE

Martyrdom and Asceticism

Have this mind among yourselves, which is yours in Christ Jesus, who, though he was in the form of God, did not count equality with God a thing to be grasped, but emptied himself and became obedient unto death, even death on a cross. Therefore God has highly exalted him and bestowed on him the name which is above every name, that at the name of Jesus every knee should bow, in heaven and on earth and under the earth, and every tongue confess that Jesus Christ is Lord, to the glory of God the Father.

Philippians 2.5-11

THIS CHAPTER turns its focus toward the relationship of ascesis to the divine *kenosis*[1] of the incarnation. Christian ascesis teaches a kind of kenotic *mimesis*; that is, it renders the Christian theology of the incarnation concrete through witness, or martyrdom, within and as the Christian body. Following Hans Urs von Balthasar, this witness is a participation in the witness of Christ to the love of the Father. As already explored in the above chapters, the economy of salvation directly corresponds to the divine missions, to the economy of the

---

[1]   Throughout this book, use of the term *kenosis* must be distinguished from Jürgen Moltmann's famous kenotic theology. See Jürgen Moltmann, *The Crucified God*, trans. R. A. Wilson and John Bowden, (New York: Harper and Row, 1974). Moltmann's kenotic theology understands the crucifixion of Jesus Christ to be the rejection of God by God; a rejection that entails the suffering of the Father as well. In this book, however, the term is closer to its use as a theological phrase in patristic Greek theology. The RV, renders the Greek root *"kenosis"* as "emptied" in Phi. 2:7. The Greek fathers used the term to refer to the role of the Son in the act of divine incarnation. The fathers never employed the concept of divine self-emptying to imply the impairment or loss of divine attributes on the part of the second person of the Trinity. Instead, they used the term in order to indicate humble acceptance of the limitations of being human on the part of the divine Logos. For bibliography and commentary see *The Oxford Dictionary of the Christian Church*, 3d ed., (New York: Oxford Univ. Press, 1997), s.v. "kenotic theories."

incarnation. Because of this, Christian witness and by extension, ascesis forms an analogue to the Son and Spirit's work of witness to the Father's love in their kenotic act of incarnation. This chapter explores Peter Brown's understanding of "singleness of heart" as foundational to early Christian ascesis, and asserts that, because Christian asceticism is a participatory witness to incarnation, it does not need a direct historical causal link to some "historical Jesus" to claim the essential validity of ascetic practice.

Peter Brown on Purity of Heart and the Witness of Christ against the City

AS MENTIONED in the introduction, Peter Brown traces the history of the development of ascetic practice, particularly voluntary celibacy, in Christian antiquity up to the beginning of the divergences between the Latin west and Greek east. Brown seeks to display the way ancient Christians understood their own practices of asceticism. One of Brown's central contentions is that the body was a "problem" for ancient Christians because it was to be loved and saved, not because is was "evil."[2]

Brown is not trying to describe this historical development from a position indigenous to Christianity. Nevertheless, one of his goals is a more charitable understanding of the meaning and motivation of ancient Christian asceticism:

> If my book gives back to the Christian men and women of the first five centuries a little of the disturbing strangeness of their most central preoccupations, I will consider that I have achieved my purpose in writing it.[3]

As much as Brown shows his respect to early Christian asceticism in correcting misconceptions and bringing early Christian celibacy to life for contemporary readers, he nevertheless mourns the loss of the society of the pagan city-state that he clearly believes to be a better 'arbiter' of bodies than that of the Christian church.[4]

This loss is especially evident with regards to his focus on what Christian asceticism did to the relationship between human society and human sexuality in late antiquity. In reference to Paul's letters, Brown worries that Christianity lacked

---

[2]   Brown, 425. (see Intro., nt. 17)

[3]   *Ibid.*, xv.

[4]   For an extension of Brown's argument that Christian asceticism meant the "close of antiquity," see Cameron, "Ascetic Closure." (see Intro., nt. 22)

> . . . the warm faith shown by contemporary pagans and Jews that the sexual urge, although disorderly, was capable of socialization and of ordered, even warm, expression within marriage.[5]

Although this sentiment is to be expected from thinking outside of the Christian tradition, it shows the extent to which his "sympathetic" reading is limited by lacking an indigenous approach to the material.

Before going on, recall from the introduction that the central thesis of Brown's work, that "Christian attitudes to sex delivered the death-blow to the ancient notion of the city as the arbiter of the body."[6] The ancient pagan world understood the need for children to keep the city, to keep society going.[7] Children were one's "resurrection." Sex was the vehicle of the perpetuation of human society and marriage its institution. The entire system of birth, death and the perpetuation of human society through sexual reproduction were seen as a simple continuity with the "natural" world around and outside the human city.

With the advent and cultural triumph of Christianity towards the closing of antiquity, this understanding of the relationship of the body to sexuality and human society began to shift radically. The body was no longer a simple part of the natural world, subject to human systems of civic duty:

> Sexual renunciation might lead the Christian to transform the body and, in transforming the body, to break with the discreet discipline of the ancient city.[8]

What Christianity offered was an apocalyptic and eschatological element to human nature. Sexuality as the "warm" perpetuation of human society became overshadowed by the desire for a new heaven and a new earth. In their eschatological hope, Christians lost interest in the preservation of human society by means that were "continuous" with "nature."

But how did these ancient Christians hope to transform their bodies? "Through the Incarnation of Christ, the Highest God had reached

---

[5]   Brown, 55; For an argument against first century Jewish "warm faith" in human sexuality, see Daniel Boyarin, "Body Politic among the Brides of Christ: Paul and the Origins of Christian Sexual Renunciation," in *Asceticism*, eds. Vincent L. Wimbush and Richard Valantasis (New York: Oxford Univ. Press, 1995).

[6]   Brown, 437.

[7]   *Ibid.*, 7.

[8]   *Ibid.*, 31.

down to make even the body capable of transformation."[9] The infinite God become finite human being shattered the previous meaning of human family and society. A new family and city, founded in this incarnate God, together became a new disciplinarian over the Christian body—not just the body as somehow opposed to the soul, but, according to the Hellenic-Jewish cultural matrix of the early Christian gospels—for the body is psychosomatically united with the soul. This psychosomatic unity was recognized in a key trope borrowed from first century Judaism: the heart.[10]

At this point in his argument, Brown turns back towards the first century foundations of Christian practice. Although deliberately denying an historical link with regards to ascetic practice between Jesus himself and his later followers, Brown does offer an alternative link: continuous struggle for "purity," or "singleness" of heart. The "heart" as the trope of human psychosomatic unity insured that the goal of Christian practice would not be the escape of a "pure" soul from the body, but rather the deliverance of the human body and soul from a reluctant or divided heart.

This singleness of heart "condensed a warm and eminently social ideal" which "summed up the moral horizons of the average man."[11] It was the foundation of a morality of social solidarity, stressing ungrudging loyalty to kin and neighbors in "unaffected straight dealing."[12] Such straight dealing would have been the goal and ideal of the average first century Jewish peasant. Under such a view, the real human problem was not embodiment, but alienation from God and inner strife within the family of God—the people of Israel. Thus, Jewish hope was in their deliverance by God, not just from political oppression, but also from the cause of it—lack of solidarity through divided hearts.

After setting up the scene, Brown then begins to sketch the entry of Jesus and the peculiar claims he made. The true radicality of Jesus is not to be found in his own emphasis on singleness or purity of heart—for this is a common value shared by most Jews of the day. The radicality of Jesus is to be found in his insistence that this purity of heart is not and cannot be found within the household as its pri-

---

[9]   *Ibid.*
[10]   *Ibid.*, 33.
[11]   *Ibid.*, 36.
[12]   *Ibid.*

mary and base unit, but solely within a community of disciples of the messianic prophet—that is, his own disciples.

> To that particular small group, Jesus had not preached singleness of heart within a married household. He had said, "Follow me . . ." His abrupt call had involved a break with the normal patterns of settled life. Even the strongest ties of Jewish piety were set aside: sons must no longer linger to bury their fathers. Married persons, such as Peter, could claim, "Lo, we have left our homes and followed you."[13]

Thus an odd paradox is set up in the usual teaching of singleness of heart. Society must be rejected as a goal if the very purity of heart that will save it is to be recovered. And this saved human society will no longer be merely human, but it will become the Kingdom of God.

A radical new approach to singleness of heart is clearly at the center of Jesus' ministry, but was it asceticism in general or celibacy in particular? In answer to this question, Brown brings his argument back around to his thesis. Brown explains that celibacy in first century Palestine served simply as a mark of a prophetic calling. "The fact that Jesus himself had not married by the age of thirty occasioned no comment."[14] So, prophets such as Jesus of Nazareth and John the Baptist would have been celibate, as their followers describe and maintain. But his point in making this link between celibacy and prophecy is to offer an alternative account of Jesus' own celibacy as an ascetical discipline: "It was almost a century before any of his followers claimed to base their own celibacy on his example."[15]

Brown turns next to the Apostle Paul, his celibacy, and his rationale for the same. Paul, of course, does not explicitly base his celibacy upon the imitation of Christ. However, contrary to his own contention, Brown quotes Paul when he describes how Paul believed that the Christian body could glow with "a measure of the same spirit that had raised the inert body of Jesus from the grave: 'so that the life of Jesus may be manifested in our mortal flesh' (II Cor. 4.10)."[16] The Christian body can "glow" with the Spirit of the resurrected Christ—the resurrected but nevertheless celibate Christ. But Brown rightly points out how Paul takes up Jesus' radical new emphasis on the pu-

---

[13]   *Ibid.*, 42.
[14]   *Ibid.*, 41.
[15]   *Ibid.*
[16]   *Ibid.*, 47.

rity of heart. Brown interprets Paul's opposition of the Law to the Gospel in an interesting way:

> [T]he spontaneous obedience of the upright mind served only to highlight the extent to which deep-set enmity to God lay diffused throughout the human person as a whole, blocking the wishes of the pious with the weight of spiritual impotence.[17]

Paul understood the Law, according to Brown's interpretation, simply to stir up hard-heartedness rather than alleviate it.

Understanding Paul's opposing of Law to Gospel in this way helps also to understand Paul's opposition of Spirit and flesh. This is not a soul or mind body duality, but more a phenomenological style reflection on *life* in the Spirit as opposed to *life* in the flesh.[18] Baptism allowed life in the Spirit, a life that took up the body, but left behind its fleshy orientations—orientations that led to divided and impure hearts. This Baptism entails a new social identification. The baptized is no longer ultimately identified as a member of a family or city, but of the family of God, in the Kingdom of God, as a follower of Christ. Here, Jesus' own understanding of what enables purity of heart is exactly maintained. Purity of heart grows in a new intentional community of Christ's disciples who reject previous societal definitions.[19] In light of this, the severity of Paul's sexual ethics makes sense. Strict sexual observances distinguished Christians bodily from the "warm faith"[20] in, and sometimes violent abuse of, sexuality in the pagan society around them.

Throughout the rest of Brown's monumental work he traces the lineage of Christian asceticism and celibacy, not directly from Christ's own celibacy, but almost directly from Christ's and the Apostles' paradoxical emphasis upon purity and singleness of heart. As this fledgling Christian tradition developed out of its peasant roots, physical heroism, such as martyrdom, would become for Christians a deliberate subversion to the values of Roman order. One may understand Christian ascesis, and even the entire development of the institution of Christian monasticism, as having its origin in a desire to

---

[17] *Ibid.*
[18] *Ibid.*, 49.
[19] *Ibid.*
[20] *Ibid.*, 55.

prepare for and reflect the embodied heroism of the martyrs at times when martyrdom was less frequent:[21]

> Thus, continence, though a marked feature of Christian prophecy, remained a secondary feature; it was a preoccupation that tended to rise to the fore in Christian literature at times when the prospect of violent death was less immediate.[22]

And as the above quotation makes clear, this celibacy was still linked to the prophetic calling well into the second Christian century, for prophetic celibacy was a mark of this anti-societal singleness of heart in devotion to God and God's eschatological community.

It is exactly the eschatological emphasis that true human community could only be found in devotion to God and God's promised future reign that was so subversive to late Pagan antiquity. For if true human community can only be found outside of the possibilities that nature offers on its own terms, then the old Pagan assumption of natural continuity between the city and "nature" is broken down.[23]

This eschatological orientation would allow someone like Cyprian to understand being a Christian disciple, being under Christian discipline, "following Christ," as "nothing less than a daily martyrdom"[24] where the "red wine of the Eucharist strengthened . . . [and] prepared them to endure the sight of their own blood, as it gushed forth"[25] at their own martyrdoms. At this point in the tradition, Christians like Cyprian could make a direct link between the body of Jesus and the body of his disciples, the church, such that the unjust attack of the state upon the body of Jesus entails the attack of that same corrupt state upon Christ's corporate body, his church. Asceticism kept one ready for martyrdom and clean of impurity of heart—the kind of impurity that would cause the Christian to fail at the hour of his or her trial. But this battle for purity was not a battle of the soul against an unruly body, but of a Christian Spirit-infused body against a divided will. So, for example, Abba Anthony's goal for himself and all monks

---

[21]   Gillian Clark, "Women and *Asceticism* in Late Antiquity: The Refusal of Status and Gender," in *Asceticism*, eds. Vincent L. Wimbush and Richard Valantasis, (New York: Oxford Univ. Press, 1995), 43, asserts that ascesis was understood to serve as a share in suffering of Christ and the martyrs by the fourth century.

[22]   Brown, 69.

[23]   *Ibid.*, 94.

[24]   *Ibid.*, 195.

[25]   *Ibid.*, 194-195.

was the purity of heart that would achieve "total transparency to others."[26]

The consistent thread concerning celibacy and ascesis among the "fathers" of the "great church" that Brown discusses is Jesus' own paradoxical emphasis on a purity of heart that requires "total transparency" in love of neighbor but at the same time radically and eschatologically opposes the structures and means of perpetuating current human society. But Brown's final analysis of this radical shift due to the growth and popularity of the Christian religion is that of disappointment that the old Pagan understanding of the "continuity of city and nature" is "sapped" away by the Christian "death-blow" delivered to the Pagan city as the ancient arbiter of the body.[27]

Von Balthasar on the "Moment" of Christian Martyria

THE WORK OF the twentieth century theologian Hans Urs von Balthasar, particularly as found in his short book, *The Moment of Christian Witness*,[28] stands in contrast to Peter Brown's methodologically immanent historiography. This work by von Balthasar represents an argument against any kind of compromise between the logic of traditional Christianity and the ideologies of modernity. Von Balthasar presents the reader with a criterion for authentic Christianity, which he calls the *Ernstfall*. "Ernstfall" is the German word for "emergency," or "case of emergency," and the emergency that von Balthasar refers to is that of martyrdom, willingness to die for Christ. Thus, the translator gives an English title of *The Moment of Christian Witness* from the actual German of *Cordula oder der Ernstfall*. The *Ernstfall* is the moment of Christian witness, where witness translates the Greek *martyria*.

The *Ernstfall*, by its nature, cannot be an objective or historical criterion; it must be an *existential* criterion. But this, in itself, says something about the nature of Christian truth. Insofar as von Balthasar has hit upon an authentic guide to Christian verity, Christianity as a religion will seek "existential," and not modern, objective styles of veracity, be they either ideological or empirical. Von Balthasar describes the point of his work in the following words:

---

26 *Ibid.*, 226.

27 *Ibid.*, 437.

28 Hans Urs von Balthasar, *The Moment of Christian Witness*, trans. Richard Beckley (San Francisco: Ignatius , 1994).

One can die for various causes. But to die for the love of the One who died for me in divine darkness: this face-to-face encounter is one of a kind, and it characterizes (this is the thesis of the book) the uniqueness of Christian truth and existence.[29]

This uniqueness is existential, not empirical or ideational. Further in this same paragraph von Balthasar refers to Kierkegaard and his diaries with the same point in mind. In the case of the nature and veracity of the connection between Christ and ascesis, following von Balthasar's suggestion here, Christianity, by its nature, seeks for an existential, formal causal connection, rather than an historical or even ideological one.

Von Balthasar defines martyrdom as witness. But it is witness primarily through action, not verbal testimony, and that action takes on three basic shapes according to von Balthasar:

Martyrdom means bearing witness. It is not so very important what form this finally takes—the physical sacrifice of one's life by a bodily death, the surrender of one's whole existence to Christ by vowing to live according to his commands, or by dying to the world in baptism together with Jesus in such a way that this death and resurrection may truly enable one to live one's life for the sake of that other, immortal life.[30]

The three kinds of martyrdom von Balthasar delineates above are death, existential surrender to the "evangelical counsels," and Baptism as entrance rite to New Covenant worship. So, according to von Balthasar, one joins oneself to the perfect witness of Christ through actual identification with Christ's death, but also through other less immediate but still formal identification with that death. Existential surrender through the traditional catholic evangelical counsels[31] that lead to the commitment of the monastic is a death to the world, a lived death. Finally, Baptism, as ritual participation in the death and resurrection of Christ, is the criteria of entrance into the rite of worship under the New Covenant established in Christ.

Von Balthasar extends the sense of martyrdom in all of the traditional directions that Christians acknowledge sanctification and sainthood. The martyr is a saint through the death that perfectly identifies the martyr, body and soul, with Christ. Thus, Christian theology of saints is *martyrology*. But sanctification is also begun at Baptism and

---

[29] Von Balthasar, 143—44.

[30] *Ibid.*, 141.

[31] The traditional catholic evangelical counsels are poverty, chastity and obedience. These are also the root vows of any western Christian monastic society.

the ritual and participatory inclusion of the convert within the Christian corporate body. Literal martyrdom is, in fact, simply the completion of one's baptismal vows. Finally, however, one's martyrdom can be daily, existential death in Christ. And this is where ascesis finds its logical place within Christian doctrines of sanctification and martyrology.[32]

Finally, it is also worth noting that, following the meaning of the above quotation, this Christian *Ernstfall* is not simply willingness to die for a *cause*, but it is a *personal* criterion for actual faith in God because it is dying for a particular *Person*—God in Christ.[33] This willingness to die, according to von Balthasar, means, existentially speaking, the willingness to *already be dead*:

> As Luther so rightly realized, the Christian strives for and attains his freedom in his confrontation with death, with Christ's death for him as an individual. And the only valid response I can make to this is to be prepared to die for him, and even more, to be dead in him.[34]

That willingness to be dead amounts to the pursuit of classical Christian ascesis, or *mortification*.[35] Indeed, Christ, in his death for the sake of the world, reduces all valid human response to the evangelical counsels:

> This . . . way of life has as its most pregnant form the love-death that took place both on the cross and beside it [in the person of Mary]. In the face of death everyone is, of course, reduced of necessity to obedience, poverty and chastity.[36]

---

[32] In the earliest centuries of the church, as a rule, only martyrs would have been accorded the status of "saint." Only later, as persecution and the chance for martyrdom faded, did monks and ascetics begin to receive this title after death. But it is for the above reason that such a move fit the logic of Christian faith.

[33] And, as discussed below in chapter seven, this willingness to die for the Person of God in Christ puts the Christian in greater existential proximity to the authors of Christian scripture, and, therefore, allows for the possibility of more accurate biblical exegesis.

[34] *Ibid.*, 37.

[35] Daniel Boyarin points out the inherent paradox that the Christian is called upon to die with Christ, while Christians are actually promised to live with Christ forever (467). This paradox corresponds concisely to the practice of death, or, mortification, in ascesis as an opening out to a share in the life of God through theoria.

[36] Von Balthasar, 46.

Von Balthasar here links valid human existential response to Christ's martyrdom to the classic institution of Christian asceticism: monasticism.

This form of personal discipleship makes sense and finds its life within the worship established by God in the New Covenant. As with the Old Covenant, so with the New, valid worship of the living God takes place in the Temple and according to a proper liturgy. Von Balthasar uses the biblical analogy of Christ as the new living Temple of the New Covenant together with its concomitant ramification that salvation of human worship entails being grafted, through Baptism, into Christ's corporate body, the church and living Temple of the Holy Spirit.[37]

> The result of this willingness is that the single stones [of the Temple] take on something of the character of the pillars of the Church and themselves become a "holy priesthood" offering "spiritual sacrifices" (1 Peter 2:5)—that is, presenting their bodies as a living sacrifice (cf. Rom. 12:1). In so doing, they have in their spiritual temper a share of the life of those who teach the message of Christ (cf. I Cor 7:29-31).[38]

For the purposes of the current argument, this analogical structure of the corporate body of Christ as a temple whose individual stones are Christians "built" atop the "foundation stone" of Christ and the apostles means that it is the formal structure of this corporate body, whether in time or in space, that defines the indigenous logic of Christian life, rather than modern historical causality. Von Balthasar continues:

> [T]he Church can be described morphologically only when she is at the same time seen from a genetic point of view. Only her growth and development out of the *morphe* of Christ can explain her nature and being.[39]

The development of the corporate Christian body, especially with regards to her practices and what they existentially entail, follows, on analogy, more the logic of biological genetics than that of historical contingency. And because of this, von Balthasar rejects those modern German ideologies that would place Christianity as a subordinate (even if necessary) step on the way to a greater human evolution that eventually goes past Christianity:

---

[37] Ephesians 2:19—22.
[38] Von Balthasar, 47—48.
[39] *Ibid.*, 48-49.

It is therefore impossible to speak of a "tendency towards incarnation" on the part of God, as a development taking place in world history, without first accepting the purpose of this development.[40]

That "purpose" of the incarnation that must first be accepted is the salvation of the world by death on the cross. World history cannot progress beyond the cross, for through the incarnation God has made the cross—a contingent historical event—the eternal and necessary criterion of love.[41] So, instead of contingent historical development, the church experiences an almost fractal and recursively genetic growth or unfolding within its life of practice (and, therefore, within its life of thought, insofar as thought is a Christian practice):

> If she is the tree that grew out of the "grain of mustard seed" of the Cross, then she is also the tree that will herself bear the same seed and, as a result, repeat the pattern of the crucifixion. In bearing this seed the Church returns to the point of her origin.[42]

The logical conclusion of this line of thinking leads von Balthasar to assert that the normal condition of the Christian church is that of persecution. One must understand this to mean theological, and not necessarily demographic or sociological normativity. So too, and by natural entailment, the normal condition of the Christian person is that of martyrdom:

> Christ himself calls men to martyrdom, and it is this that makes it a special sign of grace . . . Persecution constitutes the normal condition of the Church in her relation to the world, and martyrdom is the normal condition of the professed Christian.[43]

Because martyrdom is the theological norm of Christian life, "all the transfiguration and transparency of Christian existence stream from the darkness of death."[44] But this norm, again, cannot be construed under the conditions of German ideology: "World history by no means represents a progressive Christianization of the cosmos."[45] And this is because Christian existence within the death and resurrection of Christ, although participated in over the extension of temporality,

---

[40]   *Ibid.*, 49.

[41]   Von Balthasar develops this notion of the contingent historical manifestation of the eternal criterion of love in his section "We Anonymous Atheists and Our Dialogue," *Ibid.* 119ff.

[42]   *Ibid.*, 49.

[43]   *Ibid.*, 21.

[44]   *Ibid.*, 51.

[45]   *Ibid.*, 52.

is not progressive in the modern sense, but final in the Christian sense of the eschatological:

> Such a view of history fails to take into account two things—namely, that the sign of those "last things" (*eschaton*) in this world is Christ's death by crucifixion, and, consequently, that both the Church and the individual Christian are rooted in and sustained by the double mystery of his death and Resurrection . . .[46]

So the limits of Christian life are delineated by the eschatological events of the passion and resurrection; the Christian life, therefore, is a "race that is run within the limits set by Christ himself and judged according to the extreme standards of his struggle against the sin of the world."[47] Following such a line of reasoning, the Christian can say, "that death is what gives life its form and shape."[48] This means that whether Christ is the *material* cause of the tradition of asceticism within Christianity is really immaterial to the point from the indigenous reasoning of the Christian. Christ is, instead, the immediate and *formal* cause of all *martyria*, whether by death or by self-denial (that is to say, ascesis), through *participation* in Christ as the *form* of being fully human.

Incarnation, Kenosis and the Restoration of Mimesis

BROWN CLEARLY PAINTS a picture of ancient Christianity where the body under Christian ascetic practice becomes the gift of God to be returned to God in love. In this way it is clear that Brown understands ancient Christian ascetic practice as performed, embodied theology. And this theological performance is the practice of a political stance within the world that itself makes claims about reality. Over the course of this broader argument on Brown's part, he also argues that singleness of heart is one of the major historical and "ideological" points of continuity within the Christian tradition from the "Jesus Movement" to the close of antiquity. Brown almost contradicts himself, however, when in the face of this argument for a kind of *ideological* continuity within the Christian tradition, he argues that there is no *historical* connection between Christ's celibacy (and, by possible extension, any other behavior that may look ascetical, such as his fasting in the wilderness) and later Christian asceticism.

---

[46] *Ibid.*

[47] *Ibid.*, 54.

[48] *Ibid.*, 136.

Following, therefore, the lines of von Balthasar's argument, Christianity (together with most ancient world-views) needs no immanent structural pattern for history because it has a transcendent hierarchy of meaning for which the immanent and contingent sprawl of history is rich with types. Modernity in its systematic rejection of transcendent modes of reasoning (by means of analogy, for example) must find an immanent means for the structuring of history. Thus, modern history and historiography were born.[49] So too, also, the "historical critical method" of exegesis finds its birth.[50] Because of this, whether or not historians using modern critical methods can discern a causal connection between Jesus as the "founder" of Christianity and later ascetical developments and movements within later Christianity is immaterial. There need not be a direct historical chain of causality for asceticism to make sense within Christianity and for it to be logically coherent with its "founder," Jesus Christ, because ascesis is a *formal* and *logical* extension of the practice of Christian witness, or, *imitatio Christi*. The narrative of the life of Christ does not have to give *literal* warrant to ascetic practice when it gives overwhelming *formal* warrant.

Von Balthasar also helps theologically to ground this understanding of the connection between Christ and Christian ascesis because, over the course of his argument, he continually returns to the Trinity and the incarnation in his discussion of the *Ernstfall*:

> Christian belief means the unconditional resolve to surrender one's life for Christ's sake. Just as the triune God acquired an ascendancy over the God in one person through an unfathomable love that itself had to be founded on love (for he did not need us), and as a result fell from eternal life into the world of death and was forsaken by God, so Christian belief can be only an ascendancy that man, responding gratefully and showing himself thankful

---

[49] Here is where Foucault, then, is right in his critique of traditional modern historiography and where his 'archaelogy' is actually compatible with a Christian and transcendent participational reasoning structure. Of course, Foucault would hate his being connected in any positive way with Christianity; nevertheless Christianity always integrated *Fortuna* into a non-competitive transcendent scheme. For more on *Fortuna* in ancient and medieval Christian thought, see C. S. Lewis, *The Discarded Image: An Introduction to Medieval and Renaissance Literature* (London: Cambridge Univ. Press, 1964), especially 176—77.

[50] For a thoroughgoing discussion of the birth of the historical critical method from a postcritical point of view, see Hans W. Frei, *The Eclipse of Biblical Narrative: A Study in Eighteenth and Nineteenth Century Hermeneutics* (New Haven: Yale Univ. Press, 1974).

to God, acquires over himself by giving evidence that he has understood God's action.[51]

This quotation is far from perspicacious. But what von Balthasar means is that the passion, as Christ's witness, opened out the possibility of knowing God as triune, rather than simply unitary. And, furthermore, that true Christian response is to give up oneself for God, and thereby participate, through Christ, in God's own self-giving.

The Christian mysteries recursively perform this kenotic *mimesis* found in the Christian's willingness to die for, as, and in Christ. For example, recall Peter Brown's description of the radical transformation of "singleness of heart" in the Christian tradition, where what was once a "warm" ethic of filial piety was transformed into a radical ethic of adherence to one's new family of faith among the disciples of Jesus. Regular human community is rejected for the sake of a share in the true eschatological community. Given that community is at the core of being human, von Balthasar notes that death is the most profound point of separation from human community, for "[d]eath manages to suspend this law of community for an a-temporal moment."[52] Von Balthasar then connects martyrdom to the Trinity through the mystery of Baptism:

> The baptismal rite, by which the Christian is immersed in water and which bears a strong symbolic likeness to the threat of death, cuts him off from every other kind of communication in order to bring him to the source where true communion begins.[53]

The Christian, therefore, in undergoing Baptism, shows a willingness to die to all *human* community for the sake of being re-grounded in *ultimate* community, and the source of all true community—the community of the Persons of the Trinity.

So von Balthasar further eschews any kind of historicism with regards to the Christian relevance of martyrdom and ascesis when he plunges their meaning into the depths of the triune God. Fullness of meaning, fullness of (at least formal) causality, is to be found in God the Trinity. The incarnation and passion of Christ

---

[51]   Von Balthasar, 27.
[52]   *Ibid.*, 30.
[53]   *Ibid.*, 31.

is a human and genuinely historical event because God became incarnate, and at the same time it is an event that transcends history, which comes just as immediately to me as to everyone else.[54]

The incarnation and passion of Christ become, therefore, the historical and contingent events that re-open for alienated humanity that reality that transcends history and contingency. And human being makes her entry into this opening through sharing in the manner in which God made this opening—through a share in Christ's *witness*—in the Christian acceptance of martyrdom as a gift, and in the ascesis that prepares the Christian for martyrdom.[55]

Ascesis, therefore, understood as practice for and a participation in *witness*, can be "pushed back" into Christian Trinitarian reflection. The Spirit and Son give the world, through the incarnation and passion of Christ, back to the Father, as the gift of a saved world. This is the "True Witness" Christ and the Spirit give in the economy of salvation. The Spirit grants a body to the Logos, providing for his *kenosis*, his pouring out of himself for the sake of creation. Thus Christ and his body are "poured-out" in witness to the Father's love for the world.

The Christian body witnesses to this same love of God, in and as Christ's corporate body, upon receiving the gift of the Spirit from the Father. Thus the Spirit grants somatic conformity to Christ, the true witness, and, thereby, grants true witness to fallen human beings. By integrating human being back into true witness of the Father, in the Son, by the incorporation of the Spirit, true *mimesis* of God is restored to Christ's corporate body. Ascesis thereby forms an analogue to the Son and Spirit's economy of witness, when the Christian is incorporated in this somatic *kenosis*, into this witness of the Father's love.

Insofar as Christian witness means incorporation into the economy of salvation by means of a kind of narrative participation, martyrdom no longer simply represents dying in witness to the one God, but dying in participation of the one True Witness to the one-ness of God, in he who is one with God, Jesus Christ. This transformation in the meaning of martyrdom from simple witness to imitation of the divine life and the divine economy of salvation means that martyrdom is more than simply a witness against the city of humanity, but is

---

54   *Ibid.*, 54.

55   Gregory Collins (see ch. 1, nt. 29) asserts that ascesis is the anticipation of the Christian's future life in God. In this regard it is a program of *witness* through participation in and manifestation of the mystery of Christ. Collins describes this emphasis on witness as "fundamentally Johannine," 352.

also a participation in the city of God—it is a eucharistic "site"[56] that grounds within human space and time the coming city of God. Ascesis, as the daily practice of *martyria*, participates, in turn, this witness to the coming city.[57]

Because Christian witness, and, therefore, ascesis, entails direct ontological participation in the reality of the incarnation of God in Jesus Christ, Christian asceticism does not need a direct historical causal link to Jesus in order to claim the essential validity of ascetic practice within Christianity. Christ is the formal, not necessarily historical, cause of ascetic practice in Christianity. In indigenous terms, Christian witness, and, by extension, ascesis, forms an analogue to, and allows participation in, the kenotic act of divine incarnation. Ascesis therefore teaches incarnation as divine *kenosis* insofar as it teaches kenotic *mimesis*.

---

[56] See William T. Cavanaugh's theology of the sacramental nature of the martyr's body in *Torture and Eucharist: Theology, Politics, and the Body of Christ* (Malden, MA: Blackwell, 1998), especially pp. 58-68.

[57] Gregory Collins describes Simeon the New Theologian's approach to ascesis as a program of *witness* through participation in and manifestation of the mystery of Christ (Collins, 352).

CHAPTER FOUR

Grace is Ascetic and Ascesis is a Gift

And when Jesus was baptized, he went up immediately from the water, and behold, the heavens were opened and he saw the Spirit of God descending like a dove, and alighting on him; and lo, a voice form heaven, saying, "This is my beloved Son, with whom I am well pleased." Then Jesus was led up by the Spirit into the wilderness to be tempted by the devil. And he fasted forty days and forty nights, and afterward he was hungry. And the tempter came to him . . .

Matthew 3.16-4.3b

SO FAR this book has presented Christian asceticism as a given within Christian practice. Some Christian traditions, however, especially Protestant ones, may well worry whether or not an ascetic approach to Christianity might lead to the ancient heresy of Pelagianism, or, in more popular terms, a "works gospel." On the other hand, there are scholars that would say that insofar as Christianity is no longer a challenge to culture through radical ascetic behavior, it has actually betrayed its own essence.[1] This chapter therefore argues that, in indigenous terms, Christian ascesis not only teaches salvation as divine gift, but that, in turn, ascesis itself is a divine gift.

By understanding ascetic practice as itself a gift, one may lay aside worries that Christian asceticism is the expression of a heretical "works gospel." This chapter describes Christian ascetic practice as the manifestation of the freedom of the Spirit himself, enabling human freedom. The ground of this assertion has its foundation in the triune life. The Spirit is able to offer real human participation in the

---

[1]   J. Duncan M. Derrett (see Intro., nt., 48) represents this position keenly: "Asceticism was not the object of the Way, it was the Way; it was a route to its goal" (93).

divine life because, in the economy of salvation, the Son allowed the Spirit to give him perfect humanity. Ascesis is simply an aspect of the gift of the Spirit because the Spirit enables real human participation in God's life. In terms of the goals of the first part of this book, therefore, this chapter asserts that ascesis teaches the Christian reality of "salvation by grace alone," through a subjective appropriation of "active passivity" before God.

As discussed briefly in the introduction, Gavin Flood, in his work *The Ascetic Self*, shows a postcritical openness to the possibility that the immanent practices of a given religious tradition may well open out the ascetic to transcendent reality or realities only accessible through those indigenous practices. Because of his recognition of this possibility, Flood asks whether an indigenous theology could understand ascesis itself as a divine gift. Flood's postcritical reflections on this theme lead him to describe a certain paradox or ambiguity, across various religious ascetic traditions, that he names the "ambiguity of the self." This postcritical description of the ambiguity of the self corresponds, in Christian thought, to the Christian paradox of full human salvation by divine grace alone. So, in response to Flood's invitation to theological reflection on this postcritical observation, this chapter argues that Eugene Roger's constructive Pneumatology, in his work *After the Spirit*, provides an indigenous account of Christian life as the gift of the Spirit that may easily be extended to include Christian asceticism as also a gift of that same Spirit. This chapter now turns to Flood's description of the ambiguous self.

Flood on the Ambiguity of the Ascetic-self

FLOOD ARGUES that what he calls the "ambiguity of the self" is a paradox represented in all of the scriptural and cosmological ascetic traditions. In these "ascetico-cosmological" traditions the goal of the eradication of individual self-will is nevertheless achieved, paradoxically, through an individual act of the will, and that usually as over and against the body, which is perceived as disobedient:

> My general claim is that asceticism can be understood as the internalization of tradition . . . the performance of the memory of tradition. Such a performance contains an ambiguity or distance between the general intention to eradicate the will or in some sense to erase the self, and

expression, the affirmation of will in ascetic performance such as weakening the body through fasting.[2]

Flood's observation that there is a certain ambiguity or paradox to the self in the various ascetic traditions is closely linked to both his project and his thesis. His thesis that tradition is "internalized," subjectively, through ascetic practices necessarily entails this ambiguity, for it is by what seems to be an individual act of the will that the ascetic appropriates what may be considered a greater, more collective "will," and subjectivity. By sketching the shape of this "ambiguity" found in the subjective appropriation of tradition, Flood achieves a cross-cultural religious comparison, which represents the chief end of his project.

But Flood also pursues a certain criticism in his work with respect to his intellectual tradition within the various approaches to academic religious studies. Flood places himself within his own academic tradition: "I would place myself at the confluence of a number of intellectual traditions, especially the phenomenological and hermeneutic."[3] But Flood immediately distances himself from some of the assumptions of this tradition: "I do not inherit [my tradition] uncritically, and the present text can be seen as an implicit corrective reading to much of the work that has 'compared religions,' often in an egregious way."[4]

Flood "locates" himself, and his "corrective reading," "within a hermeneutic tradition that is open to postcritical developments within the academy."[5] These postcritical developments entail that the academic discipline of comparative religion must withhold from making any kind of claims to absolute truth, for "[r]eligious truth . . . must be understood in tradition-specific ways." Secular academia, claiming freedom from such religious traditions, therefore has no place making (religious) truth claims. But Flood's commitment to the development of postcritical scholarship also requires him to go one step further. As mentioned above, in the introduction, postcritical scholarship requires the researcher to be open to the possibility that the truth-claims of the

---

[2]   Flood, ix.
[3]   *Ibid.*, xi.
[4]   *Ibid.*
[5]   *Ibid.*

various religious traditions may have actual positive content—they may actually "open out"[6] reality to their respective practitioners.

The "ambiguity of the self" that Flood discerns across ascetic traditions is just such a postcritical observation. It represents an attempt to make a claim about religious traditions that does not, in the end, entail their reduction to immanent and human institutions and forces. Flood's "ambiguity of the self," at the same time that it makes no particular religious commitments, still allows for the possibility of truth within a religious tradition—of contact with something transcendent through a religious tradition and its practices. In the introduction, Flood reveals a possible way to misread his approach:

> The book might therefore be open to the criticism that it is implicitly theological in taking seriously the writings of ascetics and [sic] about asceticism, and in taking seriously the claim about what the ascetic self hopes to become. In the sense that I do intend to take very seriously ascetic claims about the nature of the self and world, then the book is certainly implicitly theological, although it is not theology because it does not stand directly within a theological tradition of discourse.[7]

Flood openly recognizes that such postcritical observations may be taken as a kind of covert attempt at making theological claims. He even goes so far as to admit to engaging in "implicit" theology. But that "implicit" theology can only be found when "theology" is taken in such a broad sense as to render the word almost meaningless. Flood's work does not represent anything like theology "proper" because, by his own qualification, he does not speak within or from any given, concrete "theological tradition of discourse." There is a difference between claiming and speaking for and within a theological tradition and remaining open, as a scholar, to the possibility that such traditions may speak truth. One of the goals of this chapter, therefore, is to describe, in indigenous Christian terms, the reality "opened out" by the ambiguity of the ascetic self.

The possibility that these traditions and their practices may have access to truths about reality leads Flood to comment on the direction into which a *theology* of asceticism, within a given ascetic tradition, might delve in terms of other academic conversations:

> I do not explore the theological implications of asceticism, although this is a very rich theme, especially in relation to contemporary concerns about 'the

---

6   *Ibid.*, 249.
7   *Ibid.*, xi.

gift.' Could asceticism be understood not only as voluntary discipline but as acceptance of suffering seen as divine gift?[8]

A scholar of asceticism may discover the point upon which postcritical religious studies crosses with theology proper, in the possibility that ascetic discipline is, itself, a gift from the divine. As commented upon in the introduction, one may construe this entire project in general, and its first part in particular, as an attempt to answer Flood's question, "could asceticism be understood . . . as divine gift?" This chapter best represents such an answer to Flood's question within this work as a whole, because it works out the nature of Christian asceticism as the gift of the Spirit, the manifestation of the Spirit in human habituation. But before discussing this connection, further exposition upon Flood's "ambiguity of the self" is requisite.

Flood's description of the ambiguous ascetic self is one of four significant postcritical observations that form the foundation of his overall argument. These four follow: 1) the ascetic performs his or her self, 2) in this ascetical practice the ascetic performs the memory of his or her tradition, 3) the ascetic self thus formed performs itself as ambiguous, 4) these postcritical observations allow insight into problems of universalism and method in religious studies.[9] The movement of Flood's argument, therefore, is from understanding the ascetic self as performative, through the context and result of this ascetic performance, to conclusions about the nature of religious studies in a postcritical vein in light of these observations. The first two observations lead logically to this "ambiguity of the self," the final represents something more like a "meta-" observation on the discipline that discerned these aspects of ascetic behavior. Although the final observation represents the goal of Flood's project, it is out of the scope of this chapter. The focus now turns to Flood's argument up to, and including, the ambiguity of self.

Flood's ascetic self is not a substantial, disembodied *cogito*. Flood's emphasis on the nature of "self" as performed prevents such a view. "The central contention of the book can be stated quite simply: that the ascetic self is performed."[10] But this performed self is "not a disembodied self, but a historical, language-bearing, gendered person

8   *Ibid.*
9   *Ibid.*, 3-4.
10   *Ibid.*, 2.

within their [sic] own name and story."[11] The performance or performances engaged in the practice of asceticism consist largely of practices that, according to Flood, "reverse the flow of the body:"

> [A]sceticism is the reversal of the flow of the body . . . Asceticism refers to a range of habits or bodily regimes designed to restrict or reverse the instinctual impulses of the body and to an ideology that maintains that in so doing a greater good or happiness can be achieved . . . To reverse the flow of the body is both to perform the memory of tradition and to perform the ambiguity of the self.[12]

This "reversal of the flow of the body" entails concrete practices, because the ascetic self is concrete:

> A key feature of the reversal of the body's orientation is the renunciation of food and sexual practice along with the attempted eradication of sexual desire . . . [A]scetic cultures often renounce aesthetic pleasures as well, such as music and dancing . . . The performance of asceticism can also incorporate mental disciplines, including the cultivation of humility and detachment.[13]

Such practices form the ascetic self as the "memory" of its ascetic tradition. Asceticism represents a set of practices whereby the realities taught by a given tradition are subjectively appropriated. Thus the ascetic self is a tradition-defined subject, and keeping this in mind allows the scholar "to separate subjectivity from modern notions of individuality."[14]

Flood argues for the possibility of a "traditional" self that retains subjectivity without individualism. This subjectivity performs, with the collective body of those who share his or her ascetic tradition, a collective "memory" of the tradition, forming thereby, "a shared or collective subjectivity."[15] This memory of tradition "is more than the passive conserving of information, it is the active enlivening of the present through links with the past."[16] This collective memory and subjectivity is embodied and discursive:

---

11   *Ibid.*
12   *Ibid.*, 4.
13   *Ibid.*, 5.
14   *Ibid.*, 7.
15   *Ibid.*, 8.
16   *Ibid.*

> The important point is that ascetic traditions are forms of collective memory
> enacted in the body through *praxis* and enacted in language through
> discourse.[17]

Flood then describes what he observes as the key features of ascetic
traditions:

> Firstly, ascetic traditions are always set within or are a part of a *religious*
> tradition, moreover a *cosmological* religious tradition. Secondly, cosmological
> traditions interiorise cosmology . . . Thirdly, ascetic traditions are the
> enactment of the memory of tradition, which is also the expression of
> cosmology, for tradition is understood as an expression of the cosmic
> structure.[18]

The three elements are obviously interrelated, in that each subsequent
one depends upon the first. The motion is that of a cosmologically
committed religion subjectively interiorized by performing its own
"memory."

One discovers the ambiguity of the self in the process by which
the tradition is made interior, that is, made formative of subjectivity.
Before the face of tradition, the ascetic actively pursues passivity for
the sake of transformation:

> Indeed, any ascetic performance entails the possibility of change. Such an
> inscribing of the memory of tradition on the body is both an act of will and a
> consequence of passivity.[19]

Flood's ambiguity of self arises out of the seemingly ambiguous
relationship of the individual ascetic to the ascetic tradition as a
whole. For the individual must assert will in order to appropriate the
will of the "tradition" (or, in tradition-bound language, the will of the
god of that particular tradition), thereby affectively obliterating
individual volition:

> The self becomes passive and God active. This passivity is indeed seen as a
> consequence of the activity of the divine, yet that passivity is achieved
> through the assertion of the will in ascetic action.[20]

Ascetic traditions therefore bind their members to the performance of
a kind of "active passivity."

---

[17]   *Ibid.*, 9.

[18]   *Ibid.*

[19]   *Ibid.*, 13.

[20]   *Ibid.*

But this bizarre and seemingly contradictory assertion of will for its own annihilation actually intensifies subjectivity, rather than diminishing it:

> It is almost as though the restriction undergone in asceticism is a necessary condition for the intensification of subjectivity that transcends desire and individualism. This intensification of subjectivity is spoken of in terms of freedom from restriction . . .[21]

Each tradition defines "restriction" and "freedom" differently. The Indian religious traditions will define "restriction" in terms of the cycles of karma, the western traditions in terms of "sin." Freedom means, therefore, not simply freedom in terms of freedom from bodily desires—as much as ascetic traditions may actually stress this aspect—but also freedom from the restrictions caused by individual subjectivity. But the paradox, or perhaps even contradiction, of the eradication of individual subjectivity by individual effort goes to the heart of Flood's ambiguity of the self.

In this process of performing the tradition, "the narrative of the ascetic becomes an index for the narrative of tradition."[22] So ascetic selves "become indices of tradition,"[23] that is to say, the ascetic becomes a point of reference for discerning the nature of the ascetic tradition as a whole—an example of its actual instantiation. Flood concludes the development of his particular observations about asceticism by admitting to the influence of Kierkegaard on his own thoughts. Because "Kierkegaard wishes to privilege existence, the particular existence of a lived life, over abstract system and to privilege person over world-historical dialectic,"[24] Flood recognizes the ascetic self as a kind of "Kierkegaardian," existentially authentic, self. Flood confirms Kierkegaard's description of truth as subjectivity, as subjective appropriation through *repetition*.[25] In the case of asceticism, that repetition is both embodied and traditionary. Insofar as it is somatic and traditional, however, the ascetic self deviates from the kind of authentic self that Kierkegaard envisioned.

Throughout the course of *The Ascetic Self*, Flood continues to identify this "ambiguity of the self" in the particular subjectivities formed

---

[21] *Ibid.*, 14.
[22] *Ibid.*, 15.
[23] *Ibid.*
[24] *Ibid.*, 19.
[25] *Ibid.*

within the various ascetic and cosmological religious traditions he explores. Within his analysis of the Christian tradition, Flood discerns the ambiguity of the self within the *imitatio Christi* of traditional Christian discipleship.[26]

Flood's description of the "ambiguity of the self" is a postcritical observation because it is *both* critical *and* open to the possibility of truth in tradition. It is "critical" insofar as it names, at a critical distance from ascetic traditions, an aspect of ascesis that seems at best paradoxical and at worst contradictory—the attempt to eradicate self-will through acts of the will. His description remains open to "truth in tradition" insofar as his word-choice, "ambiguity," implies something that seems contradictory to the outsider, while recognizing the possibility that inner-traditionary performance of the same "active passivity" may not be encountered as illogical, irrational or contradictory, but may, in fact, open out contact with reality. These postcritical observations of the "ambiguity of the self," which Flood discerns across ascetic traditions, also crosses with that set or region of Christian theological issues concerning "active passivity," the "problem of grace and free will," and the heresy of "Pelagianism," etc. Turning to Eugene Rogers' recent Pneumatology provides a Christian theological context for playing out the implications of this crossing.

Rogers on the Gift of the Spirit

EUGENE ROGERS SEEKS to make up for the lack of robust Pneumatology that he perceives in recent Trinitarian revivals in his constructive work *After the Spirit*. The problem as Roger's sees it is that the "Spirit, who in classical Christian discourse 'pours out on all flesh,' had, in modern Christian discourse, floated free of bodies altogether."[27] Rogers spends some time exploring the history of recent Trinitarian revivals in Christian thought, pointing especially to the seminal role Karl Barth has played in this theological development. While acknowledging the centrality and importance of Barth's contribution, Rogers points out that Barth's theology seemed to make the Spirit unnecessary—there was nothing the Spirit could do that the Son could not do better, so to speak.[28] This uneven weight upon the Son hindered a full revival of the Trinity.

---

[26] See especially pages 194 and 200.

[27] Rogers, 1. (see Ch. 1, nt. 27)

[28] *Ibid.*, 9.

Rogers' solution to this problem is found in returning to biblical narrative. Rather than deal with the doctrine of the Trinity in terms of abstractions or as if it were a kind of divine mathematical problem, Rogers looks to the biblical narrative wherein one confronts the concrete persons themselves. It was as an attempt to make sense of whom God must be in light of these narratives that the church formulated the doctrine of the Trinity in the first place. One must therefore return to these texts if one is to truly "revive" the doctrine of the Trinity:

> Because the acts of the Trinity towards the world are indivisible, the only time one could distinguish the Spirit from the Son would be when the narratives give glimpses of their *intratrinitarian* interaction.[29]

Without a divinely revealed narrative, the triune nature of God would remain unknown, for when God acts with relationship to what God creates, that action is as singular as God is one. Without a glimpse of the inner life of God that the biblical narrative intimates, there is no way of knowing God as triune.

So, through reflection on central New Testament narratives, such as the resurrection, the annunciation, the Baptism of Christ, the transfiguration, the ascension and Pentecost, Rogers discerns and asserts his central constructive thesis: "doctrinally, the Spirit alights, abides, or comes to rest on the Son."[30] Rogers asserts this constructive thesis, analogically (or, perhaps, "totemically"[31]) moving from the inner life of the triune God, through the incarnation to the integration of human and even inanimate material into the triune life. Because in God's inner triune life the Spirit rests upon the Son, in the act of the incarnation the Spirit rests upon the *body* of the Son. In so doing, this action on the part of the Trinity as a whole opens out the possibility that other fleshly things—e.g., human creatures—may also share in the life

---

29   *Ibid.*, 7.

30   *Ibid.*

31   In his commitment to engage theology in a postcritical manner, Rogers engages social theory and anthropology through Durkheim's totemic theory of the nature of religion. Rogers concedes that religion—including Christianity—is a totemic construct. But in a postcritical move he claims, nevertheless, that totemic structure opens the human participant out to the possibility of contact with actual transcendent reality. Rogers particularly likes engaging this model because it simultaneously allows for coherent logical structure in indigenous religious thought, while asserting that this logic cannot be determined beforehand; "you have to do field work first" (55—56). Ascetic practice is (at least an essential part of) the "fieldwork" necessary for unfolding the logic of the Christian "totem."

and relationships that obtain within the triune God. Therefore the Spirit may rest on human bodies and incorporate them into the corporate body of the incarnate Son. Here, of course, Rogers means the church. Finally, the Spirit may rest on non-human, or even inanimate, physical matter as a means of accomplishing this community of relationship. Chiefly, here, Rogers intends the ritual mysteries, or, sacraments, of the church.[32]

In his first chapter, Rogers cites the patristic maxim *"opera trinitatis ad extra indivisa sunt."*[33]

> That means that not only is the Father the creator, but also is the Spirit; not only is the Son the Redeemer, but the Spirit also . . . The Persons are differentiated by their actions among themselves, not their actions toward us.[34]

But he goes on to assert a commitment to another "thesis," where, "in the New Testament we see human being in transition from being exterior to being interior to the trinitarian life."[35] This confuses matters, he admits, for the very narrative that describes the life of God exterior to God's interactions with creation involves the ultimate interaction with creation—its integration into God's interior life. If the word *"theosis"* represents the Christian belief that God, in Christ, has opened out to allow human beings a share in the divine life, and yet God's actions towards creation are undivided, then, paradoxically, the one and united divine action of the economy of salvation is the one instance where God's interior life is opened up for the creature to know and share.

Throughout the course of his constructive argument concerning the Spirit, Rogers takes up a theological exegesis of Romans chapter eight. Rogers begins to enter into the debate concerning the so-called "problem" of grace and free-will by asserting, with respect to Romans chapter eight, that there is no *prayer* proper to human being, but that only God prays to God. When human beings pray, truly pray, it is by virtue of their being swept up into the "prayer" that is internal to the intelligible relationships that obtain within the triune life of God. But Rogers quickly anticipates the possibility of a charge of Pelagianism.

---

[32] For Rogers' connection of the ritual mysteries to his *ad hoc* use of Durkheim's totemic logic, see pages 57-58.

[33] *Ibid.*, 11.

[34] *Ibid.*

[35] *Ibid.*, 14.

If prayer is what joins human words and life to the triune life of God, and prayer is something that human beings choose to do or not to do, then is it not the case that one has simply turned prayer into a saving work?

> [I]s there no danger that transformative prayer will come to seem a human achievement, a "work" in the negative sense of the word? The Spirit protects against this, too, in that the Spirit prays "for" human being, on their behalf, and by taking them up into a Trinitarian prayer that is not originally their own, however much the Spirit may make it so. The pattern is that the Spirit changes them by prayer, not that they change themselves and earn the Spirit.[36]

So the fear that prayer itself will become a new "works gospel" is dispelled by recognizing that, in Christian prayer, the Spirit actually grants the person praying a share in a prayer that is not, originally, his or her own prayer. The human person is added to, taken up into, the "prayer," the mutual intelligible communication of communion in love that is inherent to the divine life of the Trinity.

Rogers then anticipates the next possible worry, that of the Arminian: "If every human response to God is credited to God again in the Spirit, does that not destroy the human person's distinctive, personal response?"[37] In answer to this, Rogers begins fairly conceptually, and then zeroes in on the concrete triune life. More conceptually, Rogers answers that this is not a problem if one understands the Spirit as the "very principle of distinctiveness in love."[38] For all human distinctiveness is a participation in the Spirit, according to Rogers. But Rogers quickly links this more abstract proposal to its concrete context. That the Spirit brings distinction . . .

> presupposes the Trinitarian mystery at the heart of absolute Being: the wonder of the mutual indwelling (*circumincessio*) of the divine Persons in a way that does not restrict their personal distinctiveness.[39]

So, just as the divine persons of the Trinity perfectly dwell within each other without compromising the integrity of their distinctive personhood, so too the Spirit may grant divine prayerful response to God in such a way as to preserve distinctive human personhood.

---

36   *Ibid.*, 212.

37   *Ibid.*, 214.

38   *Ibid.*

39   *Ibid.*, quoting Hans Urs von Balthasar, *Prayer*, (trans. Graham Harrison, San Francisco: Ignatius, 1986), 76.

Following Thomas Aquinas, Rogers asserts that the way in which the Spirit grants this distinctiveness that is simultaneously the distinctiveness of divine life and truly human, personal distinctiveness, is through the infusion of new patterns of decision-making, or, *habits*: "[G]race, as a gift that does not violate human nature, is always habitual."[40] This is the Thomistic notion of "infused grace,"[41] where the grace, or gift, of God is properly appropriated as fully human by its infusion or integration into human reason and will through Christian patterns of decision-making. But part of Rogers' argument, following in the line of this Thomistic theology of grace, is that habits are formed through the corporeal integration of corporate culture or *habitus*. If this is the case, then which is it? Do human habits find their Christian transformation through the human activity of conforming to the cultural habits of the Christian community and its tradition, or through a straightforward supernatural "infusion" of grace?

Again, this is not a problem when salvation is viewed as both a temporal process and a communal, participatory activity. For if this is the case, then there is not "that much of a paradox: In the work of the Spirit, the practice of gratitude [as one example of a Christian habit] was a habit of others before it was a habit of [any individual Christian]."[42] Just insofar as the Spirit grants prayer, grants a share in the triune life that is still properly human, then the Spirit grants to human bodies, wills, habits, communal practices, etc., a share in that divine life through re-patterning them in such a way that they may "resonate," at their ontological level, with the "frequency"[43] or pattern of life that is the Trinity at the ultimate ontological level.

Turning again to Thomas Aquinas, Rogers ties infused grace to *meaning*.[44] "As Aquinas would put it, grace is the meaning that God

---

[40] Rogers, 216. This section represents Rogers' interpretation of Aquinas.

[41] For more on this notion, see Joseph P. Wawrykow, *God's Grace and Human Action: 'Merit' in the Theology of Thomas Aquinas* (Notre Dame, IN: Univ. of Notre Dame Press, 1995) for a good account and appropriate bibliography.

[42] Rogers, 216.

[43] Musical analogies abound in Christian theology. Henri de Lubac develops his exposition of the classic four fold sense of scripture with just such a musical analogy. *Medieval Exegesis*, vol. 2, *The Four Senses of Scripture*, trans. E. M. Macierowski (Grand Rapids: William B. Eerdmans, 2000), see especially p. 187.

[44] The connection of ascesis to the formation of the body as a signifier is a vast and important part of this argument. One notable connection can be found in Patricia Cox Miller, "Dreaming the Body: An Aesthetics of Asceticism," in *Asceticism*, eds.

bestows, by which God arranges not primarily words, but states of affairs (*res*) or forms of life (*habitus*) to signify."[45] These states of affairs and forms of life signify divinity through analogical participation in the divine life. And that is what the Spirit gives when God gives a Christian person the Spirit.

Notice, however, that at this point the Person of the Spirit has dropped out of the conversation and the word "grace" has taken priority. It is at this point that Rogers names the problem in the (Western) Christian tradition that was the fall-out of the Pelagian and Augustinian debates of the fifth century.[46] Quoting Vladmir Lossky, Rogers asserts that after Pelagius: "Grace and liberty . . . are transformed into two mutually exclusive concepts which then have to be reconciled, as if they were two objects exterior to one another."[47] The gift of the Spirit and human freedom are set up as mutually incompatible realities when one speaks of the concept of grace before talking about the *concrete* person of the Spirit.

Here is the question: "who saves human being, God, or human beings?" When set in such stark, dichotomous terms, there can be only one Christian answer—God alone. But somehow, the tradition finds this answer to be too simple. What about the Trinity and relationships among persons? There must be some form of human involvement for salvation to be *human* salvation, and not merely conceptual salvation. The problem is the dichotomous terms in which the debate is set. "Grace" becomes the word used to mediate these two radical positions: all God, or all human. "Grace" becomes a "suspect *tertium quid*,"[48] a "third thing" between the divine life granted by the Spirit and the human life of habitual choices. And, as with every *tertium quid*, the distance between the two terms that this third term is supposed to mediate is actually widened, rather than truly bridged. So, as

---

Vincent L. Wimbush and Richard Valantasis (New York: Oxford University Press, 1995), 282, where she asserts that ascesis is the manipulation of the body to drive it as close as possible to the vitality of the "exemplary body," (in the case of Christianity, this body would be Christ's) in an attempt to control the play of the body as a signifier.

45   Rogers, 217; Rogers references Thomas Aquinas, *Summa Theologica* I.1.10.

46   An excellent resource for the nature and history of this debate is J. Padout Burns, ed., *Theological Anthropology* (Philadelphia: Fortress Press. 1981).

47   Rogers, 217, quoting Vladimir Lossky, *The Mystical Theology of the Eastern Church* (London: James Clarke, 1957), 198.

48   Rogers, 218.

with most theological uses of a *tertium quid*,[49] "the way forward is sometimes to omit rather than obtrude the troublesome term."[50]

It is at this point in his argument that Rogers delivers the most pertinent constructive proposal for the point of this chapter. Grace, among other things, means gift. And the gift of God in Christ simply is God—God the Spirit. The Spirit is God's gift; the Spirit is God's *grace*. The solution to the "problem of grace and freewill" is simply to omit the word "grace" and, whenever possible, replace it with the word "Spirit."[51] The point: keep Christian theology personal and Trinitarian, rather than conceptual and mechanical.

With reference to the scripture, "the love of God has been shed abroad in our hearts,"[52] Rogers takes up Augustine's exegesis,[53] claiming that the Spirit is the love of God, and by the Father's gift of the Spirit, human being loves God with the same love—that is, the Spirit—with which God loves himself. So, in one sense, the Christian habit of love of God is simply the fact that the Spirit has *rested upon* the Christian person, and, therefore, the habits of the Christian person. But what makes that love still *proper* to the human person who possesses it is the fact that the Spirit, by means of alighting upon the human person, grants the human will and its habits the opportunity to "resonate" with the "frequency" of the Spirit. That resonance may be in tune with the Spirit, but it is the human person who actually resonates, and therefore it is truly a property of the human person as well.

Rogers proposes a way to put this exercise into action by recommending Aquinas' exposition of the eighth chapter of Romans

---

[49]   In the early Christological debates of the Church, Christ as a "third thing," a kind of hybrid between God and human being provides the chief example of the theological problem of the *tertium quid*.

[50]   Rogers, 218.

[51]   As a qualifier on what may seem an extreme suggestion (given the importance of the word "grace" in the Western Christian tradition), Rogers does admit that it is not possible to go without the word "grace" in Christian theology altogether. But because the use of this word has "distracted" Christian thought for so long, Rogers offers his extreme suggestion as a kind of exercise of righting Christian discourse back towards a clearer course of direction (*Ibid.*, 219).

[52]   Romans 5:5

[53]   Augustine, *de Trinitate* 15.36

wherein he identifies God's law with the Spirit.[54] This is God's law as a way of life and not as a code set in writing. The Spirit fulfills the prophecy that God will write the law upon human hearts.[55] The law and the Spirit are one insofar as the Spirit issues habits in those upon whom he alights. For just as the Trinity is a "ruled community,"[56] so too the Christian community and those who participate in it become "ruled" as they begin to participate in this divine life upon receiving the Holy Spirit.[57]

Rogers claims that, just as the Spirit rests on the Son in the eternity of the triune life, and also upon the body of the incarnate Son in the incarnation, so too "the Spirit rests on the Son in the habits of the law."[58] For "grace just is the effect of the Holy Spirit dwelling in [Christian] hearts and writing a new law upon them."[59] Again, following Aquinas' exegesis of Paul, grace simply is the "law of the Spirit," and that as the Spirit of life in Jesus Christ.[60] This is "law," not in the written, prescriptive sense (for that would simply be the *nomos* that is the Logos), but in the "natural," almost empirical, descriptive sense, of the way things normatively function under certain conditions. Thus the law of God is "written on the heart" of the Christian because a *habit* represents an internal law of self-governance (autonomy, in its true sense).

Grace, as that which God gives the human being that the human being may properly call his or her own, is a *"structure that liberates."*[61] Rogers points to James (1:25), and names grace "the perfect law, the law of liberty." This law is the "law" of behavior that habituation en-

---

[54] Eugene Rogers here refers to Thomas Aquinas' *In Romanos*, in the *Super epistolas, Pauli lectura*, 8th rev. ed., ed. Raphael Cai, 1953.

[55] Jer. 31:33: But this is the covenant which I will make with the house of Israel after those days, says the LORD: I will put my law within them, and I will write it upon their hearts; and I will be their God, and they shall be my people.

[56] Rogers, 221.

[57] This is not unlike the direction that Richard Hooker takes in his *Laws of Ecclesiastical Polity* (I.2.2). Hooker grounds his entire treatise on the supposition that all law flows from God because, as Trinity, "The being of God is a kinde of lawe to his working." *The Folger Library Edition of The Works of Richard Hooker*, vol. 1, ed. W. Speed Hill, *Of the Laws of Ecclesiastical Polity*, ed. Georges Edelen (Cambridge, MA: Belknap Press of Harvard Univ. Press, 1977), 59.

[58] Rogers, 193.

[59] *Ibid.*, 193.

[60] *Ibid.*, 194.

[61] *Ibid.*

tails. The Spirit appropriates human reason and habit, "the structure of knowing and the reliability of love,"[62] respectively. And this is possible because will and grace, habit and Spirit are not rivals.[63] God's transcendence over what God creates is such that God does not compete, in any way, with that which God creates.[64] As Rogers points out earlier in his argument, the Spirit, at the same time that it is not material, is not non- or anti-material either, because Christianity does not contrast God and creation in a simple, dialectical way.[65] Thus the absolutely transcendent Spirit may rest upon the flesh he creates, and the freedom of the Spirit can alight upon, empower, and shape the freedom, the wills, and the concomitant habits of Christians.

An important point here that Rogers emphasizes is that habits ought not to be conceived as static, but dynamic. Habit "abbreviates a series of events,"[66] but, abbreviated or no, they are events nonetheless, and therefore active, dynamic. These dynamic abbreviations are the traces that divine intervention into human life leaves behind—if it leaves behind anything human and personal at all. And this is because of the inherent habitual structure of human action in general:

> If all human action, to be human, is habitual, then it is habitual in two ways. One, all human acting *arises* out of structures or pathways previously laid down; two, all human action *builds* or *blazes* such structures or pathways.[67]

This vision of human activity means that human being is ever building habits from previous ones. If God redeems human action, as human action, then "God habituates us."[68]

This discussion of human habit is all to say that when God the *Spirit* rests upon human beings, this active "abiding" of the Spirit results in human action. God, through Christ, involves the human person in his or her salvation by allowing a share in the good works of Christ, which, thereby, become the good works of the Christian as

---

[62]   *Ibid.*

[63]   *Ibid.*, 195.

[64]   David Burrell, *Freedom and Creation in Three Traditions* (Notre Dame, IN: Notre Dame Univ. Press, 1993). See also Kathryn Tanner, *God and Creation in Christian Theology: Tyranny or Empowerment* (New York: Blackwell, 1988).

[65]   Rogers, 58-59.

[66]   *Ibid.*, 198.

[67]   *Ibid.*

[68]   *Ibid.*

well.[69] God grants human beings, therefore, "an analogy between our goodness and God's [goodness], a participation which is already a share in God's own life and agency, since only God is self-standingly good."[70]

This share in God's life and goodness means that, paradoxically, but without contradiction, the Spirit makes participation in the life of God *intrinsic* to human nature:

> [T]he Spirit, in crying "Abba!" in sighs too deep for (this-worldly) words makes human beings capable of the divine Word, incorporates them into Christ's intratrinitarian address to the Father. Then indeed there is no need for the condescension of grace; human beings need no words if at last they possess the Word, God's own principle of intelligibility; they need no room of their own to act in, when they inhabit God's infinite roominess. Then they see God no longer by a form accidental to their nature, but by a participation become intrinsic; they see God by God's essence, or "as he is." Just that cannot, of course, be intelligibly communicated in this life, but is a radically eschatological matter.[71]

This share in the life of God that becomes intrinsic to human nature by virtue of infused habituation is only fully intelligible from the point of view of the *eschaton*. In Christ, however, the Christian asserts that "the kingdom of heaven is at hand,"[72] and in the sacramental life of the Church, the ritual mysteries, the Christian is granted a foretaste of that intelligibility.

Spirit, Gift and Ascesis

THE ASCETIC SELF is ambiguous, according to Flood, because it is unclear on the level of immanent analysis exactly how a given human "self" could simultaneously assert the self by denying the self. So far the argument has been that this ambiguity has a parallel structure in Christian thought. If salvation is by "grace alone," in what way can it truly be the salvation of human beings *qua* human? Rogers gives a theological framework for an indigenous Christian description of what Flood calls the "ambiguity of the self." By understanding ascetic practice as itself a gift one may lay aside worries that Christian asceticism is the expression of a heretical "works gospel," and learn, rather, that ascetic practice is the manifestation of the freedom of the Spirit enabling human freedom.

---

[69]   *Ibid.*, 199.

[70]   *Ibid.*

[71]   *Ibid.*, 222.

[72]   Mark 1:15 (AV).

Two things must come together for this to make sense. First, asceticism needs to be understood as fitting to the nature of a triune God. The previous three chapters outline an argument for this. This chapter is an argument for the second part: that asceticism must somehow be a necessary component to redeeming human beings as human.

Rogers argues that human nature, including human freedom, is inherently habit-forming, and that therefore salvation, if it is human salvation, must involve the transformation of human habits. This argument for the salvation of human habits illumines Rogers' Trinitarian and Pneumatological answer to the "problem" of grace and freedom—and Flood's postcritical "ambiguity of the self."

According to Rogers, it is not "grace" as something abstract that God grants the Christian; but God grants a share in God's very self, a share in God's life by granting a relationship to a Person within the Trinity: the Spirit. The Spirit rests upon the Christian body and transforms it. One key way that the Spirit transforms the Christian body is by granting it new habits that compare, analogously, to the patterned life of the Trinity.

But the Spirit does not give habits to human being such that it remains ever something foreign to human nature, extrinsic or foreign to human being. For without the ability to say that the habit is a human habit, it cannot be considered fully given to the human person. So although the source and even reality of the habit is infinitely beyond human being, the Spirit grants that it may become properly human— truly the habit of this human being who has received it as gift. And it is not only the habit that the Spirit forms, but also the very practices and events that lead to their formation. These practices are what Christians call *ascesis*.

The role of the Spirit in this regard invites a Trinitarian reflection on the divine ground of the Christian ascetic experience. Again, Rogers' construction provides this description. The Spirit is able to offer real human participation in the divine life because, in the economy of salvation, the Son allowed the Spirit to give him perfect humanity. Ascesis is fitting to the Spirit's economy of the sanctification of human will and habits, for wills and habits are formed through corporate practices with corporeal ramifications.

The Spirit does not abrogate this aspect of being human, but rather takes it up and sanctifies it in the gift of ascesis. Through this ascetic activity the Spirit grants the gift of inclusion in the body of the Son through ascetic conformation of the human body to Christ's body, because when the Spirit alights upon a human body, it is, thereby, the body of the Son, who is the Christ. Given this Trinitarian and economic description of the ground of ascesis one may discern that ascesis analogously corresponds to the divine act of incarnation itself in the life of the Christian and the Christian body—it "fleshes out" the Logos in the life and body of the Christian.

So recall how Rogers' answer to the so-called "problem" of "grace and free will" in the Christian tradition is to use the word Spirit, in place of grace, as often as theologically possible. God's grace is the Spirit, and, therefore, the Spirit brings ascesis *as a life pattern, which may be called truly human* even if not human in derivation. This paradox of ascetic action as a human endeavor that is nevertheless in its entirety a gift of the Spirit means that what Flood has seen in post-critical terms as ambiguous, may, in indigenous Christian terms, be seen as the "actively passive" self, the non-competitive self of Christian sanctification.

The indigenous Christian description of freedom is not the same as that of modern secular philosophies. Freedom is not the arbitrary self-choice of the will. Freedom is rational pursuit of the end or *telos* of one's nature. The end of being human is to share in God's life forever. Unlike any earthly creature, the goal of human nature is beyond the capabilities even of prelapsarian human nature. Therefore, human freedom must always be a gift of God, it must always be granted through divine *fiat*. Because this freedom is rational pursuit, just as soon as the will becomes arbitrary it is, for that very reason, no longer truly free in the Christian sense. So the modern secular definition of freedom and the Christian definition are actually dialectically opposed to one another.

God transcends God's creation so utterly as to be free from competitive relationship with it. That is to say, unlike the way certain creatures may "transcend" certain other creatures within creation through competition, assertion, even violence, God's transcendence does not follow that pattern, for God is not a creature. God is not just the "biggest thing around."[73] God is not a "thing" at all. Therefore di-

---

[73] David B. Burrell uses this phrase in his critique of an inadequate Christian theology of creation in the article "Creation, Metaphysics, and Ethics," *Faith and Philosophy* 18 (April 2001): 205.

vine freedom and human freedom need not be understood as set up in a relationship of competition with one another such that if God wills salvation the human will can be no part in its own salvation. Rather, it is just exactly the human will, as a necessary part of being human, that God is saving. God grants freedom to human being through a share in divine freedom upon the giving of the Spirit of God to the Christian human body.

This paradoxical, but not contradictory, relationship of the human to the divine will can be called "active passivity." This is where, although the Christian is called to be passive before God ("thy will, not mine, be done"), nevertheless, because God's will stands outside of a competitive relationship with human being, for that very passivity before God to be expressed the Christian must *take certain actions*. But even in the act of taking such truly free measures—for the first time since the fall—the Christian must attribute the power and ultimate will and source of these actions to God and to oneself only and at most secondarily and derivatively.

So ascesis is actually a paradox of the gift of forming a human will in the habit of active passivity within the context of a relationship of non-competitive transcendence between human being and God. It is therefore possible to assert that the Christian practice of asceticism existentially teaches, through subjective appropriation, the Christian paradox that, "by grace [sheer gift] you have been saved through faith," (Eph. 2.8) and that, at the same time, "faith apart from works is dead" (James 2.26). And the shape that this "teaching" takes is that of "active passivity."

Ascesis is simply an aspect of the gift of the Spirit to the Christian body. The Spirit enables real human participation in God's life because the Son allowed the Spirit to give him perfect humanity as Jesus Christ. So Flood's ambiguous ascetic self, in indigenous Christian terms, is simply the Christian disciple realizing complete dependence upon God in and through the gift of Christian ascetic practice. In terms of the goals of this first part of this project, therefore, ascesis *teaches* the Christian paradox of "active passivity," that is, the reality that human being is saved "by grace alone." These four chapters of part one converge to portray a picture of ascesis as that which teaches Christianity. The next part explores the necessarily concomitant discursive counterpart to these indigenous descriptions of Christian as-

cesis: that theology (when construed primarily as a discursive practice) is the ascesis of Christian discourse.

Part II

Theology as Ascesis: From Divine Discourse to the Discipline of Christian Discourse

If anyone makes no mistakes in what he says he is a perfect man, able to bridle the whole body also . . . The tongue is a little member and boasts of great things. How great a forest is set ablaze by a small fire!

And the tongue is a fire. The tongue is an unjust world [*ho kosmos tes adikias*] among our members, staining the whole body [*holon to soma*], setting on fire the cycle of generation, and set on fire by hell [*Gehenna*].

James 3.2b, 5, 6

CHAPTER FIVE

Theology and Contemplative Analogy

In the beginning was the Word, and the Word was with God, and the Word was God. He was in the beginning with God; all things were made through him, and without him was not anything made that was made.

John 1.1-3

THIS CHAPTER ARGUES that theology is ascetic insofar as it is contemplative, that is, caught up in the Christian ascetical practice of *theoria*. Bernard McGinn's seminal historical work on the development of "mysticism" within the Christian tradition gives an historical account of how *theoria* necessarily entails ascesis within the Christian tradition. This account of the ascetical context of *theoria*, or contemplation, provides a context wherein one can understand the work of a father such as Dionysius (or, Denys) the Pseudo-Areopagite. Denys' texts perform a mystagogical contemplation that invites the reader to engage with him in the goal of *theoria*. In this context, Denys enables the recognition of what one could call the "reversal of analogy." Through this use of analogy, Denys' text opens out the inherent connection between human *theoria* and God's own self-understanding in such a way as to display *theoria* as the discursive counterpart to *theosis* in general.

McGinn on the Unity of Ascesis and Contemplation

BERNARD MCGINN'S seminal historical work on the development of "mysticism," or contemplative prayer, within the Christian tradition, provides an account of Christian mysticism as inherently entailed in and even concomitant with Christian asceticism. McGinn explores this in his multi-volume *The Presence of God: A History of Western*

Christian Mysticism,[1] but he also provides a shorter and more concise approach in his article entitled "Asceticism and Mysticism in Late Antiquity and the Early Middle Ages."[2] His implicit thesis is that mysticism and asceticism in Christianity cannot really be separated from one another but must be understood as two phases in one motion, or two ways of looking at the same Christian activity. The real issue he explores in his article, then, is not so much how mysticism and asceticism are related, but how they ever came to be conceived separately. Furthermore, now that they have been separated, he seeks to help others see their actual historical and indigenous unity within the Christian tradition.

If asceticism represents the somatic disciplines that lead to mystical experience, then contemplation, or *theoria* is the Christian name for what that mystical experience entails. McGinn begins his narrative in earnest with a discussion of Clement of Alexandria's contribution to this history. McGinn identifies Clement as "one of the first Christians to use the term *ascesis.*"[3] In Clement, mystical contemplation, or *theoria,* is organically linked to ascesis.[4] Clement, together with his great pupil Origen, "domesticate" the term *theoria* in the sense that they borrow it from Hellenistic philosophy and transform it into the contemplation of the Christian (triune) God.

Hellenistic philosophy recognized two different ways of life: the first is that of the crowd who live in the world of *doing,* and this is called *praxis.* The second is that of gazing or watching that which is eternal—the heavens through astronomy and geometry, or, later, those pure forms that dwell in the heavens through mental meditation and contemplation—and this is called *theoria.*[5] So, even though the English word "theory" comes from this ancient philosophical term, its current English use clearly represents a semantic shift. These terms are defined by ancient philosophers with a polemical edge: they are meant to show the relative meaninglessness of day to day life

---

[1] Bernard McGinn, *The Presence of God: A History of Western Christian Mysticism,* 4 vols. (New York: Crossroads, 1991—2005).

[2] Bernard McGinn, "*Asceticism*and Mysticism in Late Antiquity and the Early Middle Ages," in *Asceticism,* eds. Vincent L. Wimbush and Richard Valantasis, (New York: Oxford Univ. Press, 1995), 58—74.

[3] *Ibid.,* 61.

[4] *Ibid.*

[5] *Ibid.*

(*praxis*) as opposed to the life of meaning and contemplation that their philosophical practices and dialogues entail (*theoria*).

Clement of Alexandria transforms this dichotomy within Christianity and uses the previously pejorative term "*praxis*" to mean the positive first step towards *theoria*. Clement describes the life of Christian discipline as a passage within Christian *praxis* (the active life of ascetical discipline) towards *theoria*, or the contemplative life of mystical experience of the Christian God. And *theoria* is not separable from the praxis, or vice versa, for they entail one another—the one is the goal of the other while the other prepares the Christian for the one. In the west the Greek *praxis* and *theoria* would become the *vita activa* and the *vita contemplativa*.[6] In thus describing the relationship between *praxis* and *theoria*, Clement does at least two things—he places Christian contemplation within the practice of Christian ascesis as part of it and its goal, and he also redeems the common Christian from being seen as less a Christian than the intellectual Christian theologian. The life of *theoria* is made more accessible to the laity insofar as all may take part, in greater or lesser degrees, in the life of Christian ascesis.

At this stage in the narrative one can see that McGinn has traced out a link within the tradition between ascesis, praxis, and the *vita activa* on the one hand, and mysticism, *theoria*, and the *vita contemplativa* on the other. Agreeing with Pierre Hadot,[7] McGinn asserts that ancient philosophy was more like Christian monasticism than like a modern academic department of philosophy.[8] Moving on in his narrative to the figure of Origen, McGinn continues to discuss the Hellenistic philosophical distinction between *praxis* and *theoria*. McGinn explains the historical transition between the roots of Hellenistic philosophy in someone like Plato, to the appropriation and explosion of these categories within Christian practice. In the teachings of someone like Plato, philosophy ought to focus on contemplating the true nature of reality. Later philosophers in the Platonic tradition also teach philosophy as this contemplation—but mediated initially through a meditation upon the texts of the great philosopher.[9] Christianity adopts this developed and text-tradition based model but inserts a

---

6   *Ibid.*

7   Pierre Hadot is discussed at more length in the next chapter.

8   McGinn, "Asceticism and Mysticism," 63.

9   Ibid., 64. More detail on the importance of text and scripture to the task of philosophy and theology follows in chapter seven, below.

new text—the scriptures—in place of Plato (or whichever classic philosopher a given school looks back to as its authority).

McGinn moves on in his discussion to Evagrius of Pontus, and it
is here that McGinn identifies what could be considered the foundation for the later split between the "mystical" and the "ascetic" in
Christian thought. Evagrius describes the Christian life according to a
series of binaries that are related to one another in developmental
terms. First, the Christian undergoes purification through *praktike*, or
the practical life of everyday Christian asceticism. This purification
leads to the clarity of soul that is necessary for *gnostike*, that is to say,
knowledge or contemplation of the way things really are. Within
gnostike, Evagrius suggests another developmental binary between
physike, which is contemplation of the nature of created reality, and
theologike, which is the contemplation of God. Although both *physike*
and *theologike* are *theoria*, their object and, therefore, their content are
different and hierarchically related to each other. Proper contemplation of God's creation leads to deeper knowledge and contemplation
of God. Evagrius would never have conceived of ascesis and the mystical contemplation it leads to and enables as possibly separable from
one another in Christian practice—but he is the first clearly to deline-
ate them from one another conceptually and to describe them as two
phases in a process.[10]

More importantly for this project, however, is McGinn's emphasis
that it is with Evagrius of Pontus—a major and early figure in the development of Christian practice and thought—that the word "theology" (*theologike*) is used explicitly to mean the ascetic contemplation
of God. Evagrius is not innovative here but merely describing a tradition that he inherits, a tradition that subsumes the Hellenistic philosophical goal of *theoria* into the Christian rubric of worship and love
of God.[11] This ascetical tradition that Evagrius' contemporaries simply
understand as Christian discipleship assumes that the love of God entails mystical contemplation, that ascesis is the foundation of this *theoria*, and that *theoria* is indeed the goal of all ascesis. For it is these
somatic disciplines that open out the ascetic to the reality for which
they discipline themselves. The experience of "being opened out" to
Christian reality is what the Origen-Evagrian tradition names *theoria*.

---

[10]   *Ibid.*, 65.
[11]   *Ibid.*, 66—7.

Furthermore, McGinn points out, when Augustine takes up the Evagrian tradition in his monastic practice in the west, he emphasizes the unity and progressive relationship between asceticism and "mysticism," ascesis and contemplation. Augustine receives the tradition with its hierarchical understanding of the relationship between ascesis and contemplation, but he expands the *vita activa* to include not just ascesis, but actual neighbor-love, and he seeks to find their consummation and completion in their harmonious co-existence:[12] contemplation of the divine leads to love of neighbor, while the purgation of ascesis that leads to true love of neighbor also allows for the clarification necessary to enjoy the contemplation of God. At the end of this vast historical survey, McGinn draws attention to the truth that, at least in the west, this monastic calling is not something that only the monk may enjoy. Gregory the Great emphasizes that the contemplative life is the call and within the grasp of every Christian.[13]

McGinn also has something to add to the discussion of the relationship between ascesis and Christian theology as Christian teaching. In his work *The Foundations of Mysticism*, McGinn argues that the development of what would later be called "mysticism" in the Christian tradition was bound up together with the development of what would be called "orthodoxy," for both were concerned with the relationship of Christianity to *gnosis*, or saving knowledge. Both Christian "mysticism" and orthodoxy were forged together in the crucible of the controversy over "Gnosticism" in the second and third Christian centuries. The nascent "great church" on the one hand, and "Gnostics" on the other, overlapped with regards to many shared goals, however, "on several crucial issues the debate over gnosis produced significant reactions against views held by those we today call Gnostics."[14] McGinn describes these crucial issues in terms that would be important both to Christian ascetical practice and the development of orthodoxy; such as, e.g. the goodness of physical creation, the unity of the Old and New Covenant revelation of God, the incarnation of the Word, "but also issues more directly involved in what came to be called mystical theology."[15] The issues that are directly involved in "mystical theology" are also concerns of orthodoxy because the de-

---

[12] *Ibid.*, 67—8.
[13] *Ibid.*, 69.
[14] *Ibid.*, 60.
[15] *Ibid.*

velopment of orthodoxy corresponds with the developing articulation of the practices that bring Christians in contact with their God.[16]

One important possible ramification of McGinn's line of thought that McGinn himself does not explicitly explore is that this simultaneous development of the Christian ascetic tradition and Christian orthodoxy is not merely coincidental but actually intimately related. And this is because the *form* of teaching Christianity and the *content* that is taught cannot be separated. Without proper ascetic training the Christian simply lacks the contact with reality necessary for discerning valid Christian teachings, or, orthodoxy. Without straightforward or orthodox teachings of Christianity as its content, one's approach and practice of ascesis would be skewed.

Coming full round, how then did these so obviously intrinsically connected realities of mysticism and asceticism ever become separated in western Christian thought and to a lesser degree, practice? McGinn points to two figures that represent the beginning and end of the modern era of catholic "spirituality." The Italian Jesuit Giovanni Battista Scaramelli published the *Direttorio ascetico*[17] in 1752, and then in 1754 his *Direttorio mistico*[18] was published posthumously. Here for the first time what would have been considered the two phases of one Christian ascetic motion were clearly separated as different kinds of Christian "spirituality" to be directed differently and treated in different books.[19] In the years of 1923-24, the Sulpician Adolphe Tanquerey, receiving this dichotomy through the work of the likes of Scaramelli, perpetuated it in his *Abrégé de théologie ascétique et mystique*,[20] which "remained a basic textbook in Catholic seminaries down to Vatican II."[21] Without intending to malign either of these figures, McGinn is only pointing out that the unified tradition of Christian ascetical contemplation was received and passed on in modern times in a way that seemed clearly to divide the two. What began with Evagrius as a bi-

---

[16] *Ibid.*, 60.

[17] Giovanni Battista Scaramelli, *Direttorio ascetico in cui s' insegna il modo di condurre l'Anime per vie ordinarie della grazia alla perfezione christiana, indirizzato ai direttori della Anime* (Naples, 1752).

[18] Giovanni Battista Scaramelli, *Il direttorio mistico indrizato a' direttori di quelle anime che Iddio conduce per la via della contemplazione* (Venice, 1754).

[19] McGinn, "Asceticism and Mysticism," 58.

[20] Adolphe Tanquerey, *Abrégé de théologie ascétique et mystique* (Paris: Société de S. Jean l'Évangéliste, 1927).

[21] McGinn, "Asceticism and Mysticism," 58.

nary opposition of development within a single way of monastic life becomes, in modern Roman Catholicism, two different subjects of study.

Some of the immediate ramifications of this division in actual practice in the Christian west included the notion that mystical experience could be pursued not only in a separate book from asceticism, but without the need of ascetic practice. With mysticism directly dissociated with everyday concrete Christian discipleship, it began to be seen as the strange, unexplainable—and usually unwanted—experiences of the "touched." For "theology" as an intellectual activity to remain legitimate, it needed to be dissociated from such a "fanatical" and "ungrounded" pursuit. So theology became no longer the contemplation of reality in and of God, nor even the description of the experience of such contemplation as Christian "teachings" (*Sacra doctrina*), but a scholarly activity that goes on in academic departments of "theology," a discipline pursued in a manner not unlike what Augustine would have denounced as *curiositas*.[22] This is a far cry from the approach of the church mothers and fathers to theology in general, and of that pseudonymous, or, perhaps, anonymous father, Denys the Pseudo-Areopagite, in particular.

Denys' Guided Contemplation and the Reversal of Analogy

THROUGHOUT Denys the Pseudo-Areopagite's corpus, he is interested in removing all conceptual idols that keep people from actual union with God. God is not a concept, and Denys wished to secure a mental state where no concept was substituted for actual knowledge of God, for knowing a concept is not knowing God. Denys' works, especially the *Divine Names*, are an invitation for the reader to "participate" in contemplating along with Denys, via *apophasis* (the path of negation or the *via negativa*). In this *apophasis*, the contemplative reaches a cessation of discursive thought that grants the possibility of actual and intelligible participatory union with the divine. Within this contemplation, the ascetic discovers a kind of "reversal" of analogy wherein human discourse participates in the (discursive) life of God. Denys approaches theology, therefore, not as a "system" of representations, but as the composition of a text that both invites and is itself a performance of *theoria*. Here the culminating ascetic discipline of contemplation, as meditation upon scripture, becomes the end and definition of "theology."

---

[22]　Paul J. Griffiths, "The Vice of Curiosity," *Pro Ecclesia* 15 (Winter 2006): 47—63.

Denys' works are all, according to him, biblical expositions. And this exposition takes the form of guided meditation. The Divine Names, according to Denys, is an exegesis of the concepts attributed to God throughout the scriptures:

> I come now to an explication of the divine names, as far as possible. Here too let us hold onto the scriptural rule that when we say anything about God, we should set down the truth [given by the authors of scripture].[23]

Not only is it an exegesis; more importantly, it is a guide to the proper exegesis of these attributions. That is, given that God is the absolute transcendent, the proper exegesis of these "divine names," which for Denys refer to the conceptual "symbols" attributed to God in the scriptures, must be in accord with the fact that, as the transcendent, God is above all names. Therefore, Denys explains:

> We learn of all these mysteries from the divine scriptures and you will find that what the scripture writers have to say regarding the divine names refers, in revealing praises, to the beneficent processions of God.[24]

This passage is pregnant with much of Denys' purpose in writing this particular work. The mysteries that one learns from are the mysteries of the church, that is, those ritual acts performed by the corporate body, the sacraments.[25] The Divine Liturgy itself being *Eucharista*, thanksgiving, and the highest form of "revealing praises," addresses those praises to the "beneficent processions" that are the triune God.

Through these mysteries, Denys would have the Christian discover God as the one who transcends every reality in a superlative way. That is, God is to be contemplated as infinitely beyond even being itself. The divine names are those predicates attributed to God in the scriptures that come from the realm of the intelligible rather than

---

23   Pseudo-Dionysius *Divine Names* I.1. Unless otherwise noted, all quotations from the writings of Pseudo-Dionysius are taken from *Pseudo-Dionysius: The Complete Works*, trans. Colm Luibheid, Classics of Western Spirituality (Paulist Press, New York: 1987).

24   *Ibid.*, 51.

25   Current scholarship on Denys' thought assumes that it is deeply influenced by the church's liturgy. See, for example: John Barnett, "Mysticism and Liturgy in Denys the Areopagite," *Downside Review* 118 (Apr. 2000): 111—36; Kenneth Paul Wesche, "Christological Doctrine and Liturgical Interpretation in Pseudo-Dionysius," *St. Vladimir's Theological Quarterly* 33 (1989): 53—73; Paul Rorem, "Moses as the Paradigm for the Liturgical Spirituality of Pseudo-Dionysius," *Studia Patristica* 18 (1989): 275—79.

the sensible. These attributes must be given in the context of ecstatic praise, not systematic theology.

Denys is working within a radically different world-view than the one to which modern thinkers are accustomed. A characterization of the modern post-Kantian world-view might be that the most basic reality is the material. The human mind, epiphenomenon of certain complex physical structures in the human brain, abstracts from the senses what become representations of reality in human brains. These representations then help one recognize things, and these are the "concepts" that constitute the raw material of human knowledge. This "theater of representations" is the basic starting point for much modern epistemology. Denys' world-view is as close to the opposite of this as possible.

In ancient thought, and particularly the Neo-Platonic version thereof, what is most real is not "stuff," but that which is intelligible, the realm of "intelligence." This intelligence, when expressed "outward" (so to speak), results in physical manifestations. That is, in the Platonic world of form and matter individual subjects receive their reality as forms impressed upon, or more accurately, manifested "outward" in matter. The human body is shaped as it is because its soul, that is, its form, is such that when "pressed outward" toward the material, the soul simply manifests as the human body. Epistemology begins, therefore, as the realization (in both senses of the word) of this participation of concrete realities in their respective forms. That is, true knowledge comes when one contemplates, or discerns intelligibly through a kind of mental participation in those self-same forms, those forms in which given concrete realities participate.

There is another difference between modern thought and this "participatory" world-view. The neat modern distinctions between epistemology and ontology are collapsed in what can be called a "gnoseological reduction," after the archaic word for "theory" of knowledge and reality.[26] Of course, what seems to be a reduction to the modern mind is simply perceived to be a unified reality within the

---

[26] For more on this use of the word "gnoseology," see the introduction to the volume *Radical Orthodoxy*, eds. John Milbank, Catherine Pickstock and Graham Ward (London: Routledge, 1999). Also Catherine Pickstock's essay, "Music: Soul, City, and Cosmos," in the same. Finally, see also John Milbank and Catherine Pickstock, *Truth in Aquinas* (London: Routledge, 2001), 20, on gnoseological dualism in the interpretation of Thomas Aquinas.

ancient Neo-Platonic frame of mind. Specifically, when knowledge is the intuition, or realization of the fact of participation, then knowledge is intellectual participation in the realities that be. So too, knowledge is participatory just insofar as reality itself is the manifestation of various levels of participation. The intellect or human mind is one of those levels of reality that participates in and is participated in by other aspects of reality. The "gnoseological reduction" is nothing more than the realization that being is the (ontological) ground of knowledge, and knowledge is a (or, an intelligible) manifestation of being.

Denys' first task, therefore, is that of contemplating the possible intelligibility of predicating the divine at all, especially insofar as God is construed as "super-abundant" transcendent reality. This is the movement of his contemplations in the *Theological Representations*.[27] Then he must take into account, given that God is God (that is, utterly transcendent of any name or description), what these *theologians* (that is, for Denys, the inspired authors of scripture[28]) could mean by employing such predications. These predications are derived from creation. But within the realm of creation there is a divide between the realm of the intelligible and the realm of the sensible, or material. There is also a hierarchy here. The intelligible is greater, perhaps even more "real" than the material. In light of this, therefore, there are two possible realms within creation from which to ascribe names to God, namely, the intelligible and the material.

This, then, is the context of Denys' work. The *Divine Names* progressively develops upon his first, now nonextant work, *Theological Representations*.[29] It seems that this first work was a meditative justification of cataphatic predication of divinity, in opposition to possible Neo-Platonic criticism (of, say, the literal attributions to God found in Christian scripture). The *Divine Names* also, in many ways, rehearses this meditation and is dependent upon it. The main purpose of *Divine Names*, however, is to properly contemplate divine attribution, particularly those attributes which come from the realm of the intelligible, rather than the sensible.

---

[27] Pseudo-Dionysius, *Mystical Theology* III (138).
[28] Pseudo-Dionysius, *On Divine Names* I.1 (50).
[29] It is not known whether these should be considered fictional, or simply lost. See footnote to *On Divine Names* I.1 (50) in the edition translated by Luibheid.

The *Divine Names* starts at the top of this hierarchy and meditates upon the meaning of the names derived from the realm of the intelligible, that is to say, conceptual names. It is important to keep in mind, however, that these concepts are not to be understood as part of a "theater of representations" within an individual sentient being's brain. Rather, these concepts are participated *external* realities, if not more real, then at least as real as the individual subjects they instantiate. The next logical link in Denys' corpus leads to the *Symbolical Theology*,[30] which deals with those symbols of the divine that are derived from the realm of the sensible.

Why this downward motion from the intelligible to the sensible, rather than vice versa? Denys explains that he must treat the *Divine Names* first because, as part of the superior realm of the intelligible, the human mind is more likely to mistake these with the divine and thereby turn concepts into idols. Denys therefore insists that utmost care and diligence be taken in order to obtain proper contemplation of the divine nature. Likewise, the *Symbolical Theology* follows close behind in order to point out by their obviously inferior ability to refer to the divine, that all creaturely attribution must be laid aside for the *via negativa*. This "way of negation" is the subject of the next text within the flow of his thought, the famously influential *Mystical Theology*.[31]

Setting these key works side by side in terms of their logical flow one to the other makes it clear that Denys' theology is not systematic in the modern sense. Denys' religious thought most closely resembles the genera of "devotional" or "spirituality" in contemporary literature—but without its resolute lack of theological depth or analytic thought. This is because a system is simply not a goal, or even a viable option for Denys:

> Cause of all existence, and therefore itself transcending existence, it [God] alone could give an authoritative account of what it really is.[32]

His goal as a theologian is not that of summing up Christian discourse about God and showing its conceptually systematic inter-related-ness, no matter how much he may well be committed to the notion that Christian doctrine is organically interrelated.

---

[30] Again, this text is now nonextant, and scholars debate whether it is fictional or simply lost.

[31] Pseudo-Dionysius, *Mystical Theology* 3 (138—40).

[32] Pseudo-Dionysius, *Divine Names* I.1 (50).

A system is the proper work of one who is committed to a "theater of representations" epistemology. That is, if knowledge is the result of abstractions on the part of the individual subject, then the goal of Christian teaching is the delivering of the proper abstractions in a totalizing and harmonizing way, that is, a "systematic theology." However, if one is committed to a participatory model of epistemology, and in particular a gnoseological reduction of epistemology and ontology, then theology necessarily has a different goal—participatory, intelligible union with God through *theoria*, contemplation.

This leads to two key approaches to theology to keep in mind when reading Denys' works. The first is in regards to his corpus as a whole. Denys' general Christian practice conforms to a soteriology of *theosis*, or "deification," as discussed above, in the first chapter of this work. That is to say, he upholds an ancient patristic understanding that the goal of Christian salvation is a sort of "union in communion" with God, which grants human beings unity with divine nature, by grace, while fully retaining their particular and created status. Denys speaks of this "deification" (or divinization) in Neo-Platonic vocabulary. That is, Denys makes use of Neo-Platonic categories and their "gnoseological reduction." This participatory epistemology and ontology easily lends itself to this kind of soteriology. Namely, if reality is such that things exist as participants in the reality of things of a higher cosmological or even ontological status (e.g., individual concrete subjects participating in their conceptual forms) then the notion that human nature should ultimately participate in the divine is not absurd.

With this in mind, it is easy to see that Denys' goal in the composition of these theological texts is not *system*, but *journey*. He does not want his work read in order to *abstract* "facts" from it and add them to some theater of representations. Denys desires that, through a meditative reading of his works, his readers may *participate* with him in his "God-talk," his theology, his contemplation of God, and thereby leave behind with him the merely rational (indeed, all of created reality, for that matter) for union with God. For Denys, just as the realm of the intelligible almost completely transcends the realm of the sensible, such that the material has no grasp of the realities going on in the realm of the intelligible, so too, then, by perfect analogy, the Divine transcends all of created reality, both intelligible and sensible together, but in an altogether superlative and infinite way. Just as a stone cannot "intuit" the Good but nevertheless participates in it, so too even the highest realities within the realm of the intelligible cannot conceptually "grasp" God, but they participate in God. The human mind cannot grasp God, but God most certainly "grasps" human thought. Union with God then is not so much an ontological problem as an ontological reality. The goal of theology is *theoria*, contemplation, as the intelligible realization on the part of the believer of God as ontological ground of reality. Such contemplation leads to increasing love, devotion and holiness on the part of the believer—which in turn leads to still greater degrees of union.

The second key to understanding Denys is the approach to God as primordial archetype. Again, this understanding of God and God's relationship to reality is simultaneously borrowed from, and a transformation of, Neo-Platonic thought. Here is a passage where these two approaches actually come into direct play with one another:

> Furthermore, since there are many who are by his gift raised, so far as they can be, to *divinization*, it would seem that here there is not only differentiation but actual replication of the one God. In fact he is nothing less than the *archetypal* God, the supra-divine transcendentally one God who dwells indivisibly in every individual and who is in himself undifferentiated unity with no commixture and no multiplication arising out of his presence among the many.[33]

The "differentiation" referred to by Denys in the text is that which exists within the godhead manifest as the three Persons of the Trinity. The "replication" of God refers not to the making of little "gods;" rather it is Denys' way of dealing with multifarious personal participation in God, without making it in any way a multiplication of the divine Persons. By "divinization" human persons are not made divine Persons. They remain human persons and are divinized by this "actual replication of the one God."[34] This can be so because of the following: God is the archetypal font and source of creation, its patterns and created personhood. This concept of "the archetypal God" is also what allows Denys to claim, contrary to some of his Neo-Platonic contemporaries, that affirmative predication of God is

---

[33]   *Ibid.*, II.11 (67); italics mine.

[34]   In this one finds something similar to Florensky's speculation about the nature of divine persons as three and the possibility of created person's participating in the divine.

appropriate. This paradoxical justification of cataphatic theology is the central theme of the *Divine Names*.

Denys also uses the term "exemplar" in reference to these "archetypes" (*paradeigmata*). In speaking of these exemplars, Denys says:

> The exemplars of everything preexist as a transcendent unity within It [God]. It brings forth being as a tide of being. We give the name "exemplar" to those principles which preexist as a unity in God and which produce the essences of things.[35]

In Platonic parlance, that which "produces the essences of things," is the forms. What has already changed by Neo-Platonism is that this "heaven of forms" has been transferred into the primordial "One." The forms that necessarily pre-exist those things formed by them, indeed *produced* by them, are conceived to "pre"-exist in the unnamable transcendent. But Denys is a Christian and committed to the scriptures, so even this thought is "taken captive for Christ:"

> Theology [which, for Denys, is the scriptures] calls them predefining, divine good acts of will which determine and create things and in accordance with which the Transcendent One predefined and brought into being everything that is.[36]

Words such as "act," "will" and "create," are not Neo-Platonic theological terms. They are Christian words derived from reflection upon the way that the Christian scriptures describe God.

In Denys' contemplations, the Platonic forms that have been shifted into the "One" by the Neo-Platonists have been transformed into the preexistent "thoughts" of a personal God who by divine "thought" "wills" creation. Gone is emanation; gone is being as a "bubbling forth" of the "One." Of course, Denys would never say God is a "person" in a straightforward sense. But neither would he say that God is good in a straightforward sense. This is a transformation, a Christianization, of the Neo-Platonic through contemplation of scripture.

God creates all things in accordance with the divine unified archetypal "thoughts." This understanding of God is another aspect of the divine that allows for divinization. If human being is created as an impression and expression of divine archetypes, then her "natural," or at least perfect state, is union with that archetype by which she is formed and in which she participates in order to have her being. But it

---

[35]   *Ibid.*, V.8 (102).

[36]   *Ibid.*

is also because of the primordial archetypes that Christians may predicate creaturely things of God. Here is where Denys transforms his Neo-Platonic background:

> And so it is that as Cause of all and as transcending all, he is rightly nameless and yet has the names of everything that is. Truly he has dominion over all and all things revolve around him, for he is their cause, their source, and their destiny.[37]

While affirming the divine transcendence over all creation, and therefore over all predication (again, because of the "gnoseological reduction" of ontology and epistemology) he nevertheless asserts that predication, indeed infinite predication, is due him as creator, and archetypal progenitor, of all:

> [The divine] actually contains everything beforehand within itself—and this in an uncomplicated and boundless manner—and it is thus by virtue of the unlimited goodness of its single all-creative Providence. Hence the songs of praise and the names for it are fittingly derived from the sum total of creation.[38]

These "names" and "songs of praise"[39] are prayerful notes (doxology), prayerful notes of contemplation, not systematic theology. It is only fitting for a being who exists as formed by an archetype, and who possess not only the capacity to understand this but even the capacity to participate directly in this fact, to "praise" the source of all archetypes. So Denys' argument throughout the text, but especially in its introductory chapters (namely, those coming before chapter four), traces this development: God is identified as the nameless transcendent, even above the name "God." This nameless transcendence is identified as the source of all that is, as the *scriptural creator* of everything that is. Everything within creation is created in one divine act. Therefore, creaturely names may be used for the nameless because the nameless is their source, destiny and sustenance—chiefly by being contained within this nameless transcendent reality before their creation.

The *Divine Names* has three major divisions. Chapters one through three comprise the first division and lead the reader into the contemplation of the object at hand. They summarize his previous work, the *Symbolic Theology*, they introduce the topic of conceptual attribution of God, and then they establish a Christian, Trinitarian foundation to

---

37   *Ibid.*, I.7 (56).
38   *Ibid.*
39   *Humneitai kai onomazetai.*

such contemplation. All subsequent chapters apply this pattern to meditation upon the conceptual predicates derived from scripture. The last portion of the book can be divided in half conceptually: chapter four deals with the attribute of the "Good." This discussion of the Good becomes the archetypal interpretive key for all the subsequent attributes of God, the discussion of which comprise chapters five through thirteen. That there are many divine names, for Denys, is due to the fact that God may be given the chief of created names: Good. All forms exist because of the form of the Good, including even "being" itself. Therefore the "Good" becomes Denys' chief contemplative category.[40]

The body chapters follow a clear logical order. Chapter one reconfirms the Neo-Platonic vocabulary of God as the nameless transcendent. Chapter two establishes that no predication of God can be established outside of a Christian conception of a triune God; that is, none of the divine names make any sense unless God is conceived to be triune and (super-) Personal, as the Christian scriptures narrate. Chapter three reminds the reader that the purpose of all of the above is not to add to conceptual knowledge but actually to pull the mind away from concepts and thought and into union with this triune and incarnate God. In chapter four Denys contemplates the intelligible reality of the "Good" through a meditation upon scripture and sets up the pattern that will be his approach throughout all subsequent chapters.

Each of the chapters describing the divine names of God follows a similar contemplative pattern. Each approach a certain predicate (e.g., "Good," "Being," "Life," "Wisdom") with a contemplation of the meaning of that particular "name" within the created order. From there Denys reasserts that God transcends this order and therefore this predication. No analogy between God and the created order can be made from this side of the ontological divide. In light of this, Denys provides an exegesis of what the predications properly mean: God's super-abundant transcending of all names. In other words, God is denied these names not by simple negation, but by the divine super-abundant transcendence over these names that allows for the *assumption* of these very names on the part of divinity. This re-

---

[40] This is in contradistinction to other great theologians within the tradition, such as St. Thomas Aquinas, who will assert "Being" and therefore *simplicity* as God's chief attributes.

appropriation of creaturely derived predication is then confirmed on account of the ontological fact that *all things*, and therefore the predicates that are proper to them, "pre-exist" in the divine nature as archetypes.

So, what begins as a warning against the false attempt to predicate by analogy from the created to the creator, transforms, after its simple negation, into the reverse-flow of analogy from the archetypal God to that which God has made. God is not called "good" because creaturely goods may be used as analogies for God. Rather, creaturely realities may be identified as good only insofar as they may be shown to participate, at an (infinite) analogical remove, in the Goodness that God *is*. Here, Denys moves from the *apophatic denial of analogy* to the *apophatic reintegration* of cataphasis *through analogy*. Analogy is here reconceived with God rather than creation as its starting point.

Given this over-all pattern of reversing the discursive flow of analogy from God to creation, chapter four (concerning God as superabundant goodness) provides the key example of the contemplative trajectory of Denys' work of scriptural meditation. Chapter four begins with a discussion of the conceptual content of the name "Good." As stated above, the "Good" is Denys' chief name for God among the conceptual, and therefore among all created names. He begins chapter four thus:

> Let us move on now to the name "Good," which the sacred writers have preeminently set apart for the supra-divine God from all other names. They call the divine subsistence itself "goodness." This essential Good, by the very fact of its existence, extends goodness into all things.[41]

The good is not merely a concept within the created order, nor is it a removed Platonic heaven within a transcendent "One." Goodness is now identified with God as the source and participated reality of all created goods:

> Given that the Good transcends everything, as indeed it does, its nature, unconfined by form, is the creator of all form. In it is nonbeing really an excess of being . . . Whatever partakes of the Good partakes of what preeminently gives form to the formless.[42]

The good also establishes the hierarchy of created existence. Just as Denys assumes a "gnoseological reduction" of knowledge and reality,

---

[41]   Pseudo-Dionysius, *Divine Names*, IV.1 (71).
[42]   *Ibid.*, IV.3 (73).

so too he dwells within a conceptual framework in which goodness precedes being. Things exist in so far as they are good, they are not good because they exist. The more something participates in the form of the good, the more "real" it is. This establishes a hierarchy within which goodness moves certain operations:

> The Good returns all things to itself and gathers together whatever may be scattered, for it is the divine Source and unifier of the sum total of things.[43]

There is a pattern within created existence, for Denys, that is both caused by, and the result of, the good. Insofar as all things exist because of the good:

> All things desire it: Everything with mind and reason seeks to know it, everything sentient yearns to perceive it, everything lacking perception has a living and instinctive longing for it, and everything lifeless and merely existent turns, in its own fashion, for a share of it.[44]

All things "yearn" for the good in proportion to its ability, that is, its share within the good. In this way all things are therefore on a certain progress towards the divine, which is their source. This *exodus / reditus* is clear in passages such as the following where Denys describes a sort of "dance" within the cosmos:

> Because of it and for its sake, subordinate is returned to superior, equal keeps company with equal, superior turns providentially to subordinate, each bestirs itself and all are stirred to do and to will whatever it is they do and will because of the yearning for the Beautiful and the Good.[45]

Here the "Beautiful" and the "Good" are linked together by the harmony that the good produces in the cosmos. But new words— words derived from scripture—have been brought to bear on the subject: "yearning" and "will."

Denys develops the word "yearning" into a key term where this "yearning," both on the part of the creator and the creature, leads to ecstasy. "This divine yearning brings ecstasy so that the lover belongs not to self but to the beloved."[46] Created subjects are taken "out of themselves" in order to participate in their creator. So too, then, the creator "moves" ecstatically "out of" himself in order to create the world out of nothing:

---

43   *Ibid.*, IV.4 (75).
44   *Ibid.*
45   *Ibid.*, IV.10 (79).
46   *Ibid.*, IV.13 (82).

> And, in truth, it must be said too that the very cause of the universe in the beautiful, good superabundance of his benign yearning for all is also carried outside of himself in the loving care he has for everything.[47]

The created actually participates in the yearning of the creator within the triune godhead. The same ecstatic yearning of the creature which leads the creature out of itself into God is that ecstatic yearning which led the creator to create outside of the divine life in its primordial completeness. So, the analogy is reversed: yearning is something of God, granted to human being, not a mere analogy from being human. The Christian ascetic is invited to share, through contemplating along with Denys, and not through "systematic" exposition, this super-abundant yearning of God.

It is with this beautiful and paradoxical vision of God that Denys leads his reader through the rest of this chapter and, indeed, through the rest of his work. Denys next discusses whether God is "love" it-self, or the object of love. He reduces this distinction by way of divine transcendence. God is super-abundantly both lover and beloved. It is from here that the "problem of evil" is proposed. Denys first delivers the traditional "Augustinian" theodicy, explaining evil as a mere lack. Here he struggles with his participatory "gnoseological" world-view. The epistemological category of abstraction, in this case, would have served him well in explaining the meaning of evil. Evil does not exist; it is merely something one perceives by abstraction in things that are deficient in the goodness appropriate to their actual nature.

Finally, however, he provides a more contemplative answer to this issue. God needs no justification, no "theodicy." The problem is not "evil;" the problem is *sin*. The question is not "how can a super-abundantly good God allow evil within creation?" Rather, the question is "how can the human will choose anything but the super-abundantly good God?" The answer to that question, as always, is not to be found in systematic propositions. There can be no reasonable ac-count of the quintessentially unreasonable event, the Fall.[48] Further-

---

[47]   *Ibid.*

[48]   No system is both coherent and complete. A system must either forfeit coherence for completion, or completion for coherence—unless it is purely notional and therefore of no help in describing the nature of reality. The problem of "why did rational beings ever sin in the first place" (notice, this is not the so-called "prob-lem of evil") is the incoherence of the Christian "system" of teaching that keeps it complete and in contact with reality. Even this incoherence is, nevertheless, co-herent by means of paradox. Sin, as "ungood," is also unreal and senseless. It

more, Denys implies through the performative nature of his work that the "answer" to such a "problem" is rather demanded of the reader, existentially. That is to say, the problem of "why choose evil over God" is not a logical puzzle but an existential crisis: choose this day, reader, evil or the loving contemplation of the triune God.

Through an exposition of Denys' *Divine Names* it is clear that Denys is committed to the culminating ascetic discipline of contemplation, practiced as meditation upon scripture, as the end and definition of "theology." Denys approaches theology, therefore, not as a "system" of representations, but as the composition of a performative text that invites the reader to join in *theoria*. Denys invites the reader to "participate" in *theoria* via *apophasis* (the path of negation or the *via negativa*). In this *apophasis*, the contemplative reaches a cessation of discursive thought that grants the possibility of actual and intelligible participatory union with the divine. The discussion now turns to how *theoria*, or contemplation, discovers a kind of "reversal" of analogy wherein human discourse participates in the (discursive) life of God.

God's Discursive Self-knowledge and Human Contemplation of God

DENYS UNDERSTANDS theology to be ascetic because he understands it to be *theoria*—the culmination of the ascetical "project." Denys performs theology as an ascesis of discourse, moving from the apophatic, through a participatory reversal of analogy, to *theoria*. Through this use of analogy, Denys opens out the inherent connection between human *theoria* and God's own self-understanding. This section expounds the discursive analogy of God's triune nature found in Christian scripture. When this analogy undergoes the same "reversal" that one finds in Denys' work, *theoria* emerges as the discursive counterpart to *theosis*.

There are at least two key analogies given in Christian scriptures for God as Trinity of persons. The first key analogy given in scripture for the nature of the Trinity is what one might call the "paternal analogy." The paternal analogy is centered on the filial relationship of the first and second persons of the Trinity to one another, and the actions of the Trinity are described in terms of filiation and begetting. Scrip-

---

therefore *makes sense* that choosing evil *makes no sense*. It must be remembered, nevertheless, that Denys is not concerned with making a Christian *system* that comports with the rules of logic. Denys is concerned with guiding the Christian ascetic in a meditation that allows actual contemplative contact with what is ultimately real, that is, God.

tural examples for this analogy abound and do not need rehearsing. This analogy clearly has to do primarily with the relationship between the Father and the Son. The role of the Holy Spirit, on the other hand, seems almost an afterthought with respect to this analogy, seemingly within the scriptures themselves and certainly within the tradition, although there are a few examples of constructive attempts to include a more robust understanding of the role of the Spirit in the paternal analogy.[49]

But the other analogy for the nature of the Trinity is what one could call the "discursive analogy." What is interesting about this discursive analogy is that it seems to make more sense of *all* three persons of the Trinity, Holy Spirit included. So what is this discursive analogy? The Son is not only the Son but also the Word, that is to say *Logos*—a discursive analogue *par excellence*. Although the Spirit as the Breath of God might not clearly fit within the paternal analogy so often used in discussions of the Trinity, God as Breath fits well within the context of a discursive analogy that also calls God *Word*. It seems, at least initially, that the discursive analogy for the Trinity, often treated as secondary, may well provide for a richer account of the Trinity in terms of the relationship of all three persons to one another. Words are spoken on breath and the Word of God is spoken upon the Breath of God.[50]

If this analogy of discourse within the Godhead is so much more robust than the more typical paternal analogy, why not use it exclusively? Despite the richness it adds, it has problems for which the paternal analogy is the solution. Put quite simply, "word" does not convey a strong sense of individuated personhood in the way that "son" does. "Word" and "breath" seem to be impersonal realities at the control of a given *speaker* within the natural order. Naming the second person of the Trinity "Son" avoids that problem by granting that person a name that implies full personhood. The Spirit, of course, does not escape this problem, really, in either analogue. The answer to granting the discursive analogy a fuller sense of personhood, and accounting the Holy Spirit a richer personhood in both analogues, is Denys' reversal of analogy—one must make the internal dialogue of

---

49   See, for example, Eugene Roger's *After the Spirit*, and the recent history of this issue he traces in its introduction.

50   For a patristic example of the exposition of this particular Trinitarian analogy, see John of Damascus, *De Fide orthodoxa* I. 6-8.

God *the native environment of discourse*, wherein created discourse becomes a mere, but participating, analogue.

God the Father speaks forth and in so doing shares intelligible divine being in eternity as his Word. This Word, the divine Logos, is the intelligible *Name* of God the Father. God the Father receives a Name, a sign of himself, which is fully worthy and able to convey the infinite and divine depths of the Father's intelligibility. Only something equally divine and equally infinite can comprehend the Father, because like all signs, only that which is *other*, and, indeed, in this case, *infinitely* "Other," can perform the function of a *sign*. God the Son is the perfect reflection of God the Father and is that sign which is other than the Father by which the Godhead is recognized as intelligible.

What then is the role of the Holy Spirit within this particular analogy? God the Spirit is the *Breath* of God upon whom the Father's *Word* is spoken. The Breath of God, then, is the one who resides and rests within that Word as the intelligible witness and seal of the Word. Just as breath simultaneously sustains life as respiration and allows human being, through the use of signs, to share discourse with one another, that is, to share in intelligible communion with one another, so too God's Breath is the Lordly and Life-giving One[51]—the very life of the Living God—and he who is "breathed"[52] forth, infinitely, from the Father as the one upon whom the Father utters his infinite Word.

In the case of finite human being, human breath serves as the medium for conveying words and sharing in intelligible communication. In the case of the infinite God, the divine Breath, who is infinite, bears the infinite divine Word for the sake of the infinite Father in a divine and perichoretic "immediacy." In this infinity of mutual ecstatic "outpouring" for the sake of the other, the Son, as Word and Name of the Father, reflects the Father. And the Father speaks that Word upon the Spirit. The Spirit thereby grants the divine assent, grants the divine "Amen" to the Word of the Father as the perfect intelligible Name of their mutually and co-equally shared divine nature.

God's own "self-understanding," therefore, is "immediated" within the Godhead by means of this internal divine discourse. This is

---

[51] Jaroslav Pelikan, *Credo: Historical and Theological Guide to Creeds and Confessions of Faith in the Christian Tradition* (New Haven: Yale Univ. Press, 2003), 541. Pelikan offers an excellent English translation of the Nicene Creed.

[52] This refers to what is traditionally called "spiration" in Latin Christian terminology.

a kind of internal discursive and intelligible contemplation of the divine nature by divinity itself. So this discourse is the internal *theoria* of God. God's own self-contemplation, the foundation of God's eternal beatitude, is itself a Trinitarian motion. It is, therefore, something that may by analogy and participation be shared at the level of creation—insofar as a created rational being may be taken up into this triune pattern.

The word *theoria*, or "contemplation," is not employed by the Christian tradition chiefly to describe an activity of the Godhead but in order to describe a certain kind of human participation in the Godhead—in this case, an intelligible and discursive one, albeit a discourse between the divine and human which exceeds all possible *inter-human* propositional communication. God's gift of human *theoria* is an analogous part of the Word and Breath's intelligible share in the naming and witnessing to the Father. That is to say, just as the Word and the Breath of God constitute God, together with the Father, in the divine act of mutual contemplation and self-grounding of the intelligible being of the Godhead, so too then in the economy of salvation the Word incarnate, together with the inspiration of the Breath of God, lift up human discourse into this same shape of divine contemplation—enabling human being a share in the life of the divine discourse as *theoria*, contemplation.

Just as discourse enables human being to share intelligible noetic content among one another, so too, in God, discourse allows the sharing and mutual grounding of the intelligible divine being itself. God's discourse, as an analogy for Trinitarian *perichoresis*, may undergo a Dionysian reversal and serve as the model for human communion *through communication*. This description of the analogous parallel between divine and human contemplation of God makes clear that, just as *theosis* describes how God takes up human life into the divine life so too here, with regards to the salvation of human discourse in particular, *theoria* describes how God takes up human discourse into God's own life of discourse.

Upon this understanding, *theoria* grants a temporal share in the eternal discourse, the eternal contemplation that constitutes the divine nature. The Christian contemplation of God is nothing less than that of God taking the Christian mind up into God's own contemplation of God. What would be impossible for human being by nature, that is, knowledge of God, becomes possible by *gift*. Only that which is infinite may understand the infinite. By participating in the infinite God, the Christian mind may share God's knowledge of God's own nature.

Because Christianity understands human being to be the psychosomatic unity of body and soul, such a taking up of the mind inherently entails the taking up of the entire human being—including the body—in *theosis*. As explored above in chapter one, the means by which the Spirit grants such a gift is ascesis. The ecstatic form of theology, as ascesis, conforms, therefore, to the content of which it is the task of theology both to teach (as doctrine) and contemplate (as ascetic practice). The concrete content of Christian theology is nothing less than the ecstatic Christian God who is Trinity of persons.[53] Christian discourse contemplates God because it is taken up into God's contemplation of God, because *theoria* corresponds—within the context of discourse—to *theosis* in general.[54]

Following the discussion of Denys, above, the discursive analogy of the Trinity that began as an analogy from creation for the sake of comprehending the uncreate is reversed; God becomes the paradigm, and the creature becomes the analogue. That is to say, for Christian teaching, God is the definition and paradigm of discourse. Human discourse must be understood to be an analogue, at an infinite remove from the deity, of the divine discourse. God's ecstatic love, after the analogical reversal, is the pattern for human discourse. The discursive analogy gives a picture of what divinized human discourse might look like. The necessarily apophatic element in all Christian theological analogy helps to make sense of the importance of apophaticism and the use of analogy within the development of the Christian tradition.[55] Following Denys, this chapter argues that *theoria* is the goal of Christian prayer and the pith of *theosis*. The *theological* means to reaching *theoria* is found in the paradox of contemplation wherein the initial apophatic denial of discourse returns as the gift of a use of analogy that begins within the life of the triune God and spills over the ontological divide into created discourse.

Therefore the apophatic reversal of the discursive analogy of the Trinity that was implicit above and now made explicit, is *a perform-*

---

53   So, in Christian theology, form follows content at the level of the Christian body as a whole (the church universal), while, at the level of the individual theologian, form enables, through *conformity*, the contemplation of content.

54   See chapter one.

55   Louth, "Place."(see Ch.1, nt. 28).

ance of the thesis that theology is the ascesis of human discourse. Following Denys, words are denied in *apophasis* then re-grounded in God, rather than their immanent and arbitrary human and created source. One may extend this to the attempt to define theology. The goal and context of theology is *theoria*, that is to say, prayerful contemplation of God. Theology is therefore ecstatic and perichoretic; it involves mutual denial for the sake of mutual grounding. This chapter defines theology as ascesis, in part, by showing how human discourse may also be added to divine discourse in *theoria*.

So *theoria*, or contemplation, is the discursive[56] aspect of *theosis*, or divinization. The denial of discourse, then, is the first step to the *theosis* of discourse. This chapter argues that, from the point of view of Christian dogmatics, this *theosis* of human discourse is what the Christian tradition calls *theoria*. Just as the denial of the body is the first step towards its hope of a share in Christ's resurrection body,[57] so too, denial of discourse is not simply for the sake of its denial or because discourse is evil or incompatible or incapable of being a part of the economy of God's manifestation among human beings.[58] Denys helps one to understand this. Human words, by means of analogy, can no more express the divine nature than a finite human body can contain it. But, as Gavin Flood puts it, the body is denied *in order to reverse its flow.*

After the fall, human orientation to the body is perverted—human being hopes to find fulfillment in something finite. The Christian denies the body in order to regain the body as a part of the economy of God's good creation. The same holds true for human discourse. It is denied in order that its "flow" may be reversed. Instead of attempting to breach the ontological divide with human ideas, Denys guides the reader's contemplation upwards to the super-abundantly transcendent God, who is the source of all reality as its creator. Therefore, *the native context of predication is the interior* discursive *life of God.* It is not by analogy from creation that one predicates the creator. Through the ascesis of discourse that is called *apophasis*, Christians discover that it is only analogy from the divine that enables the predication of anything *real* to creation at all. Something is good, insofar as it is good at

---

[56]   Discourse is essential to rational and therefore human nature.

[57]   But this is not denial for the sake of denial itself or because the body is evil, etc.

[58]   "Whereof one cannot speak one must remain silent," is secular, not Christian theology.

all, only by analogy to its creator. So just as the flow of the body is reversed in ascesis in order to attain the divinization of the body, so too in *apophasis* analogical discourse is reversed so that human discourse may be shot through and transfigured by the *original environment of all predication*—the divine life of Father, Word and Breath as the triune discourse of the living God. *Theoria*, as this transfiguration of human discourse, performs the discursive aspect of the process of *theosis* for the whole human being.

This chapter began as a study of Bernard McGinn's historical account of how *theoria* necessarily entails ascesis within the Christian tradition. This account of the ascetical context of contemplation makes sense of Denys' texts as contemplative performances that invite the reader to engage with him in the goal of *theoria*. In this context, Denys enables the reader to recognize the "reversal of analogy." Through this use of analogy, Denys' text opens out the inherent connection between human *theoria* and God's own self-understanding in such a way as to display *theoria* as the discursive aspect of *theosis*. Christian theology is, therefore, ascetic, insofar as it is caught up in the Christian ascetical practice of *theoria*, contemplation.

CHAPTER SIX

Theology and the End of Philosophical Dialogue

The heavens declare the glory of God, and the firmament shows his handiwork / One day tells its tale to another, and one night imparts knowledge to another / Although they have no words or language, and their voices are not heard / Their sound has gone out into all lands, and their message to the ends of the world.

Psalm 19.1-4

ANCIENT CHRISTIANS often construed Christianity to be a philosophy among other competing philosophies—but the one that was their goal and completion. Christian theology is ascetic as the discourse inherent to Christianity when Christianity is construed as the philosophy that ends all other philosophy. Pierre Hadot's work, especially his *What is Ancient Philosophy?*, shows how Christianity put an end to all other ancient philosophy in his historical discussion of the relationship of ancient philosophical practice to the discourse it generated. Hadot's work helps one to understand the approach of many of the fathers of the church and especially someone like Gregory Nazianzus. Nazianzus' assumption, in his *Five Theological Orations*,[1] of the deep connection between ascetical knowledge of God and God's infinite self-gift, allows him to see the end of philosophical discourse to be union with the Christian triune God. This understanding of dialogue

---

[1] All Nazianzus quotations are from the English translation in *The Christology of the Later Fathers*, Vol. III, The Library of Christian Classics, ed. Edward Rochie Hardy (Philadelphia: The Westminster Press, 1954). For a recent critical edition, see Frederick W. Norris, ed., *Faith Gives Fullness to Reason: The Five Theological Orations of Gregory Nazianzen*, trans. Lionel Wickham and Frederick Williams (New York: E. J. Brill, 1990).

as union with God makes sense in indigenous Christian terms when dialogue is understood as the gift of an infinite and discursive God.

Hadot on Philosophical Practice and Discourse

FOR THE ANCIENTS, philosophy is primarily a *way of life*, and this way of life is to be achieved by transformational and *ascetical* spiritual disciplines.[2] "Above all, philosophy is viewed as an exercise of wisdom, and therefore as the practice of a way of life."[3] Hadot identifies six major ancient philosophical schools: the Academy, the Lyceum, the Garden, the Stoa, and, in a loser sense, the "schools of life" found among those subscribing to Pyrrhonism and Cynicism. According to Hadot, it is important to identify each school according to the existential choice of life that it demands, and not through an abstraction of its various doctrines. Each school identifies differently the problem of living without peace of mind and each offers a different solution. All of the ancient philosophical schools say that ignorance destroys freedom and peace of mind and that new values will lead to the knowledge necessary to overcome this ignorance. The choice of a radical philosophical way of life that includes concomitant ascetical practices is the only way to acquire these life changing and mind altering virtues. Philosophy is therefore primarily a therapeutic way of life and not a system of abstract theories.[4]

But Hadot has another significant contribution in his *What is Ancient Philosophy?* and that is his discussion of the relationship of philosophical discourse to the philosophical life after granting that ancient philosophy is indeed primarily a way of life. It is here, also, that Hadot has the most to contribute to this project. According to Hadot's position that philosophy is primarily a way of life, philosophical discourse is always derived from the "authenticity" (to use a modern existentialist term) of the philosophical life over other ways of living. Philosophical dialogue thus begins with this practice, and the philosopher's speculations are that of discussing what the nature of reality is ("what reality is like") given that the philosophical life places the philosopher in closer contact with reality. Thus, each particular philosophy speculates on the nature of reality given its own various nuances—what reality is like given the practices of Stoicism, Aristotelianism, etc.

---

2   Hadot, *Way of Life*, 82 (See Intro., nts. 43-46).
3   Hadot, *Ancient Philosophy*, 49.
4   *Ibid.*, 102.

The relationship of discourse to practice in ancient philosophy is the main problem that Hadot pursues in this work. His thesis is that "philosophical discourse is a *part* of this [philosophical] way of life."[5] And the exploration of this assertion shows two major ramifications on the relationship of discourse to the philosophical way of life. The first is that it is the existential choice of life that determines the nature of philosophical discourse and not the other way round. The second is that this way of discourse is not an end in itself but exists for the philosophical way of life. The main way in which this particular description of the relationship between philosophy as a way of life and the discourse that is concomitant to it is shown to be the case is found in the philosophical practice of dialogue. Dialogue, when practiced correctly, leads to spiritual transformation and is therefore part and parcel of the overall way of life demanded of by philosophy.[6]

Hadot describes all six ancient philosophical schools in terms of the peculiar existential choice demanded by each school and how that choice determines that school's particular mode of discourse.[7] So, for example, he points out the atomism and materialism of the Epicureans and their decision to enjoy things as they are without hope of divine intervention, or the fatalism and cosmic recurrence of the Stoics and their decision to patiently endure all things and be happy with the structures of the universal logos.

Although philosophical discourse is inherently derived from the philosophical way of life, nevertheless discourse is only philosophical if the discourse itself leads to transformation of one's way of life. There is a danger in what Hadot describes as "the ambiguity of philosophical discourse."[8] This ambiguity consists of the fact that at the same time that philosophical discourse and philosophy as a way of life are "incommensurable" and "completely heterogeneous"[9] in nature (because mere discourse is not a way of life), nevertheless it is impossible to have a way of life divorced from discourse: "There is no discourse which deserves to be called philosophical if it is separated

---

[5]   *Ibid.*, 5.

[6]   *Ibid.*, 6.

[7]   Hadot covers this especially throughout chapters six through eight.

[8]   *Ibid.*, 174.

[9]   *Ibid.*, 173.

from the philosophical life, and there is no philosophical life unless it is directly linked to philosophical discourse."[10]

Hadot describes three ways in which discourse exists for philosophy as a way of life—three ways in which the philosophical life is directly linked to philosophical discourse: "First, discourse justifies our choice of life and develops all its implications."[11] This first and probably weakest link of discourse to way of life in philosophy is that discourse justifies and persuades others to pursue the philosophical life.

> Second, in order to live philosophically, we must perform actions on ourselves and on others; and if philosophical discourse is truly the expression of an existential option, then from this perspective it is an indispensable means.[12]

The actions that must be performed on others and on oneself are those of *ethics*, construed in its ancient sense of pursuit of the good life. Here Hadot is hinting at the use of language as a means of social action and not mere signification. As the medium of speech-action, discourse must be used philosophically as part of the overall way of life of philosophy. But the third and strongest link between discourse and way of life in philosophy is also the most germane to the topic of this book: "Finally, philosophical discourse is one of the very forms of the exercise of the philosophical way of life, as dialogue with others or with oneself [in the practice of meditation]."[13] Of the various life-changing ascetical practices to which the various philosophical schools are committed, dialogue itself is one of the most important formative ascetical practices—for although it has to do with the intelligible, it is ascetic insofar as discourse is embodied.

Dialogue is one of the disciplines of ancient philosophy, among others. The goal of the practice of philosophical dialogue is not systematic doctrine or the discovery that reality may be perfectly rendered through discourse. On the contrary, the goal of dialogue was to bring about personal transformation on the part of those engaged in it.[14] Dialogue demands submission to the "other"—that is, concretely, to the other member of the dialogue, it demands mutual submission to recognized norms of reason (*logos*) and recognition that only the

---

10   *Ibid.*, 174.
11   *Ibid.*, 175.
12   *Ibid.*
13   *Ibid.*
14   *Ibid.*, 177.

good is absolute.[15] Hadot speaks in particular with regards to Platonic dialectics:

> Platonic dialectics was not a purely logical exercise. Instead, it was a spiritual exercise which demanded that the interlocutors undergo an *askesis*, or self-transformation. It was not a matter of a combat between two individuals, in which the more skillful person imposed his point of view, but a joint effort on the part of two interlocutors in accord with the rational demands of reasonable discourse, or the *logos*.[16]

This ascesis is practiced with something in mind that is beyond dialectics:

> A true dialogue is possible only if the interlocutors *want* to dialogue. Thanks to this agreement between the interlocutors, which is renewed at each stage of the discussion, neither one of the interlocutors imposes his truth upon the other. On the contrary, dialogue teaches them to put themselves in each other's place and thereby transcend their own point of view. By dint of a sincere effort, the interlocutors discover by themselves, and within themselves, a truth which is independent of them, insofar as they submit to the superior authority of the *logos*.[17]

Therefore, even lectures at the Academy would have been understood as large swaths out of an even larger, on-going dialogue.[18]

"[A]ll philosophies of antiquity . . . shared the aim of establishing an intimate link between philosophical discourse and way of life."[19] But they all also share a desire to make use of ascesis—including dialogue as one particular ascetical discipline—to come in touch with what is real. And those ancient philosophies that seek the good as ultimate reality agree that knowledge of the Good comes only through similarity with the Good. Similarity with the good is the development of virtue, and that development comes through ascesis. For someone like Aristotle, this similarity with the good that allows contact with the Good comes, chiefly, through the ascetical discipline of *theoria*, or contemplation.[20] For Aristotle, the Good is the first cause that contemplates itself in serenity forever, with no thought of the outside world. The philosopher, therefore, is one who contemplates the na-

---

15   *Ibid.*
16   *Ibid.*, 62-3.
17   *Ibid.*, 63.
18   *Ibid.*, 164.
19   *Ibid.*, 55.
20   *Ibid.*

ture of reality, and finally its first cause, in imitation of the Good, and thereby achieves contact through contemplation.

Later Neo-Platonists adopt this understanding of *theoria* but transform it as they reconcile it with their Platonic theory of forms. *Theoria* is not mere ratiocination but the rendering of the philosopher similar to what the philosopher contemplates. "[T]hose who contemplate must render themselves similar to what they contemplate . . . Thus, contemplation is not abstract knowledge but self-transformation."[21] Hadot emphasizes that both action and discourse transforms the philosopher to make the philosopher more like that which the philosopher desires to know. And this is especially the case because discourse *is* an action.

For the early Christians, beginning at least with the Apologists and continuing through someone like Nazianzus, Christianity provides the ultimate, final, and only true philosophy—way of life.[22] If philosophy is the conforming of one's life to that of the universal Reason or *logos*, then Christianity is a philosophy for it is conformation to Jesus Christ as the incarnation of the universal *logos*.[23] Thus, discussion based upon and of this way of life is the only means by which human discourse can authentically participate in reality. And for Christian "philosophy," ultimate reality is the God of Abraham, Isaac and Jacob. True knowledge of God requires the true philosophy of God. Philosophy is a way of life. That true way of life is given only in Christianity.

Like the various ancient schools of philosophy, Christianity practiced a form of ascesis, that is, discipleship.[24] Hadot provides an interesting note of comparison by describing some of what it meant for individuals to commit to one of the ancient schools of philosophy:

> They entered into a community, under the direction of a spiritual master, in which they venerated the school's founder and often took meals in common with the other members of the school. They examined their conscience and perhaps even confessed their misdeeds . . . They lived an ascetic life . . . [some] followed a vegetarian diet and devoted themselves to contemplation, seeking mystical union.[25]

---

21 *Ibid.*, 158.
22 *Ibid.*, 237.
23 *Ibid.*, 239.
24 *Ibid.*, 241.
25 *Ibid.*, 247-8.

This description sounds familiar, and it is supposed to. Hadot directly compares the ancient philosophical schools with Christian monasticism[26] as it developed from the third through the fourth centuries.

In fact, Hadot is doing more than a mere comparison. Hadot wants to make the historical argument that not only did Christianity enter into the world of antiquity in competition with the various pagan philosophical schools but that it ultimately both integrated what insights it deemed acceptable into the structure of Christian teaching and emerged as the only major philosophy[27] by the end of antiquity and the beginning of the middle ages, thus ending (in both senses of the word) ancient philosophy. In this history Hadot provides an answer to the question: why is philosophy no longer understood, by and large, among modern scholars, as a way of life?

Hadot points out that Christianity rejected other philosophies as ways of life because it claimed to be an exclusive way of life for its adherents. One could not practice, for example, Christianity and Stoicism, for Stoicism allowed for taking part in pagan festivals and sacrifices, among other things. Even so, from the beginning of Christian thought, Christian thinkers made use of the *discourse* of ancient philosophical schools *but divorced from their respective practices.*[28] They did so not because they considered philosophical discourse separable from its way of life, but because Christianity was the one true way of life that could make sense of all previous philosophy—either by dispelling its errors, or by taking on the relative truths it had discovered outside of the revelation of the God of Israel.

There are then two Christian approaches to "philosophy" which are not in competition with each other but are based on the two different uses of the term "philosophy." In terms of "philosophy" as a way of life (its truest sense, according to Hadot), Christianity reacts in *competition* as the one true philosophy. In terms of "philosophy" as the various doctrines and theories developed in the context of the practice of the discourse inherent to the practice of philosophy as a way of life (its merely subordinate sense, according to Hadot's argu-

---

26 *Ibid.*, 242.

27 The chief final competitor to Christianity as a philosophy was Neo-Platonism— and it too sought to be a kind of summation and "end" of ancient Hellenistic thought and religion.

28 *Ibid.*, 254.

ment), Christianity looks to philosophy as the "handmaid" of its own discursive practice: *theology*. Theology as a practice is therefore nothing less than the dialogical ascetical practices of Christians who understand Christianity to be (the one true) philosophy and, if one concedes to Hadot's point, subject to all of the requirements of the relationship of philosophical discourse to philosophy as a way of life.

But Hadot's history does not end there. After the triumph of Christianity as the one philosophy of the west during the middle ages, the various schools of philosophy as ways of life are forgotten and the word "philosophy" is used only in the later sense of the discourse that these ways of life generate. Philosophy as a way of life is forgotten and philosophy is conceived of and taught merely as the logical systems and theories of great pre-Christian thinkers.[29] To make a long history short and overly simple and to leave out several other important points and qualifications that Hadot makes in his argument, Hadot concludes that when philosophy finally regains its autonomy in modernity, it nevertheless retains this fallacious separation of philosophical discourse from the philosophical way of life, at least in terms of its academic presentation.[30]

Were this book an historical project this sketch of a history could be expanded. One might argue that, in reaction to the autonomy of modern philosophy, Christian theology—in order to seem legitimate in the face of this new secular scholarly authority—began to pattern itself after this same fallacious model. That is to say, Christian theology, like secular philosophy, began to be taught as though it were the passing on of systems and theories rather than as a discursive ascesis within the general practice of the Christian way of life. But such expansion on the argument is out of the scope of this current project.

Hadot makes another important point. Hellenistic philosophy and religion do not, for the most part, compete with one another in antiquity.[31] What then is different about Christianity that suddenly puts it in competition with both pagan religion and philosophy? Pagan religion and philosophy actually cover two quite distinct aspects of ancient life. Religion concerns itself with public and civic rites and duties. Most of the ancient philosophical schools have no inherent problem with this civic and public duty on the part of their adherents.

---

[29]   *Ibid.*

[30]   *Ibid.*

[31]   *Ibid.*, 272.

They are more concerned with the individual as a project in its own right—even if, ultimately, for the sake of bettering the whole of society. Christianity, by contrast, is far more all encompassing. In terms of ancient culture, Christianity is more than a religion. It is actually a religion (concerned with public, civic and visible piety towards the gods, or God) *and* a philosophy (concerned with the discipleship and development of each adherent). Because of this comprehensive agenda, Christianity cannot but compete with both pagan religion and philosophy. With this in mind, the discussion now turns to Gregory of Nazianzus and his own practice of Christian theology as Christian discursive ascetical discipline.

Nazianzus and the Theological End of Philosophy

GREGORY NAZIANZUS assumes an understanding of Christianity as the one true philosophy, and he pits it against all other (contemporaneous) philosophies, which, in turn, must be considered false. But Nazianzus shares with his own broader intellectual culture an understanding of what philosophy *is*. Gregory Nazianzus begins his *Theological Orations*—a series of five texts wherein he defends the developing orthodox Christian teaching of the Trinity—with an entire oration dedicated not so much to God's essence and its knowability, as to the moral and spiritual state of the theologian *as the knower*. Nazianzus assumes a deep connection in the *Theological Orations* between the ascetical practices of the theologian (including theoretical discourse as part and parcel of that ascetic practice that puts the theologian in a position of more intimate knowledge of God) and God's own unbounded nature as the "giver of himself" to the knower. In making such a connection Nazianzus puts an *end* (stop) to the discourse of the various ancient schools of philosophy by making the Christian life of participation in the life of the triune God the *end* (goal) of philosophical dialogue.

Gregory Nazianzus' *First Theological Oration* must be understood more as a repudiation of false philosophical practice than as a refutation of false doctrine. In other words, in this oration, Nazianzus does not so much claim that Eunomius and Nazianzus' various other opponents are practicing poor behavior for a Christian philosopher because of their faulty beliefs, as show that their inaccurate theology is the result of their refusal to submit to the rigorous spiritual disciplines of the truly Christian "philosopher." Nazianzus makes this explicit in his discussion of how vicious people receive the arguments of genuine theology:

> How, do you think, or with what temper, will the arguments about such [theological] subjects be received by one who approves of adulteries, and corruption of children, and who worships the passions and cannot conceive of aught higher than the body. . . Will he not make your theology a defense of his own gods and passions?[32]

Of course, the answer is yes, for this is a rhetorical question. It is clear that Nazianzus sees those who are still enthralled by their passions as being unable to do anything but distort whatever valid teaching they receive. Understanding philosophical, and in this case, theological speculation is dependent upon how clear one's faculties of comprehension are. The passions and love of the creaturely are idols that prevent vision of the true God.

We can hear echoes of Nazianzus' position in the thought of an ancient Stoic such as Epictetus:

> The first and most necessary area of philosophy is the one that deals with the application of principles, such as 'We ought not to lie'; the second deals with demonstrations, for instance, 'How is it that we ought not to lie?'; the third confirms and analyzes the other two, for instance, 'How comes it that this is a demonstration? For what is a demonstration, what is logical consequence, what contradiction, what truth, and what falsehood?' The third area of study, then, is necessary on the account of the second, and the second on the account of the first. But the most necessary, and that on which we should dwell, is the first. But we do the reverse. For we spend all our time on the third topic, and employ all our effort that, and entirely neglect the first. Therefore we speak falsely, but are quite ready to show how it is demonstrated that one ought not to speak falsely.[33]

The sarcasm is biting, and it is intended to be. In fact, in terms of tone, Epictetus here and Nazianzus in his *First Theological Oration* sound quite similar. Epictetus represents a prime example of Hadot's interpretation of ancient philosophy. Philosophy is first and primarily concerned with action—how to take the precepts of a given philosophy and live by them. Epictetus' second and third "areas" are varying levels of speculation upon these precepts. The first area argues how fitting these precepts are. The second is a dialogue on the assumed principles that form the basis of logical discourse concerning such a way of life. Thus the spoken content of speculative philosophy

---

32 Gregory, *Five Orations* I. 6.
33 Epictetus, *The Discourses, The Handbook, Fragments*, ed. Christopher Gill, trans. Robin Hard (London: J. M. Dent, 1995), *The Handbook*, 52.

is organically related to, and a means for, philosophy as a way of life—but speculative thought in and of itself is useless and not the end of philosophy.

Near the end of the *First Oration*, as Nazianzus' rhetoric is mounting, Nazianzus pretends to give up arguing for the virtuous life and gives suggestions for what his opponents should discuss, if all they are interested in is talk:

> Must your tongue rule at any cost, and can you not restrain the birth pang of your speech? You may find many other honorable subjects for discussion. To these turn this disease of yours [i.e., the desire to speculate divorced from spiritual exercise] with some advantage. Attack the silence of Pythagoras, and the Orphic beans, and the novel brag about "The Master said." Attack the ideas of Plato, and the transmigrations and courses of our souls, and the reminiscences, and the unlovely loves of the soul for lovely bodies. Attack the atheism of Epicurus, and his atoms, and his unphilosophic pleasure; or Aristotle's petty Providence, and his artificial system, and his discourses about the mortality of the soul, and the humanitarianism of his doctrine. Attack the superciliousness of the Stoa, or the greed and vulgarity of the Cynic.[34]

Recall that Hadot lists what he sees as the six most important and recognized philosophies in the classical era. These are: Stoicism, Epicureanism, Platonism, Aristotelianism, Cynicism, and Pyrrhonism.[35] In the above passage Nazianzus is providing a list of false philosophies against which these talkative Christians can spend their time arguing, from the point of view of the one true philosophy—Christianity. Notice that only one of the six great ancient philosophies fails to make Nazianzus' list: Pyrrhonism.[36] Otherwise, Hadot's and Nazianzus' lists exactly correspond. Clearly, Nazianzus understands Christianity as an alternative philosophy, and, indeed, the only true one. Nazianzus suggests to those who treat Christianity as mere discourse that they use it to refute the falsehoods Christians find in other philosophical discourse.

So Nazianzus suggests to his opponents that they take this empty mode of argumentation and use their talkativeness to some productive end, rather than wasting their own time, and corrupting others'

---

[34]   Gregory, *Five Orations* I. 9.

[35]   Hadot, *Way of Life*, 56.

[36]   Why would Nazianzus exclude Pyrrhonism? Perhaps Nazianzus excludes it because at this point in the history of philosophy it would have been almost non-existent—and then only in its most exaggerated skeptical form. Perhaps Nazianzus therefore did not even recognize it as qualifying as a philosophy worth engaging. But this is only speculation.

hearts, by speculating about a God whom they do not know because their knowledge is only speculative—they do not actually practice Christianity. Christianity is the one true philosophy—but Nazianzus' understanding of the nature of philosophy itself does not differ radically from his pagan contemporaries. Philosophy is a way of life. Philosophical discourse is merely derivative. So the dialogue appropriate to Christian "philosophy" must be entered into as part of the Christian life of ascesis and not as mere theory. This "disease" of theoretical reflection absent from concrete practice, Nazianzus suggests, ought simply to be turned on false philosophies—and not used to distort Christian teaching. For without ascesis and properly disciplined Christian dialogue, these theologians have no contact with the realities they discuss—and therefore have no place in discussing them. Philosophy is primarily a discipline of spiritual exercises—a mode of ascesis. Nazianzus is sure that his opponents are misled primarily because they are not practicing, or, at least, not properly practicing the ascesis inherent to true Christian life.

One can get a sense of the nature of these philosophical and spiritual exercises as practiced by Nazianzus and his friends by reading Basil the Great's *Second Epistle*.[37] This letter was actually addressed by Basil to his friend, Gregory Nazianzus, in about AD 358. It is an attempt on the part of Basil to persuade Gregory to join him in the practice of a more monastic life. It basically constitutes a brief monastic rule, giving a glimpse at how the idea of Christianity as a philosophy with its own inherent spiritual exercises developed into, and along with, the monastic movement. Implicit in writing thus to Nazianzus is that Basil is already practicing a similar regimen[38] on his own. Basil is inviting Nazianzus to join his community, not to begin these practices in general.

But how is *ascesis* linked to the knowledge of God? In order to discuss that, and to put Nazianzus' *First Theological Oration* into proper perspective, it is necessary to discuss the end of Nazianzus' *Fifth Theological Oration*. The second through the fourth *Orations* comprise an

---

[37] Basil the Great, Basil to Gregory, in *St. Basil: Letters and Selected Works*, Second Series, Vol. VIII, trans. Blomfield Jackson, *Nicene and Post-Nicene Fathers of the Christian Church*, eds. Philip Schaff and Henry Wace (Grand Rapids: Wm. B. Eerdmans, 1983), 110—12.

[38] Further clear evidence of his dedication to a life of ascesis may be found throughout his *Letters*, especially 31 and 153.

argument about the nature of God in general (the Second) and the Person of the Son in particular (the Third and Fourth). One finds an ongoing development of an understanding of the theologian as one, along with all other Christians, who is being divinized by the restoration of the *imago Dei*. In the *Fourth Theological Oration*, Nazianzus describes the "best theologian:"

> But we sketch [God] by his attributes, and so obtain a certain faint and feeble and partial idea concerning him, and our best theologian is he who has, not indeed discovered the whole, for our present chain does not allow of our seeing the whole, but conceived of him [that is, God] to a greater extent than another, and *gathered in himself more of the likeness* or adumbration *of the truth* . . .[39]

The "Truth" for Nazianzus is the Christ. And the Christ is the incarnation of the eternal image of God. The theologian thus, according to Nazianzus, gathers "in himself more of the likeness . . . of the truth." Like is known by like. Distorted human nature has obscured the fact that it is created in God's image.[40] With the process of *theosis*, "the image shall have ascended to the archetype, of which it has now the desire" to be made one.[41] The image is restored to the Christian by transformation in the God who is willing to stoop down to rescue human being. Such restoration to the likeness of God allows the theologian accurate, existential knowledge of God. It is in the "God made capable of suffering [to strive] against sin,"[42] that human *theosis* is made possible. Human *theosis* is that which corresponds, at the level of the individual Christian and the Christian community as a whole, to the incarnation of Christ who:

> by himself [is able to] sanctify humanity, and be as it were a leaven to the whole lump; and by uniting to himself that which was condemned may release it from all condemnation . . .[43]

Nazianzus understands the theologian as a philosopher who, meditating upon Holy Scripture, ascends to and regains the *imago Dei* and is thereby assimilated to the "Truth," who is the Christ, the

---

[39] Gregory, *Five Orations* IV. 17; Italics mine.

[40] This discussion of the *imago Dei* ought to recall the discussion above in chapter two concerning Pavel Florensky. The end of this chapter argues that such Christian philosophical dialogue is the discursive counterpart to Christian *mimesis* in general.

[41] *Ibid.*, II. 17.

[42] *Ibid.*, IV. 1.

[43] *Ibid.*, IV. 21.

eternal image of God. Ascesis is that gift from God that enables human return to its true image. Human being is created in the image of the infinite giver and indweller; therefore human being must relearn to give of herself completely—and that is the goal of spiritual discipline.

"I have been unable to discover anything on earth with which to compare the nature of the Godhead."[44] Nazianzus asserts an apophatic approach to Christian discourse, and therefore to Christian philosophical dialogue, at the very end of his *Theological Orations*. Nazianzus fully accepts the (ascetical) apophatic imperative of Christian theology.[45] That typical and usually acceptable mode of knowing God—analogy from creation—finally breaks down when confronted with the mystery of the Trinity, for there is no created analogue to the life of the uncreate. In Nazianzus' conclusion, he reemphasizes the apophatic both for rhetorical and theological reasons. The rhetorical goal is to silence the impious speculation of his opponents. The theological goal is to affirm that God is unknowable in purely human terms. But does that mean that God is ultimately unknowable for Nazianzus?

Earlier in the *Fifth Theological Oration*, Nazianzus builds his argument for the divinity of the Spirit. Here one begins to grasp how Nazianzus views the difference between divine and human persons—and thereby the difference between divine and human knowing. Nazianzus writes:

> When, then, we look at the Godhead, or the first cause, or the *monarchia*, that which we conceive is one; but when we look at the Persons in whom the Godhead dwells, and at those who timelessly and with equal glory have their being from that first cause, there are three whom we worship.[46]

The divine persons share in Godhead fully and in timeless and equal glory. But could this not simply be polytheism? No, Nazianzus asserts, for

> In this case the common nature has a unity which is only conceivable in thought; and the individuals are parted from one another very far indeed, both by time and by dispositions, and by power. For we are not only

---

[44] *Ibid.*, V. 31.

[45] This apophatic imperative recalls Denys' use and transformation of *apophasis* described above, in the previous chapter.

[46] Gregory, *Five Orations*, V. 14.

compound beings, but also contrasted beings, both with one another and with ourselves . . .[47]

The pagan polytheists conceive their many-personed divinity after a human fashion—where each god limits another in the way human beings are "contrasted" against one another. But Christianity teaches that in the Godhead there is both simplicity and the absence of contrast as well. There is no competition for "space" or "time" in the Godhead, for God is beyond those creaturely limitations. Human "unity" in "humanity" is abstract and conceptual. God's unity is not simply abstract or conceptual, but actual—the Persons share in one another *infinitely* for God is bound by nothing.[48]

As Nazianzus develops his argument for the divinity of the Spirit, he leads his reader to the "unwritten" sources of Christian knowledge of God. That "unwritten" source is the shared Christian worship of the liturgy:

> For if He is not to be worshiped, how can he deify me by baptism? But if he is to be worshiped surely he is an object of adorations and . . . must be God.[49]

It is clear that, for Nazianzus, the Christian is related to God by deification, by union with God. That is not even questioned. It is assumed that both he and his opponents share such a view. And it is because of this deification through worship that Christians receive knowledge of God:

> From the Spirit comes our new birth, and from the new birth our new creation, and from the new creation our deeper knowledge of the dignity of Him from whom it is derived.[50]

In this process of *theosis* Christians come to recognize the God in whom their deification is granted. The God who is bound by nothing is able to take up the finite into the infinite divine life. *Theosis* through the gift of liturgical and ascetical practice becomes the environment for knowledge of God and dialogue about the divine.

In Nazianzus' works, and many other works of the fathers, there is a direct relationship between knowledge of God and ascesis. The

---

[47]   *Ibid.*, V. 15.

[48]   This point demands caution because Nazianzus does not use the word "infinite" (unbounded)—it would be Gregory of Nyssa who would explicitly unfold this attribute of the Christian God. But surely it cannot be doubted that it is exactly God's *infinity* that is the operative concept here, if only implicitly.

[49]   Gregory, *Five Orations*, V. 28.

[50]   *Ibid.*

broader implications of this study point to the fact that, insofar as knowledge of God is a participation or sharing in God's own self-knowledge,[51] then ascesis, as that practice within the overall *theosis* of Christian life whereby God draws human being into participation with the divine nature is the foundation of actual contact with God, and therefore the basis of any theology—"God talk" or Christian "dialogue"—of any substance. If Christian thought assumes an integrated anthropology (where human being is a psychosomatic unity of body and soul), along with an understanding that truth is ontological (the gnoseological reduction), then participation in Christ through *ascesis*, as human *ontological* transformation (*theosis*), is also the source and ground of *knowledge* of God (epiphany / *theoria*). This chapter argues with Gregory the Theologian that any theology worthy of the name is grounded in actual "contact with," or participation in, God—and is therefore knowledge *of* God, insofar as that is humanly possible,[52] and not merely discursive knowledge *about* God.

For Nazianzus, mere human knowledge based upon an analogy from creation[53] is inadequate to what is actually revealed in true, Christian, philosophy. Thus, Nazianzus' opponents' speculations are pernicious because they assume a human mode of knowing to be adequate to a divinely inspired gift. Mere speculative discursive analogies from creation cannot contain the depth of the knowledge of God granted to the Christian in worship because, unlike these analogies, the infinite God actually gives the divine nature, pours the godhead out upon the worshiping, ascetical body. That God whose Persons mutually indwell one another, infinitely, in the divine *perichoresis* is the same God who gives the divine nature to those who worship the Father "in Spirit and in Truth." And it is this self-giving of God that enables the Christian to know God, and engage in discourse concerning God, in a way that no other philosopher can—and that no mere speculation can achieve.

---

[51] This participation in God's self-knowledge echoes the discussion of the same pattern found in Denys' thought, above, in the previous chapter.

[52] "That is why a man should make all haste to escape from earth to heaven; and escape means assimilation to the deity insofar as it is possible; and one assimilates oneself by becoming just and holy, together with intelligence," Plato, *Theatetus*, 176 b.

[53] That is, one that has not undergone the reversal of analogy discussed above in chapter six.

Clearly worship is shared between Nazianzus and his opponents. Why is the liturgy of the church not sufficient to guide his opponents into truth as it is for Nazianzus? *Ascesis* is the means of preparing oneself truly for the worship of the true God. Ascesis includes, of course, within its regimen, properly regulated philosophical dialogue. As God gives the divine nature to the Christian, the Christian must be prepared to give herself fully and truly to God. In the current condition of being human, due to the fall, this involves *ascesis*. Nazianzus' opponents are misled, not by the liturgy, but because they approach it *unprepared*. Thus, Nazianzus' understanding of the knowledge of God in his *Fifth Theological Oration* is logically linked to his understanding of the nature of the theologian in his *First Theological Oration*.

The degree to, and sense in which, God is knowable for Nazianzus corresponds directly to the fact that, according to Nazianzus, there is a proper moral and spiritual state for the theologian, made possible only by the Holy Spirit as made manifest in worship and through the spiritual exercises of Christian "philosophy," and these practices comprise ascesis in general, and philosophical discourse in particular. There is a deep logical and organic connection in the *Theological Orations* among the ascetical practices of the theologian that puts the theologian in a position of more intimate knowledge of God and God's own unbounded nature as the "giver of himself" to the knower. In making such a connection Nazianzus puts an *end* (stop) to the discourse of the various ancient schools of philosophy by making the Christian life of participation in the life of the triune God the *end* (goal) of philosophical dialogue.

Christian Dialogue and God's Unbounded Self-giving

GREGORY NAZIANZUS assumes that knowledge of God is directly proportional to the spiritual progress of the theologian. And, as discussed, he also connects this spiritual progress to the infinite self-giving of God to the Christian in worship and ascesis. This vision of the connection between practice and knowledge is directly parallel to the previous chapter's exploration of the connection made by Denys between human *theoria* and divine self-knowledge. The dialogue that is essential to the practice of Christianity as a philosophy is the shared human discursive counterpart to contemplation. This position makes sense, in terms of Christian teaching, when the practice of dialogue about God is received as a gift from the infinite—and inherently discursive—God.

Following Nazianzus' connection between the ascetic knowledge of God and God's infinite self-gift, the difference between divine and human persons is essential here. The divine Persons indwell one another infinitely for God is infinite. God indwells creatures in their finitude, because they are forever, as creatures, finite. But, and this is important, *the mode of knowing is the same*. God knows God infinitely in the infinity of the mutual indwelling. The worshiper knows God *finitely* in the finitude of created being, but it is *by the (mutual) indwelling of God* that the worshiper knows God. Like is known by like. Just as God's own self-knowledge is part and parcel of the infinite mutual indwelling of the divine Persons, so too human knowledge of God comes about through *ascesis* and during worship when the ascetic prepares to give herself fully to God, and God, in turn, graces the ascetic with the indwelling of the divine nature.

The last chapter discussed the "discursive" analogy of God, wherein the mutual indwelling, or *perichoresis*, of the Trinity may be understood in terms of the intelligible communion available through discursive communication. In this analogy, the Father is the speaker, the Son is the Logos or "Word," and the Spirit is the Breath of God whereon the Father speaks the Word. On this analogy, discourse has the potential of being ecstatic *apropos* to whatever level or register of reality it is found. So the divine discourse at the level of divinity is actually one of the chief analogues for discussing the nature of *perichoresis* itself. So too then, for human being as the *imago Dei*, discourse is ecstatic and perichoretic insofar as human beings commune with God and one another in *dialogue*. Dialogue, then, corresponds within the context of discourse to *mimesis*.[54]

Dialogue, in this sense, is the human communication of the Logos through one another as human beings (*dia-logos*). It is about communicating among one another in such a way that the Logos is transparent within the discourse as its background and goal. And dialogue is ecstatic. Human embodied discourse, insofar as it allows communication and a share in the transcendent (the Logos), performs a *mimesis* of the discourse that constitutes the mutual indwelling of the persons of the Trinity. God makes the divine nature manifest through human discourse by means of *transparent* communication.[55] It is important to

---

[54]   Chapter two explores the nature of Christian *mimesis*.

[55]   One might call this "transparency," or straightforwardness, "orthodoxy" (*orthos*, straight, *doxa*, praise or opinion).

note for the general thesis that this transparency is made possible, on this side of the fall, through *voluntary self-denial*. Following Hadot's account, dialogue opens out the ascetic to the "other."

Even though divine discourse is the source and model of human discourse, nevertheless human discourse is not *in spite of* the human body. That is, discourse as chiefly an *intelligible* activity is not so contrary to somatic existence as in fact to oppose it. With regards to being human, the intelligible is made manifest through the human body. Discourse, for human being, is impossible without the body. Discourse is simply an inherently embodied reality for human beings in both senses of the body as corporeal and as corporate, for there is no discourse without tongues, lips, vocal cords, ears, eyes, hands, limbs, and brains. Furthermore, discourse itself, mediated through the body, is for the sake of and sometimes even constitutive of (the) human body/ies. Discourse, therefore, for human being, is already and always mediated through the human body.

Though human discourse is always mediated by the somatic structures of being human, the temptation to reductionism must be avoided in this case. Human discourse is not reducible to the body. Although human discourse is made possible by the mediation of the human body, nevertheless, on the order of logic, human discourse is actually the gift of being able to take up and transfigure the human somatic environment by means of human being's intelligible nature (that is, the human soul). So the body is actually transfigured by the soul in the act of discourse. This intelligible transfiguration of the somatic also takes place at both the level of the corporate body and the corporeal body. This transfiguration, then, includes even the various academic and empirical scientific disciplines, as well as the various bodies and "canons" of literature.

The human body is, therefore, the concrete medium of human discursive *ecstasy*—human beings "get outside of themselves" and actually share communion and communication with others *through* their bodies and with their bodies—and this somatic discourse includes, indeed it *must* include, for human being, human communion with God. Already always (somatically) mediated, human discourse is also the ecstatic transcendence of that very mediation. Therefore, given the importance of discourse in constituting human being *qua* human, one must also avoid reducing human nature as a whole to discourse in a sort of over-affirmation of the essential nature of discourse to being human.

Human discourse is to the *imago Dei* as the life of divine discourse is to the perichoretic life of the Persons of the Trinity. Human discourse is as essential to the *imago Dei* as the discursive analogue is to understanding God as triune. With such a view in mind, one could say that God creates human being to be invited into, and enabled for, dialogue with the Father through his Word and Spirit.[56] One must avoid reducing discourse itself to its explicit and verbal forms. Human embodied discourse goes far beyond the use of signs. The very fact that children are born from the act of intelligible and *sexual* intercourse shows that, for human nature, children are the gift of *discursive* union. The nine months in the womb, the process of birth—these basic physical facts—all wed being human somatically and intelligibly to other human beings. Human being is born in community, in somatic community, and in intelligibly transfigured community.[57]

In terms of the Christian teaching of the Trinity, when the practice of dialogue *about* God is received as an embodied and ascetic gift *from* God, then the *perichoresis* of divine discourse becomes the reality in which Christian theology participates. For human being as the *imago Dei*, discourse is ecstatic and perichoretic insofar as human beings share in their imitation of the divine discourse and commune with God and one another in *dialogue*. Dialogue is discursive *mimesis*. Embodied human discourse performs a *mimesis* of the discourse that constitutes the mutual indwelling of the persons of the Trinity insofar as it allows communication and a share in the transcendent (in this case, the Logos as "reason"). Like (the *imago Dei* embodied through human

---

[56] But one must not assume then that there are no other aspects to being human. Human being is essentially discursive, but it is not simply discursive.

[57] Therefore one may dismiss any claims that infants, the severely mentally retarded (that is, in this case, those who lack the capability to use human sign-systems or language), the comatose and the dumb (that is, those who are physically incapable of speech) are somehow sub-human. This must be stated explicitly in order to deal with any possible objection to this portion of the argument on the grounds that it is an overly exclusive definition of being human that rules out whole people-groups in an ethically questionable way. Given how broadly this book has defined discourse, and how, although rightly expounding its importance, it relativizes its status as defining human nature, these possible objections are untenable.

discourse) is thereby known by like (the eternal discourse of the triune God).

This chapter shows how Christian theology is ascetic as the discourse inherent to Christianity when Christianity is construed as the philosophy that ends all other philosophy. Hadot's work on the relationship of ancient philosophical practice to the discourse it generated guides an understanding of the approach of Gregory Nazianzus in his *Five Theological Orations*. Nazianzus assumes a deep connection between ascetical knowledge of God and God's infinite self-gift which allows him to see the end of philosophical discourse to be union with the triune God. This understanding of dialogue as union with God makes sense in Christian terms where dialogue is understood as the gift of an infinite and discursive God.

CHAPTER SEVEN

Theology and the Ascetic Performance of Sacred Text

The Counselor, the Holy Spirit, whom the Father will send in my name, he will teach you all things, and bring to your remembrance all that I have said to you.

John 15.26

All scripture is God-inspired and profitable for teaching, for reproof, for correction, and for training [*paideian*] in being just [*dikaiosune*], that God's human being may be complete, equipped for every good work.

2 Timothy 3.16

THE CHRISTIAN tradition binds up what it calls "theology" with the practice of the interpretation of its sacred texts. Insofar as exegesis is discursive, theology is ascesis, for exegesis is an ascetic discipline. To argue this, this chapter first describes how several recent scholars (including Pierre Hadot, Gavin Flood and Geoffrey Harpham)[1] paint a picture both of ascesis as always bound up in the exegesis of a given scriptural tradition and of exegesis as itself an ascetical performance. Next, and in light of this recent scholarship, this chapter presents how Augustine assumes that "teaching Christianity" means teaching the performance of a way of life and that this performance is nothing less than the *teaching*, that is, the performative interpretation of Christian scripture in and as the ascetic life of imitation of the saints. Finally, this chapter claims that exegesis as ascesis makes sense in terms indigenous to Christianity because Christians interpret the scriptures according to the "rule of faith."

---

[1] In passing and footnotes mention will also be made of Bernard McGinn and Douglas Burton-Christie.

The Textuality of Ascesis in Some Recent Scholarship

CHAPTER SIX, above, presents Pierre Hadot's argument that philosophy is an ascetic way of life that wrestles with the relationship of its necessarily concomitant life of discourse. In that same work, Hadot describes a shift from the earlier philosophical practice of dialogue to the development of commentary and the rise of scholasticism in the philosophical practice of late antiquity. Hadot describes the situation of late antique philosophy as that of a divorce from the living tradition of various schools of philosophy due to their slow dissolution over time:

> The situation called for a return to the sources. From this point on, instruction would consist in explaining the texts of the "authorities"—for instance, the dialogues of Plato, the treatises of Aristotle, or the works of Chrysippus and his successors.[2]

In a situation where the sources of philosophy seemed to be divorced from the current life of their schools, philosophers sought a return to the sources. In doing so, the writings of the now "ancient" philosophers took on a new authority as revealed texts.[3] In fact, the older the text, the more "true" it was often esteemed to be—including texts of the "barbarians" and therefore of the Jews.[4]

This shift from dialogue to exegetical commentary on authoritative texts should not, however, be read as a shift away from philosophy as a way of life or away from philosophy as ascetic practice. For "throughout this period, philosophy continued to be conceived as an attempt at spiritual progress and a means of inner transformation."[5] Indeed, commentary itself is a form of spiritual discipline:

> [T]he exercise of commentary is already formative, just as the exercise of dialectics had been—for it is an exercise of reason, an invitation to modesty, and an element of the contemplative life.[6]

Commentary is itself ascetic in the sense that it engaged the philosopher in a physical (vocal or written) activity of denial of the self before an authoritative text:

---

2 Hadot, *Way of Life*, 148.

3 *Ibid.*, 152.

4 *Ibid.*, 153. Much late antique philosophy—especially Neo-Platonism—consisted of the attempt to reconcile ancient philosophies and various revealed religious texts and practices.

5 *Ibid.*, 149.

6 *Ibid.*, 153.

> Moreover, each commentary was considered a spiritual exercise—not only because the search for the meaning of a text really does demand the moral qualities of modesty and love for the truth, but also because the reading of each philosophical text was supposed to produce a transformation in the person reading or listening to the commentary.[7]

In fact, according to Hadot, this shift to commentary ought not entirely to be taken as a shift away from the more ancient philosophical discipline of dialogue. Dialogue continued, but transformed into dialogue concerning philosophical issues as the discussion of authoritative texts.[8]

This scholastic method of commentary on texts survives into, and forms, the Christian scholastic era in the west. When Hadot goes on to describe the relationship of Christianity to philosophy, he makes the obvious connection between the philosophy of the day and Christianity with regards to commentary as a shared root practice.[9] Nevertheless, Hadot qualifies this description of Christianity as parallel to ancient philosophy through exegesis:

> Yet although some Christian authors might present Christianity as a philosophy, or even as the philosophy, this was not so much because Christianity proposed an exegesis and a theology analogous to pagan exegesis and theology, but because it was a style of life and a mode of being, just as ancient philosophy was.[10]

Christianity identifies itself as a philosophy primarily because it is a way of life, and only secondarily because it follows practices of commentary on authoritative texts. Still, this parallel was seen as naturally compelling and is an important, even if secondary point.

Gavin Flood, whose work *The Ascetic Self* is discussed at length above in chapter four, also weighs in on the relationship of ascesis to commentary or scriptural exegesis and describes how in various ascetic traditions the body is understood as a text—something written—as a way of empowering the body.

---

[7] *Ibid.*, 155.

[8] *Ibid.*, 156.

[9] Bernard McGinn also makes this obvious but important connection. He describes the pattern of ancient thought moving from the ancient philosophers and their study of the cosmos, to the late antique philosophers and their study of authoritative texts, leading finally to Christian "philosophers"—theologians—and the study of sacred scripture. McGinn, "Asceticism and Mysticism," 64.

[10] Hadot, *Way of Life*, 240.

[P]ower is *inscribed* upon the body through the *habitus*. The ascetic conforms to the discipline of the tradition, shapes his or her body into particular cultural forms over time, and thereby appropriates the tradition. This appropriation of tradition is a form of remembrance, the memory of tradition performed through the body, and is also the vehicle for change or transformation.[11]

Within the particular context of the Christian scriptural ascetic tradition, Flood reflects upon the writings of Maximus the Confessor and succinctly describes the world-view generated by such ascetic-exegetical practices:

[T]he *logos* is reflected or incarnated not only in Christ himself but also in created beings (*logoi ton onton*) and in scripture. The 'intelligences' or *logoi* that are pre-existent in God are held together, although differentiated, within the *logos* and manifested in the world. These three incarnations, in Christ, in creation and in scripture, are also recapitulated within the ascetic who becomes, as it were, a further site of the incarnation.[12]

The Christian body is transformed into the Christian scriptures, and, in turn, undergoes the *theosis* of unity with the incarnate Word embodied in those texts.

At this point it is important to note that Flood stresses that all ascetic traditions are to be found within religious traditions that have a robust cosmology that the ascetic internalizes through the embodied performance of this given tradition:

In the cosmological religions we shall be viewing, cosmic time is reflected in subjective time partly through the medium of the text. . . The world envisioned by a text is [therefore] our prime focus of inquiry.[13]

Again, according to Flood, ascetic traditions that allow for internalization are always *scriptural* traditions insofar as they are always bound to an authoritative text or set of texts that the ascetic attempts to embody, that is, that the ascetic attempts to "write" upon herself.

How exactly, then, is the body "turned into" writing? Scripture is appropriated to the body through *mimesis* of the content of scripture. Flood uses Kierkegaard's term "repetition" to describe this: "we can develop an existential understanding of the scriptural traditions as the appropriation of tradition and the repetition of the tradition's goals

---

[11]   Flood, 6. Italics mine on "inscribed." It is important to remember here that for Flood, any ascetic tradition is a scriptural tradition.

[12]   *Ibid.*, 158.

[13]   *Ibid.*, 25.

enacted in ritual."[14] Ritual, as both liturgy and ascesis, is the bodily action through which the tradition inscribes its scriptures upon the body of the ascetic:

> The ascetic self is created through the integration of both inner [private] and outer [e.g., liturgical] aspects of the ascetic path, fostered over long periods until the self is transformed in tradition-specific ways. The habit inscribes the body with the text and, through an act of will, the ascetic self loses that will in order that the Kingdom of Heaven should become the indwelling truth of the ascetic's being.[15]

This kind of ascetic exegesis is a *performative* interpretation of the scriptural text into the life of the ascetic-cum-saint. In the case of the desert fathers, the founders of Christian monasticism, "Word *events* transformed their lives."[16]

Geoffrey Harpham, whose work *The Ascetic Imperative* is discussed above in chapter two, further develops this theme of embodied textual appropriation. The ascetic becomes iteration, a copy of the text of scripture readable even by the illiterate:

> [T]extuality enables such imitation. In his illiteracy, Anthony exemplifies a way of reading that is enacted in life, a hermeneutics that tries to overcome the gap between (divine) intention and (human) understanding through the "reader's" recreation or rewriting of the text not on paper but in his own being—a way of reading that sees, as Gregory of Nyssa comments, "activity as a kind of imitation." The reception of the Biblical text becomes a form of ascesis, of self-overcoming in which the reader or hearer aspires to an identification with the text that is simultaneously original and derivative.[17]

Through liturgical and ascetical emersion into the texts of the scriptures the ascetic can "become a new text."[18] The *saint* is therefore the highest "form" of scriptural interpretation and its goal.

The "spiritual sense" of the scriptures is the reading of scripture for existential appropriation (at either a corporate or corporeal level)

---

[14]   *Ibid.*, 19.

[15]   *Ibid.*, 178.

[16]   Douglas Burton-Christie, *The Word in the Desert: Scripture and the Quest for Holiness in Early Christian Monasticism* (New York: Oxford University Press, 1993), 19; italics mine. Despite what seems to be a great lack of scriptural references in the collected sayings of the desert fathers, Burton-Christie discerns that it was "their continuous rumination upon Scripture, their desire to embody the texts in their lives, [that] was a primary source of the compelling spirituality that emerged from the desert (297)."

[17]   Harpham, 42; Nyssa quote from *On Perfection*, III.

[18]   Burton-Christie, 20.

and transformation. The tropological sense is usually taught to represent the reading of scripture for morality or life-application, even in places where this is not the obvious first meaning of the text. In his exploration of the conversion of Augustine, Harpham describes how the tropological sense should not be understood so much as the *use of scripture* as a trope for (proper) human behavior, but as the *use of human behavior* as a trope for scripture—scripture representing a level of reality in some ways more real than the human person:

> Situating himself within the community of imitators, Augustine understands the text when he understands that it is a model for himself; and he understands himself when he grasps his own "tropological" nature, that is, when he sees not only that he can imitate the text but that he has in fact been doing so all along. The "new life" of the convert is an old and borrowed life, authentic because aesthetic.[19]

Just as the "reversal of analogy" above, in discussing Denys, turned analogies about God derived from creation to analogies about creation derived from the divine life, here is a so-called "figurative" reading of scripture "reversed" into the figurative reading of one's own life and body in terms of the text of scripture.

Another recent scholar describes the ascetic interpretation of scripture as the affects of a "new world of possibilities" in the lives of the desert fathers: "Holiness in the desert meant giving concrete shape to this world of possibilities stretching ahead of the sacred texts by interpreting them and appropriating them into one's life."[20] The ascetic practice of exegesis opens up a new world to the ascetic by expanding previous finite and fallen horizons into the New Creation. The "commentaries" that guide Christian exegesis towards these new horizons are the living texts of the saints.

In these ascetic acts of spiritual interpretation of scripture into a life of imitation of the saints the ascetic actually enacts the deconstruction of any claims to non-textual reality—at least with regards to his or her life as saintly. For once the scriptures have been entirely appropriated, entirely "written" upon the body, there is then "nothing outside the text."

> The convert imitates Christ by converting himself into a textual representation which both imitates the textual imitation of Christ in the Gospels and serves as an imitable model for others. In a deeper sense,

---

[19]   Harpham, 97.
[20]   Burton-Christie, 20.

writing in general offers itself as an activity fit for one whose highest ambition has become the purging of the *"hors-texte"* from his life, the abolition of everything not textualized or textualizable.[21]

Such an approach to scripture requires the conviction that the scriptures share in cosmic reality as a microcosmic recapitulation of the cosmos itself—the text of the *logos* of God.

Harpham's key literary example of this hermeneutical circle that encompasses the life of a saint as the embodiment of scripture and the imitation of the saint as a means of induction into the life of scripture is Athanasius' *Life of Anthony*.[22] Athanasius' *Life of Anthony* was responsible for the conversion of Augustine, thus providing another link in the chain of saint-inspiring-saint to the life of scriptural exegesis into life and body. Exegesis as a *discursive* practice, then, is the *submission of discourse* to the overall ascetic practice of interpreting scripture into *the life and body* of the ascetic—discourse being a subordinate but necessary part of life as a whole. Augustine's semiotics of teaching Christianity in his *De doctrina Christiana* provides a theoretical account of this hermeneutical circle.

Augustine and the Performance of Scripture

AUGUSTINE understands exegesis to be bound up in discipleship. In his work *On Christian Doctrine*,[23] Augustine assumes that the teaching of Christianity, or "doctrine," is simply the performative interpretation of scripture as the imitation of Christ and the saints through the pursuit of the Christian life of ascesis.[24] In order to

---

[21] Harpham, 120. *"Hors-texte"* here is referring to Derrida, *Grammatology*, 158 (see Ch. 2, nt. 89).

[22] Athanasius' *Life of Anthony* is discussed extensively throughout Harpham's *Ascetic Imperative*, but with respect to Augustine's conversion see especially part two, chapter one, "The Language of Conversion," 91—106.

[23] See Augustine, *On Christian Doctrine*, trans. D. W. Robertson, Jr., Library of Liberal Arts (New York: Macmillan Publishing Company, 1958). For a recent critical edition, see Augustine, *De doctrina christiana*, ed. and trans. R. P. H. Green (New York: Clarendon Press, 1995).

[24] John Cassian is well known for bringing the Evagrian tradition to the Christian west—and therefore to Augustine. McGinn explains that in passing on this tradition he both simplified Evagrius and simultaneously bound the notion of theoria up more closely with the interpretation of scripture. "Cassian was neither so original nor so systematic a thinker as Evagrius . . . [but] Cassian's description of *scientia theoretike* differs from that of Evagrius in being directly tied to the Bible, its two parts [*phusike* and *theologike*] being described as 'historical interpretation'

understand this overall structure of knowledge of scripture through the imitation of the saints it is necessary to delve into Augustine's semiotics with some depth.

"All doctrine," Augustine says, "is about things or signs, but things are learned by signs."[25] All teachings of Christianity are about "things" themselves, or the signs that signify those things. Augustine provides some working definitions of these distinctions. Augustine explains that, strictly speaking, a "thing" is that which is not used to signify something else.[26] Some things, however, are used as signs, that is, are used to signify some other thing beside themselves. A "sign" is, therefore, a thing used to signify something else.[27] Some things that are used as signs find their whole utility in signifying something else. Here Augustine means conventional signs, such as words. "No one uses words except for the purpose of signifying something [else]."[28] It follows, then, that "every sign is a thing, for that which is not a thing is nothing at all; but not every thing is also a sign."[29]

Augustine begins, then, with a "functionalist" semiotics that is intelligible within an anthropology of human action. Signs are merely the way in which human beings make use of certain things in order to signify certain other things. So, Augustine's first distinction is that between signs and things. Signs are defined, functionally, as the way in which certain things are used to refer to other things. Not all things are used as signs, but all things potentially can be used as signs.

Starting with his basic distinction between things and signs, Augustine builds his theory of signification. Things are to be divided primarily into two classes: 1) those that are to be enjoyed and 2) those that are merely used.[30] Augustine defines enjoyment as clinging "with love to something for its own sake."[31] Love is the principle for division between classes of things. "Use" is defined as the employing of

---

and 'spiritual understanding,' which consists in tropology, allegory and anagogy" (McGinn, 68, quoting Cassian *Conl.* 14.8). For Cassian, monastic training is Biblical training—writing the scriptures, so to speak, on the body (and, thereby, the soul) of the ascetic.

25   Augustine, *De doctrina christiana* I. ii. 2.
26   *Ibid.*
27   *Ibid.*
28   *Ibid.*
29   *Ibid.*
30   *Ibid.* I. iii. 3.
31   *Ibid.* I. iv. 4.

things in order to obtain that which is loved.[32] That which is enjoyed makes the Christian blessed; that which is used helps to attain that which is enjoyed.[33]

But what is the thing or things that one is to enjoy for beatitude? God is that "thing" to be enjoyed[34] "if, indeed, it is a thing and not rather the cause of all things, or both a thing and a cause. It is not easy to find a name proper to such excellence."[35] Augustine finds it difficult to give God a proper name; nevertheless, it is God and God alone that is to be enjoyed. God is that thing placed above all others.[36] It is because God is placed above all others that God alone is to be enjoyed.[37] Only the eternal and immutable will bring true enjoyment, because transitory things will pass away and bring grief. God alone is eternal and immutable; therefore God alone is to be enjoyed.[38] However, insofar as God is triune, one may say that there are three "things" which one may enjoy: Father, Son and Holy Spirit, one God.[39]

It is at this point that the primary distinction becomes complicated with one further "sub-category." Within the category of things that are not God (i.e., all of creation), there is at least one type of creature that is made in the image of God: human being. Augustine asks:

> [W]hether man is to be loved by man for his own sake or for the sake of something else. If for his own sake, we enjoy him; if for the sake of something else, we use him. But I think that man is to be loved for the sake of something else.[40]

In all but one case, only one thing is to be enjoyed, and that for its own sake. All other things, in all but one case, are to be used for the sake of enjoying that one thing. But "man is to be loved for the sake of something else."[41] Human beings, made in God's image, constitute a third category of things that are to be enjoyed for God's sake.[42] Things

---

32   *Ibid.* I. iv. 4.
33   *Ibid.* I. iii. 3.
34   *Ibid.* I. v. 5.
35   *Ibid.*
36   *Ibid.* I. vii. 7.
37   *Ibid.*
38   *Ibid.* I. xxii. 20.
39   *Ibid.*
40   *Ibid.*
41   *Ibid.*
42   *Ibid.* I. xxii. 20.

that pertain to God by association, i.e., human beings and angels, and things that "pertain to us and require the favor of God through us,"[43] e.g., the body, may be enjoyed for God's sake. All other things are to be used for God's sake.

So Augustine's distinction between use and enjoyment brings into play an axiology of love as ascent to God.[44] Some things may be used, others enjoyed. Some things may be both used and enjoyed. The ultimate "thing"[45] to be enjoyed is God. One ought only to enjoy God, never use. Most of reality, in turn, is to be used in the enjoyment of God, usually in terms of helping to attain to such enjoyment. Those things ontologically lower than being human are not to be enjoyed at all. That is, idolatry and lust, and therefore the human problem, reside in the fact that human beings keep trying to enjoy creaturely goods in place of the Good itself. Human being constitutes a strange kind of third category.[46] Human beings are to use themselves in order to enjoy God, but may also enjoy themselves insofar as and to the extent to which human being is made in the image of God.

After making these definitions and distinctions in the realm of things considered in themselves, Augustine moves on to define and determine things considered as signs for other things. Augustine provides another definition for a sign: "a thing which causes us to think of something beyond the impression the thing itself makes upon the senses."[47] He then lists natural examples[48] but is concerned with those types of signs that bring forth or transfer "to another mind the action of the mind in the person who makes the sign."[49] Only rational creatures such as human beings can make these kinds of conventional signs, that is, signs that derive their meaning from common consent—the chief example of this type being words and language.[50]

---

[43]   *Ibid.* I. xxiii. 22.

[44]   *Ibid.* I. xxvii. 28.

[45]   Here, the fact that Augustine engages in a functional and anthropological pursuit is clear because, in referring to God as a "thing" to which one may refer by the use of other things as signs, he is not attempting to engage in ontology—although there are ontological ramifications, the exploration of which is beyond the scope of this study.

[46]   Augustine, *De doctrina christiana* , I. xxviii. 29.

[47]   *Ibid.* II. i. 1.

[48]   *Ibid.*

[49]   *Ibid.* II. ii. 3.

[50]   *Ibid.*

Conventional signs are either literal or figurative.[51] Augustine defines literal signs as signs "when they are used to designate those things on account of which they were instituted."[52] The example Augustine employs is that of using the word "ox" to signify the animal it names. Augustine defines a figurative sign as when "that thing which we designate by a literal sign is used to signify something else."[53] He gives the example of the "ox" being used by Paul to signify an evangelist. A figurative sign is the use of a sign in such a way that the thing that it usually signifies is used as a sign of something else as well. Through use of the conventional sign one is directed toward some thing. Then, if one signs figuratively, that thing signified is used as a sign of something else. So figurative signification is more *complex* (in the literal sense of the word "complex" that is, composite) than literal signification.

Augustine transitions from a discussion of his overall axiology and semiotics to practical suggestions with regards to exegesis by introducing a caveat regarding the "fear of the Lord" as "the beginning of all wisdom."[54] Augustine traces seven steps from fear as the first step to wisdom, wisdom being the seventh and final step.[55] "Knowledge" is the third step and by this Augustine means existential knowledge of Christianity through the "translation" of scripture into a faithful life. The immediate step after "fear of the Lord" but before this knowledge of scripture, is *pietas*, piety:

> Then it is necessary that we become meek through piety so that we do not contradict Divine Scripture . . . But we should rather think and believe that which is written to be better and more true than anything which we could think of by ourselves, even when it is obscure.[56]

Here Augustine means the development of humility before and obedience to the scriptural tradition of Christianity—a humility and obedience that Augustine would have practiced, and recommended, in and as ascesis.

---

51 *Ibid.* II. x. 15.
52 *Ibid.*
53 *Ibid.*
54 The "fear of the Lord" as the source of wisdom is a theme throughout the Old Testament, but directly quoted from Ps. 111.10 and Prov. 9.10.
55 *Ibid.* II. vii. 9—11.
56 *Ibid.* II. vii. 9.

Before moving from Augustine's semiotics to his approach to exegesis, it is important to note that when his axiology of use and enjoyment meets with his functional anthropological semiotic distinction between things and signs, a certain principle is generated. This is the principle that Augustine reiterates throughout his work, that the thing itself is always to be preferred to its sign. Signs are merely used, not enjoyed for their own sake. The ultimate purpose of being human is to enjoy God and fellow human beings in God. Signs merely serve the purpose, through their use, of helping to attain this goal. A certain paradox, however, becomes evident in Augustine's thought with regard to this principle. One must know the thing referred to in order to understand the sign, while things themselves are often, in turn, learned by means of signs.[57] Augustine's approach to Biblical exegesis makes sense of this paradox.

Augustine provides a few preliminary guidelines for unknown figurative signs before laying down his pivotal hermeneutical principles. Augustine accepts as obvious that the scriptures have a multiplicity of possible correct interpretations: "When . . . not one but two or more meanings are elicited, even if what he who wrote the passage intended remains hidden, there is no danger if any of the meanings may be congruous with the truth taught in other passages of the holy scriptures."[58]

In fact, that this is so is part of divine providence, for "certainly the Spirit of God, who worked through that author, undoubtedly foresaw that this meaning would occur to the reader or listener."[59] According to Augustine, God desires to give a guiding text with many layers of meaning:

> For what could God have more generously and abundantly provided in the divine writings than that the same words might be understood in various ways which other no less divine witnesses approve?[60]

Ultimately, Augustine's commitment to the possibility of infinite good interpretation of the texts of scripture is directly grounded upon his theology of God as that reality who is the very definition of "good," who is infinite and whose acts are chiefly characterized by the lavishing of this abundance on that which he creates. Scriptures

---

57   This paradox is Augustine's refashioning of Plato's paradox in the *Meno*.
58   Augustine, *De doctrina christiana*, III. xxvii. 38.
59   *Ibid.*
60   *Ibid.*

are possessed of maximal possible meanings because the God who inspires them overflows with infinite abundant goodness.

Returning then to Augustine's preliminary guidelines, a thoroughgoing knowledge of the stories and key passages of the Bible is essential for interpreting the scriptures because, through memory of less obscure passages, more obscure passages can be explained and brought to light.[61] For Augustine, the *regula fidei* itself may be understood as a sort of compiling and summarizing of the authoritative Christian narrative that may also be discerned in the more literal portions of the scriptural texts. The rule of faith is found in the "open places of scriptures"[62] and in "the authority of the Church."[63] So the last of these preliminary rules would be that any interpretation that does not contradict the rule of faith is potentially an acceptable biblical interpretation, pending his other principles.

The scriptures are filled with signs of the spiritual life. Recall that signs are either literal or figurative. In order to understand the spiritual things these signs denote, the first step in exegesis is to determine whether a passage is to be taken literally or figuratively.[64] Augustine's "principle" of figuration may be spelled out thus: if a passage may be taken literally, do so. If a passage may be taken both figuratively and literally, do so. If a passage cannot be taken literally, take it to be only figurative. It is of utmost importance to Augustine that literal passages not be taken as merely figurative and that figurative passages not be taken literally: "He is a slave to a sign who uses or worships a significant thing without knowing what it signifies."[65] This is the formal principle for Augustine's approach to exegesis.

How then does one determine whether a passage is literal or figurative? Here Augustine's most important principle finally comes in to play, the principle that drives Augustine's theory of knowledge. The "thesis" of the entire canon is *performative*. It is the love of God and human being commanded by Christ in summation of the law.[66]

---

[61]   *Ibid.* III. xxvi.

[62]   *Ibid.* III. ii. 2.

[63]   *Ibid.* III. ii. 3.

[64]   *Ibid.* III. xxiv. 34.

[65]   *Ibid.* III. ix. 13.

[66]   Mt 22.37-40: Hear, O Israel, the Lord your God is one, you shall love the Lord your God with all your heart, with all your mind, with all your strength. And the second is like the first, you shall love your neighbor as yourself. On these two laws hang all the Law and the Prophets.

This "thesis" is also, therefore, Christologically speaking, Jesus Christ himself—the incarnate God as the human and personal summation of the law. In *De doctrina*, this "principle" of charity provides the single most important tool for Augustine's approach to scriptural exegesis.[67]

The principle of charity is a guide to the content of the scriptures. Because content is privileged over form, this principle may therefore serve as a guide over the formal principle of figuration. This follows because knowledge of things is preferred to knowledge of signs. Signs are the form, but the thing itself provides the content. In answer to the above question, how does one know whether a passage is literal or figurative, the exegete should answer this question: does the given passage of scripture literally pertain to (the performance of) Christ's summation of the Law? If so, the passage is literal; if not, it must (at least) be figurative:

> [A] method for determining whether a locution is literal or figurative must be established. And generally this method consists in this: that whatever appears in the divine Word that does not literally pertain to virtuous behavior or to the truth of faith you must take to be figurative. Virtuous behavior pertains to the love of God and of one's neighbor; the truth of faith pertains to a knowledge of God and of one's neighbor.[68]

This is not to say that Augustine would have Christians take historical narratives that do not seem to have anything to do with the principle of charity as merely figurative and not literally historical:

> Whatever is so narrated is to be taken not only historically and literally but also figuratively and prophetically, so that it is interpreted for the end of charity, either as it applies to God, to one's neighbor, or to both.[69]

However, Augustine wants to say that these historical happenings were guided by providence as signs of things more spiritual for those in the New Covenant.

The culmination of Augustine's approach of Biblical exegesis, based on his semiotics, is the principle of charity. His semiotics, of course, also grounded upon an axiology of love, is derived from his Biblical word-view. Here is a statement of Augustine's hermeneutical circle: the Bible (as sign) denotes reality, and therefore an accurate

---

[67]   The next section below takes up how Augustine's "principle" of charity relates to the more traditionary criteria of the rule of faith.

[68]   Augustine, *De doctrina christiana*, III. x. 14.

[69]   *Ibid*. III. xii. 20.

knowledge of reality (as "thing") will generate greater understanding of the scriptures. Because God the Word is the Logos through whom all things were created, he who is incarnate as Jesus, and that same "Word" that was spoken by the prophets in the scriptures, knowledge of the world helps in understanding the scriptures, and vice versa. In order to enter into this hermeneutical circle and begin to make progress in any way, the Christian must enter into the life of discipleship, or ascesis. That is, the Christian must make herself available to the *things themselves* to which scripture makes reference.

According to Augustine, one cannot attempt to be a Biblical scholar, or to discern between the literal and figurative levels of exegesis, until one is living out at least the literal portions of the scriptures (e.g., those that parallel the rule of faith) in the performance of Christian charity that is the life of the Christian disciple-ascetic.[70] The student of scripture must interpret the scriptures first and foremost into the life of Christian charity through discipleship.[71] This discipleship does two things: it prepares one spiritually for discerning multiple meanings within the scriptures, and it is the best method of teaching the scriptures to those who need to learn.[72] But this still begs the question—if the scriptures alone are not a sufficient guide to the things of God until one knows those things themselves, then how is one conducted through the discipline that leads to such contact?

Augustine determines that the only way to convey the meaning of a sign without simply employing other signs is to *demonstrate* the thing itself to the learner. Augustine uses the analogy of a child learning the functional human action of language.[73] An infant listens to and imitates her parents in all the patterns of human behavior, not the least of which is human speech. By imitating her parents a child can learn both the things to which her parents refer and the signs by which her parents refer to these things. In this analogy, of course, instead of imitating natural parents, Christians are to imitate their spiritual parents, the saints.[74] This is made possible with the acceptance of the discipline of, and the disciplined life of, the church.

---

[70]   *Ibid.* II. xli. 62.

[71]   *Ibid.* IV. xxviii. 61.

[72]   *Ibid.* IV. xxix.

[73]   *Ibid.* Prologue. 5. This analogy is developed more fully in Augustine's dialogue *De magistro.*

[74]   This doubles back on Harpham's point, discussed above.

Through discipleship, Christians come in contact with the divine realities—divine things—to which the signs of scripture refer. As the ascetic comes to know the things themselves, she is better able to grasp the signs that point to them:

> If the *res* [thing-itself] of all scriptures is *caritas*, the *signa*, the communicative signs of that *caritas*, are here the monastic [and therefore ascetic] servants of God.[75]

These signs that point to divine things are also given to the ascetic in the text of the scriptures. As the ascetic pursues the life of discipleship through ascesis, she, in turn, is led to ever deepening knowledge of scripture. So, the teaching of Christianity is the teaching of scripture, and the scriptures are taught through their ascetic "translation" into the lives of saints.

Scripture and the Measure of Fidelity

EXEGESIS IS ascesis. This point makes sense in terms indigenous to Christianity because Christians interpret the scriptures according to the "rule of faith"—the measure of fidelity, the rule of faithfulness, to God. This chapter now explores some of the ascetical logic of what the Christian tradition has called the rule of faith and "canon" as measure of fidelity. To do so, it returns to von Balthasar's work *the Moment of Christian Witness* and his description of the criteria of the *Ernstfall*—the Christian existential willingness to die for Christ—as discussed above in chapter three. But before doing so, one needs a brief definition and historical note on the term "rule of faith."

The *regula fidei*, or the "rule of faith," is one of many terms used to describe brief outline-style statements of Christian belief that can be textually traced back to at least the second Christian century. These narrative summaries of Christian faith were used as guides to the interpretation of scripture[76] and to distinguish the apostolic tradition

---

[75]   Thomas F. Martin, "'An Abundant Supply of Discourse': Augustine and the Rhetoric of Monasticism," *Downside Review* 116 (Jan. 1998), 13. This article does much to connect exegesis as a way of life to exegesis as a mode of discourse. Martin points out that Augustine understood that a human life could serve as a sign, and, as with all signs, some could be eloquent. One's way of living as a Christian ascetic could therefore provide the world with "an abundant supply of discourse" rhetorically persuasive to Christian faith.

[76]   Irenaeus of Lyons, *Against All Heresies*, expounded most famously and importantly the use of the rule of faith as a guide to Biblical exegesis (see especially I. 9. 4.).

from that of "heretics." These are not formal creeds, as are those that develop and become formalized in the fourth century and following, but vary in wording and are fluid in form. The rule of faith is standardized more as a narrative structure than as a formal and unchangeable set of words. This rule of faith comes under many names that included the "rule of truth," the "law of faith," and the "norm," or "canon of truth." The point of this brief historical sketch is that Christian teaching, as the interpretation of scripture, has a standard by which it may be *measured*. So another possible rendering of this traditional Christian formula might be *measure of fidelity*—in this case, faithfulness to God in Christ.[77]

Von Balthasar is also concerned with a criterion for proper Biblical exegesis—and that as against the modern project of "demythologization" of scripture and its unchristian principles of exegesis. According to von Balthasar, the real reason for the project of demythologization, or as he calls it, the project of making Christian teaching "analogous," is that *"we want to shelve or postpone the decision of faith,"*[78] the decision to accept martyrdom—the *Ernstfall*:

> The trouble is that if the content of our belief becomes analogous, the actions that arise from this belief are also bound to be analogous, and no one who adopted a belief based on the transposed terms just described could possibly claim to possess an unambiguous faith in Christ as it has been understood by the Church for nearly two thousand years.[79]

If the content of the Christian faith is merely analogous, then the Christian act of martyrdom may be accomplished by analogy as well.

Willingness to die puts the Christian in the same existential condition as that of the "authors" of the scriptures. Because of this, the willing martyr or practicing ascetic is allowed a closer understanding of the text that actually allows for more accurate scriptural exegesis. This is not far from Augustine's criteria for biblical exegesis. In fact, if one bears in mind the connection between ascetic sainthood and martyrdom, then it is simply a contemporary restatement of Augustine's ancient position. Only (the pursuit of) actively living out the life of total

---

[77]   For more on the rule of faith, see J. N. D. Kelly, *Early Christian Creeds*, 3rd edition (New York: D. McKay Co., 1972), and Jaroslav Pelikan, *Credo* (New Haven: Yale University Press, 2003).

[78]   Von Balthasar, 97.

[79]   *Ibid.*, 98—9.

love of God—that characterizes the performative content of scripture—can open up the discursive meaning of scripture to the believer.

This description of an approach to the scriptures links the lives of the saints to the Christian canon of *scripture* through the "canon," or "measure," of the faithfulness of Christ. According to the Christian tradition, God defines that measure in the incarnation and passion of Christ. For this historical instance of divine life shows the measure of love to be that of nothing less than the infinite love of a crucified and triune God.[80] Jesus Christ is the living, personal "rule of faith," or measure of fidelity to God; or, as Augustine would have it, Christ is the living summation of the Law. The only "answer" to the existential challenge of Christ as rule, on the part of the believer, is an existential one: it is the personal love of God in Christ *to the point of being willing to die.*

Von Balthasar poses a question to which he provides a challenging answer: "can the *Ernstfall* be set aside in order for Christianity to be made compatible with the modern criteria of rationality?"

The whole question of a possible alternative to the system is, therefore, not so much a matter of choosing between a conservative or a progressive attitude, as of discovering whether it is possible for a Christian to ignore or put aside the challenge of the *Ernstfall* to follow Christ's example for the sake of an *aggiornamento* [with modernity].[81]

God gives the *Ernstfall* as the criterion of love in history by providing a perfect historical instance of the form of love: the incarnation and passion of Christ.[82] In *beholding* this form (through the *witness* of martyrdom, Baptism and asceticism), the Christian shares in the form of love.

The answer to all this, is, of course, that the Christian cannot make such an *aggiornamento* with modernity, but must bear the stamp of the form of Christ through existential participation in Christ's life, passion, and resurrection—whether by death or by ascesis following Baptism. Von Balthasar asks his central question another way:

---

80   *Ibid.*, 149.
81   *Ibid.*, 75.
82   *Ibid.*, 121.

> In other words: Is it possible for [the Christian] to make intellectual experiments concerning his faith unless his capacity for loving is fully engaged in his activity?[83]

In the logic of Christian faith, love, not speculation or experimentation, is the key factor in gaining knowledge. The criterion of *Ernstfall* is the divinely granted example and form of perfect love in the life, death, and resurrection of Jesus Christ. This, von Balthasar connects directly with Christ's summation of the law: "Every action that is not rooted in contemplation is doomed to sterility from the start."[84]

Any Christian action not rooted in Christian contemplation, that is, contemplative prayer as the chief corporeal manifestation of the human love of God, is doomed to failure on Christian terms. For without the connection to the ground of being that the love of God allows in the discipline of contemplation, no real self-sacrificial love of neighbor is possible. As discussed above, this willingness to die for the Person of God in Christ puts the Christian in greater existential proximity to the authors of Christian scripture, and, therefore, allows for the possibility of more accurate biblical exegesis.

Just exactly how does the rule of faith as the church's authoritative tradition relate to what Augustine introduces in his "principle" of charity—and von Balthasar in his *Ernstfall*? The answer is complex and "totemic,"[85] but simply put, Augustine's principle of charity, von Balthasar's *Ernstfall*, and the traditionary rule of faith actually overlap or run parallel to one another. Augustine's and von Balthasar's principles are ways of stating or describing the *narrative* rule of faith in a *performative* mode. The rule of faith parallels and provides the guide to interpreting scripture by acting like a summarization and compilation of (especially the literal portions of) scripture. It is therefore a kind of narrative formulation of the "thesis" of the canon. In Augustine's principle of charity the scriptures are about inducing the performance of the love of God and love of neighbor. Again, von Balthasar's principle of the *Ernstfall*: the scriptures are about inducing the performance of total love as lived in the self-sacrifice of Jesus Christ. In both cases Christ is the measure, for Christ is the incarna-

---

83   *Ibid.*, 75-76.
84   *Ibid.*, 119.
85   See ch. 4, nt. 31.

tion of the love of God—both God's love of human beings and proper and complete human love of God.

The triune action of God in the incarnation and passion of the Son of God performs the human measure of fidelity to that selfsame God:

> Everything the church has canonized (elevated to a standard rule) in two thousand years as sanctity according to the measure of the Gospel corresponds unequivocally to the criterion proposed in *The Moment of Christian Witness*: *every* saint has attempted to shape his life into a loving response to the crucified Trinitarian love of God and thus placed himself at the disposition of Jesus' work of establishing God's kingdom of love among men.[86]

The rule of faith as the guide to scriptural interpretation is, therefore, theologically coterminous with the imitation of the saints because in both cases fidelity to God is "measured" in terms of the *mimesis* of the life of Christ. Exegesis in its secondary and derivative sense, that is, as a discursive practice, follows from this and is a part of this "measuring up to" the life of Christ and the saints.

Again, that this performative measure of fidelity would be the criteria for the proper performance of scriptural interpretation makes sense in terms of the traditional Christian understanding of what the scriptures themselves are. For Christians understand the scriptures to be the inspired and inspiring discourse of the love of God in Jesus Christ. The scriptures are the Word of God made human *discourse*— the extension of the triune act of incarnation into (a literary body of) human discourse (and its interpretive tradition). Just as discourse and its concomitant body of written text makes human being manifest, so too then part of God's becoming fully human is the taking up of discourse, text, and text-interpretive tradition. Thus the "rule of faith" can be found in the "plain texts of scripture," as per Augustine. Exegesis is itself a self-mortifying ascetic practice of submission of the self (behavior) to the text. In this sense, then, exegesis corresponds within the context of discourse to *martyria*, or Christian witness.[87]

There is a totemic system, described in tandem by the rule of faith in narrative form proper and in the performance-oriented formulations of both Augustine's principle of charity and von Balthasar's criteria of the *Ernstfall*. It looks something like this: Christ provides the measure of faithfulness to God (personally); Christ—who is the living

---

[86] Von Balthasar, 149.

[87] Chapter three above explores *martyria* as Christian witness.

summation of the law—discursively summarizes the law in his own spoken teachings; the scriptures that "measure up" to Christ, that are recognized—canonized—by the church (the body of Christ) as inspiring true charity, provide the inspired witness to Christ as the measure of faithfulness to God; the traditionary "rule of faith" is the narrative summary of Christ's life and passion as the measure of fidelity to God and guides the body of Christ in its performance (interpretation) of the scriptures; the church "canonizes" the "saints" as those whom the church recognizes to conform to the rule of faithfulness to God—they are the rule of faith in and as a human life; the body of Christ worships the Father in the Spirit according to the measure of Thanksgiving, or the "canon of the mass;" the "canons" are those conventional laws that govern the corporate life of the body of Christ towards mutual deferral and accountability.[88] The list could go on and on but the point concerning the totemic interrelatedness of Christ, the scriptures, the saints, and the rule of faith has been made.

This chapter first describes how several recent scholars paint a picture both of ascesis as always bound up in the exegesis of a given scriptural tradition and of exegesis as itself an ascetical performance. Augustine assumes that "teaching Christianity" is nothing less than the teaching of the performance of a way of life through the interpretation of Christian scripture. This performance is, in turn, nothing less than the teaching, that is, the performative interpretation of Christian scripture in and as the ascetic life of imitation of the saints. These points make sense because Christians interpret the scriptures according to the measure of human faithfulness to God as found in the incarnation and passion of the Son of God. Insofar, therefore, as exegesis entails a discursive element in its role in Christian theology, then theology is ascesis.

---

[88] See chapter eight for the relationship of councils and their respective canon law to ascesis and theology.

Theology and the Gift of Council

The brethren, both the apostles and the elders, to the brethren who are of the Gentiles in Antioch and Syria and Cilicia: Greeting . . . For it has seemed good to the Holy Spirit and to us to lay upon you no greater burden than these necessary things . . . If you keep yourselves from these, you will do well. Farewell.

Acts 15.23b; 28, 29

With [the tongue] we bless the Lord and Father, and with it we curse men, who are made in the likeness of God. From the same mouth come blessing and cursing. My brethren, this ought not to be so.

James 3.9, 10

THE ECUMENICAL Christian tradition places "dogmatics," or the theology of Christian teachings, in service of the discursive articulation of those teachings found in the formal documents of its conciliar tradition. Theology is ascesis, therefore, because council, as an ascetic act, is its formal discursive, articulation. Virginia Burrus, in her article "Ascesis, Authority, and Text: The Acts of the Council of Saragossa,"[1] argues that, just as narrative itself may be seen as an ascetic form of discourse, so too conciliar texts and their *acta* are also ascetic. In light of Burrus' scholarship, this chapter argues that this specific insight of conciliar *acta* as ascetic texts may be broadened and applied to the doctrinal statements of (ecumenical) councils in general and Nicea in particular. To do so this chapter engages a recent article

---

[1] Virginia Burrus, "Ascesis, Authority, and Text: The Acts of the Council of Sara-gossa," *Semeia* 58 (1992): 95—108.

by Ephraim Radner.[2] Finally, this chapter claims that council as ascesis makes sense in terms indigenous to Christianity because council is the gift to human discourse of a share in the discourse of the corporate body of the incarnate God.

Virginia Burrus on Episcopal and Ascetical Authority

IN AD 380, the bishops of cities and regions scattered throughout what is now northern Spain and Aquitaine met in the city of Saragossa (now Zaragoza, Spain) in order to discuss current controversies surrounding local ascetic observance. The Council of Saragossa is usually understood as a kind of anti-ascetic council on the part of the episcopacy over against the Priscillian[3] heretics and other extreme, late fourth-century ascetics.[4] Virginia Burrus argues that Christian ascetic practice was not renounced but highlighted and articulated at the council of Saragossa.

Burrus contends that the controversy was not to be found between those who advocated asceticism and those who opposed it—for all parties would have affirmed some form of ascesis as basic to Christian practice. Rather, the real conflict was between two different views of the nature of authority and its relationship to ascesis. The *Acts of the Council of Saragossa* is not a text that is against asceticism, it is "rather a text which engages the question of the true nature of Christian discipline and authority."[5] Her thesis, like that of Geoffrey Harpham,[6] is that just as narrative itself may be seen as an ascetic form of discourse, so too conciliar texts and their *acta* are also ascetic, "the genre of conciliar *acta* [is] not only as a vehicle for the assertion of Episcopal authority but also . . . a form of ascetic discourse."[7] Ultimately, Burrus argues, these late fourth century bishops sought to unify ascetic and episcopal authority, and the genre of conciliar *acta* were key to this

---

[2]   Ephraim Radner, "To Desire Rightly: The Force of the Creed in its Canonical Context," in *Nicene Christianity: The Future for a New Ecumenism*, ed. Christopher R. Seitz (Grand Rapids: Brazos, 2001).

[3]   Priscillian was a devout Spanish layman who flourished in the 370s and who called on his fellow Christians to follow strict forms of asceticism. There is a long history here that is out of the scope of this project, but a preliminary study and bibliography may be found in the article "Priscillianism," in the *Oxford Dictionary of the Christian Church*.

[4]   Burrus, "Ascesis," 95.

[5]   *Ibid.*, 96.

[6]   Burrus makes this connection of her work with that of Harpham on page 106.

[7]   *Ibid.*, 96.

process.[8] Because of her focus on this conciliar document as an ascetic text, Burrus spends the bulk of her essay in a discussion of the text itself.[9]

In order to press their authority, Burrus points out, conciliar documents of this time echoed the formal language and procedures of senatorial decision-making.[10] The text contains eight recorded decisions. The first and last acts introduce and close on similar notes regarding women ascetics, thus adding a sense of completeness and unity to the document. The first declares that women should not be alone with men with whom they are not related.[11] Women should not be involved with male spiritual leaders and ascetic masters.[12] The eighth declares that "virgins," as an order of ascetic observance in the church, are not to be veiled, that is, formally enrolled, until they are known to be over forty years of age, asserting, as with the first act, the formal authority of the church over female ascetic behavior. Although this may be a clear instance of "patriarchy," it is also an attempt on the part of the bishops to ensure that the laity are above reproach to those who would critique the church. In both of these cases, the bishops are not interested in combating ascetic observance itself but are seeking to assert their authority over *and through* ascesis.

The second and fourth acts deal with possible conflicts between voluntary ascetic observance and common liturgical times and seasons. The second act declares that there should be no fasting on Sundays.[13] All must observe the day of the Lord, together, as the body of Christ, regardless of voluntary ascetic practices. The common life of the body always takes precedence over individual devotion. The fourth act deals with a kind of a quasi-lent that these independent ascetics had been observing before Epiphany.[14] So, again, similar to the

---

[8]   *Ibid.*, 95.

[9]   This discussion covers pages 96—102. Burrus notes that she is not concerned with the relative accuracy of this text in representing the actual proceedings of the council but in its historical *function* as an ascetic text (95).

[10] *Ibid.*, 96.

[11] *Ibid.*, 97. When Burrus refers to the acts of the council she uses the following text: J. P. Migne, ed., *Acta Concilii Caesaraugustani*, Patrologia Latina 84 (1850), 315—18, and Felix Rodriguez, "Concilio I de Zaragoza: Texto critico,"in *Primero Concilio Caesaraugustano: MDC aniversario*, (Zaragoza, 1981) 9—25.

[12] Burrus, "Ascesis," 101.

[13] *Ibid.*, 98.

[14] *Ibid.*, 99.

second act, individual ascetic devotion is not to take precedence over
the common feast days and seasons of the Church. In both of these
cases the bishops are not attempting to suppress ascetic behavior, but
rather they are working to bring it into conformity with the *communal*
ascesis of liturgical observance.

The third, fifth, and sixth acts reflect issues of discipline and especially compliance of clergy to such discipline. The third act declares
that those who refuse to attend church to receive communion will in
turn be refused communion, excommunicated.[15] Ascetic behavior
alone cannot replace or act as a supplement for regular liturgical observance and eucharistic attendance and participation. Those who are
not dedicated to participation in the church are to be expunged from
the church. The fifth act demands episcopal solidarity.[16] Bishops who
fail to recognize the excommunication pronounced by other bishops
jeopardize the authority of all bishops. This is a direct re-articulation
at the local level of canon five of the "ecumenical" council of Nicea,
fifteen years before. The sixth act deals with clergy who abandon their
cures for "vainglorious" asceticism.[17] Here, the bishops assert that the
church, as the communal body of Christ, takes precedence over individual devotion. The clergy's charge to care for this communal life
takes precedence over any of their own individual ascetical or devotional commitments. In all of these decisions the bishops are bringing
ascetic observance under the authority of the life of the community. In
their extreme asceticism the bishops' opponents fall into a kind of
false, vainglorious form of ascetic observance.[18] This conciliar document therefore addresses the problem of extreme ascetics who practice a Christianity divorced from the regular life of the institutional
church through a kind of ascetic-elitism.

In order to understand this document as representing an inner-
ascetic conflict rather than a conflict with asceticism itself, Burrus
proposes that "eremitism" and "cenobitism," as hermit-asceticism
and communal-asceticism respectively, may serve as types for understanding the conflict.[19] The conflict, therefore, is between a solitary,

---

15   *Ibid.*
16   *Ibid.*, 100.
17   *Ibid.*
18   *Ibid.*, 96.
19   *Ibid.*, 102—03.

elitist form of asceticism and a communal asceticism that is fitting to the nature of a communal religion and its common institution.

> The bishops at Saragossa oppose one set of ascetic practices. In its place, they advocate an alternative lifestyle of discipline and order focused on obedience to episcopal authority and the renunciation of personal desire and private pursuits.[20]

The bishops not only pursue a common discipline but a discipline that is communal, ecclesial. This is an ascesis that brings the disciplining of the individual Christian body into the orbit of the common disciplining of the corporate Christian body—here, chiefly, through liturgical observance. The bishops at Saragossa

> agreed that the Christian life was essentially a life of discipline . . . However, they perceived in the practices of their opponents not a praiseworthy ascesis but an acquiescence to the temptations of self-aggrandizement.[21]

Ascetics outside of the orbit of common church practice put themselves in danger of defeating the very purpose of ascesis; the denial of self may become the vaunting of self over the very community that grounds its religious and cosmological significance.

In conclusion, Burrus brings up Philip Rousseau's illustration of the significance of hagiographic biography for forging a link between the personal and charismatic authority brought by ascetic practice and the communal and institutional authority of the bishop in Gaul.[22] This concurs with Harpham's general point that narrative itself is an ascetical form of discourse—a kind of ascesis of discourse.[23] Burrus' contribution is to see these formal conciliar acts as ascetic texts also, texts that perform an ascesis of (Christian) discourse. In doing so, the bishops take on ascesis (by engaging in it), along with the charismatic authority it provides, while subjecting it to a "cenobitic" ascesis of common life.[24] This describes the general nature of councils as providing discipline for the common life of the church. But what does it

---

[20]   *Ibid.*, 96.

[21]   *Ibid.*, 103.

[22]   *Ibid.*, 106. Philip Rousseau, *Ascetics, Authority, and the Church in the Age of Jerome and Cassian* (Oxford: Oxford University Press, 1978).

[23]   *Ibid.*, 106.

[24]   "Every society has ascetic elements in the sense that it prescribes and advises certain limits on ordinary behavior for the common good." Michael L. Satlow, "Shame and Sex in Late Antique Judaism," in *Asceticism*, eds. Vincent L. Wimbush and Richard Valantasis (New York: Oxford University Press, 1995), 540.

mean when these councils also expound upon the rule of faith and make theological proscriptions, as with the various ecumenical councils, and many others? This chapter now turns to the work of Ephraim Radner in order to discuss the nature of the relationship of theological statement and conciliar authority.

Radner on Ecumenical Council

EPHRAIM RADNER, in his article "To Desire Rightly: The Force of the Creed in Its Canonical Context,"[25] argues that the Nicene Creed (and, by extension, creeds in general) only makes sense in its conciliar and canonical context. In doing so, he also describes the Christian act of council as essentially a self-ordering, corporate ascesis. Radner's position broadens Burrus' specific insight of conciliar *acta* as ascetic texts and applies it to the doctrinal statements of (ecumenical) councils in general and Nicea in particular.

At the beginning of his article, Radner turns to Athanasius' description of the purpose of the council of Nicea. In one of his letters,[26] Athanasius explains that the council of Nicea was called for one chief end, the shared observance of Easter throughout the church. Only then does Athanasius list the Arian crisis. A third and final reason for the meeting: the various schisms in the church in Egypt. So, Radner contends, contrary to what is commonly held, this council was not primarily called for the formulation of a creed but for the disciplining of the common life of the Christian body.[27] This common discipline Radner calls the "principle of Easter and order."[28] That is to say, Radner sees the practice of discerning a creed at a council to be bound up in the general practice of establishing order in and for the church, for all of these issues have to do with harmony and unity within the church.

Radner asserts that the canonical context of the creed is essential to understanding its meanings as an authoritative text within the Christian tradition. The creed was also simply called "the canon" among its contemporary adherents. "The *canon* of the creed and the *canons* of the many decrees are therefore terms that often ambigu-

---

25   Radner, "To Desire."
26   Athanasius, *De Synodis.*
27   Radner, 214-5.
28   *Ibid.,* 215.

ously overlap in the writings of the early church."[29] This ambiguous semantic overlapping[30] of the terms "canon" and "canons" deliberately calls up the more traditional phrase "canon of truth," or the rule of faith, as its intended implication. Simultaneously, this phraseology also deliberately links the creed with church *canons* in general. What Radner means by pointing this out is that the creed cannot be meaningfully separated from the other conciliar acts and canons within which it took its shape. Obedience to God is found in the concrete mutual submission of the church between her various members with regards to its common life *and discourse,* and this is the reason why there is "semantic overlap" in the use of the terms "canon" and "canons."

Radner understands Christian council as a practice of communal self-ordering among the members of the body of Christ corporate. The council of Nicea did not *create* this common body but assumed church unity. The creed is also tied to a common *discursive* community. Radner poses the question: "[i]f the creed is organically tied to a discursive community"[31] then what defines the communal life that embodies such a creed? Radner's consistent answer is that this community must be dedicated to the common imitation of Christ in the self-ordering patterns and disciplines of mutual accountability and deference. The speech of the church is also a part of the life of the church that must be self-ordered in mutual deference, for "[t]he creed is the speech of a church that acts to order itself,"[32] in terms of mutuality and accountability.

The Nicene Creed is, however, most commonly read "doctrinally" instead of "ascetically."[33] Radner understands the nature of the "self-ordering" of Christian council to be essentially ascetic. In fact, it is directly analogous to the connection between mortification (an essential aspect of Christian ascesis) and the development of the Christian virtue of charity.[34] Radner's point is that the means to Christian virtue in general is the submission to disciplines that reshape human habits. This is no different at the level of a corporate body. The Spirit forms

---

[29] *Ibid.,* 216.
[30] *Ibid.,* 221.
[31] *Ibid.,* 218.
[32] *Ibid.*
[33] *Ibid.,* 217.
[34] *Ibid.,* 225.

the corporate body of Christ through disciplines that keep the various members integral to one another. The chief manifestation of this is the self-ordering virtue of mutual deference and accountability of Christian common life. At the level of the "universal" church, this occurs with the self-ordering of bishops[35] in mutual deference to one another at church councils.

The issue at hand, therefore, is "to desire rightly." The reshaping of communal Christian desire occurs through the common Christian discipline of council.[36] The canons and creeds of Christian council are chiefly concerned with the mutual internal discipline that allows the corporate body of Christ to remain whole and integral to itself: "[t]o order truthful theological speech, therefore, is to order the church *ascetically*."[37] This practice of ordering the church is essentially a practice whereby the Spirit trains ecclesial structures in *virtue*. When this church practice entails a *doctrinal* statement, it means training common structures of *discourse* in virtue.[38]

If council forms the corporate body of Christ in the virtue that determines its own cohesion, then true (dogmatic) theology is nothing less than the ascetic ordering of the church (especially) with regards to its discursive practice.[39] Creedal meaning is not discernable theoretically or discursively but only in terms of corporate self-discipline.[40] Radner here implicitly agrees with Hadot:[41] Christianity as a way of life inherently precedes its concomitant discursive practices and dis-

---

[35] In the eastern Christian tradition, canon law has developed such that bishops themselves must be practicing monks under monastic discipline. Jaroslav Pelikan points this out in a section of his book *Credo* entitled "Orthodoxy and Asceticism" that sheds some light on Radner's article. *Credo* is a massive historical and theological commentary on and companion volume to the three-volume set *Creeds and Confessions of Faith in the Christian Tradition*, Pelikan, Jaroslav and Valerie R. Hotchkiss, eds. (New Haven: Yale Univ. Press, 2003).

[36] Radner, 228.

[37] *Ibid.*, 220.

[38] Pelikan corroborates on this point: "A special affinity between dogma-as-orthodoxy and discipline-as-askesis, and thus between creeds and a particular class of deeds, has been documented by the history of the relation of orthodoxy to Christian monasticism in both East and West" (*Credo*, 93). Further, recall McGinn's comments on the relationship between the growth of mysticism and orthodoxy in the early church as described, above, in chapter five.

[39] Radner, 221.

[40] *Ibid.*, 219.

[41] *Ibid.*, 221.

ciplines. These disciplines, both general and discursive, share the end of unity in Christian charity.[42]

Why should the corporate Christian body be concerned with developing this virtue and with this particular means to its development? Wherever virtue is invoked a narrative structure is surely present. And Radner does invoke a narrative: "the historical reality, of God's own life given to the world, to which the church is the gifted response."[43] Such discipline and virtue constitute a concrete means by which the Christian body may participate in the imitation of its creator. It restores the *imago Dei* to human being through a corporate *mimesis*. In fact, Radner holds that this life of common discipline actually mirrors divine truth itself. Radner points out that Athanasius described submission to church discipline as itself a kind of *martyrdom*.[44] This mutual deference becomes, therefore, an existential interpretation of scripture according to Christ as the living rule of faith into the life of the corporate body.

In invoking the kenotic narrative of the incarnate God, Radner makes a bold connection between the development within the Christian community of "ecclesial order" and the historical incarnation of God.[45] Radner asserts, therefore, historical and theological grounds for the development of the institutional church's commitment to its own self-ordering as, in the end, commitment to its own gospel narrative and rule of faith.

Finally, Radner would have us understand,

> the canons as structures of ecclesial mortification in that their purpose in ordering the church is to leave space, through the limiting of human pride's self-assertion in the corporate life, for the divine assertion of Christ's own gracious form upon his body.[46]

The Spirit forms the various disparate individuals who claim to be Christians into a cohesive corporate body through this corporate mortification of mutual submission. Thus council is the analogue at the corporate level to ascetic mortification at the corporeal level. Both cases prove examples of a performative reiteration, or *mimesis*, of the divine act of incarnation as an act of sacrificial self-giving on behalf of

---

[42]   *Ibid.*, 220.
[43]   *Ibid.*, 223.
[44]   *Ibid.*
[45]   *Ibid.*, 224.
[46]   *Ibid.*, 225-6.

the other. Finally, this makes sense in terms from the previous chapter, above. Christ was obedient, "even to death on a cross,"[47] and his pattern is one of obedience.[48] Jesus Christ, as the living measure of fidelity to God, is represented discursively in the "rule of faith." And that rule of faith is expanded and ordered, ascetically, in the conciliar formulation of the creed. Council, therefore, like mortification, puts this obedience into practice in the life of the Christian body—and its discourse.

Radner's crucial contribution to the goal of this work is the assertion that the creeds and canons of the church represent "structures of ecclesial mortification" and, thereby, *ascesis*. These structures limit pride in leadership, reflect the divine humiliation of incarnation, and characterize the church as essentially ascetic in its nature.[49] Thus, the focus of the first ecumenical council in Nicea upon the issues of the observance of Easter, the various schisms in the church in Egypt, and the heresy of Arianism make sense because the canons of that very council show that doctrinal division simply "mirrors" jurisdictional confusion and the moral corruption of its leaders.[50] Conciliar *acta*, whether concerning practice (canons) or discourse (creed), are ascetic texts in both senses of the term: they arise out of the shared assumption of ascesis as Christian discipleship, and they serve to enforce and encourage that very practice.

Council and the Extension of the Incarnation into Human Discourse

COUNCIL AS ascesis makes sense in terms indigenous to Christianity because in council the Spirit gives a share in the incarnate discourse of God to (the body of) human discourse. Chapter four, above, adopted Eugene Roger's discussion of the Spirit as the gift that reorders and re-habituates human habits in its description of the nature of ascesis as gift. If theology is ascetic, then it also must be a gift that re-

---

[47]   Phil. 2.8.

[48]   Again, Pelikan corroborates: "the intellectual and theological obedience or self-restraint required to be orthodox is more than superficially analogous to the psychological and moral obedience or self-restraint required to be ascetic" (*Credo*, 299).

[49]   Radner, 226.

[50]   *Ibid.*, 222. Radner provides a brief but informative synopsis of the twenty canons of Nicea and groups them according to themes he discerns: "(2, 9 and 17) deal with the moral purity of the clergy." "(8, 10, 14, and 19) deal explicitly with the reception of repentant heretics," and "(4, 5, 6, 15, 16, 18, and 20) . . . deal with the ordering and political jurisdiction of the church's leadership" (222).

habituates—in this case, the habits of human discourse. For just as ascesis in general is concerned with disciplining over-all human habits, so too theology—the ascesis of discourse—must be concerned with up-rooting poor discursive habits and ingraining new healthy discursive habits in their place. Theology, if the over-all thesis holds true, must be concerned with reforming and restructuring human discursive habits. In doing so, theology enables human discourse to become habituated to the incarnate discourse of God.

The primary form that formal "theology" or "dogma" has taken in the Christian body is that of the official creeds and statements of episcopal[51] councils. The Christian body, by virtue of its desire to be disciplined under Christ, is *conciliar*. The Spirit gives council as counsel to the Christian body—the gift of corporate and sometimes discursive re-habituation. The ramification of conciliar authority affects both practice and, concomitantly, "dogma," or formal teaching of the Christian body. This is nothing other than the mutual deferral in discipline of the various members of the body to the whole for the sake of unity and health within the whole body. The discipline of the whole is for the sake of each member, while the discipline of each member is for the sake of the whole, and therefore councils are *according to the whole* they are "*kata-holos*,"—catholic.

Councils result in texts that take the form of *acta*, or *canons*; and these canons reflect and, so to speak, refract, the over-all canon or measure of fidelity to Christ—the rule of faith. In order to play out all implications of theology as ascesis, it must be the case that there are canons guiding Christian discourse as well as Christian action in general. And, of course, there are. Canonical decisions about discourse are known as *creeds*, and they sometimes take the form of *acts* (as in the statement at Chalcedon) and *confessions*.[52] Creeds are, therefore, formal, conciliar statements that reflect and share in the rule of faith at the level of discourse.

A council, then, is a *formal* dialogue that results in just such *formal* theological statements. So, unlike the informal but *theologically formative* dialogue of someone like Nazianzus described above in chapter

---

51 The intention is not to exclude those Protestant bodies that do not have an office explicitly deemed "bishop." "Bishop" may simply mean the authority of representative pastors in some form or another.

52 Here "confession" means, of course, the narrower, non-existential sense, as with the various articles published by the disparate Christian bodies after the Reformation.

six, formal theological dialogue at a council is simultaneously *more indirectly related to theology proper* (that is to say, the *performative* teaching of the Trinity, or, *theoria*) and yet *more formally binding upon the discourse of the Christian body* as a whole.[53] Creeds are the form of discursive ascesis—the performative teaching of the Trinity and its concomitant *theoria*, or contemplation as its concrete *content*.

This mutual deference embodied in Christian council represents the kind of formative discipline that any *voluntary* corporate body must take in order to maintain itself. For people to join together into a corporate body requires the discipline or ascesis of mutual deference, regardless of whether that body is Christian or not.[54] But in terms indigenous to Christianity, the church allows herself to be formed by the Holy Spirit through following the rule of faith as mutual deference. In allowing the Spirit to grant them a shared discourse in and as the body of Christ, bishops in council thereby allow the Spirit to take up human discourse and continue the incarnation of the Word of God, for wherever the Spirit guides discourse, there is the discourse of God, the Logos.

Thus, following Radner, this discipline of council is an embodiment in the corporate Christian body of God's own self-giving to the world in the incarnation—the living measure of fidelity. This embodiment of the incarnation thereby extends God's discourse—the divine Logos—into the world through the ongoing life of discipline and mutual submission of the church.[55] And, following Hadot, this way of

---

[53] Christian dialogue in the style of Nazianzus is not formally binding on the Christian body; but it is nevertheless more directly related to the task of theology as discursive union with God in contemplation (*theoria*).

[54] And this is true in Christian terms primarily because of the fall, as discussed above in chapter two with regards to the creation of culture—cultures being shared and communal human artifacts.

[55] Mutual deference of the Christian body to each member for the sake of the whole includes deference to those who have died but who "remain in Christ"—the fathers and mothers of the church. Deference to the fathers includes deference to previous councils, canons, confessions, and formal acts of these fathers, but also to their informal insights found in their body of literature such as discourses, books, sermons, and commentaries. Deference to the fathers in the practice of theology is the discursive analogue to the ascetic master-pupil relationship. A continued share in this ongoing conversation on the part of the Christian body, as part of the ongoing unfolding of Christian teaching, also extends the incarnation of divine discourse into the life of the corporate Christian body.

life entails and includes a discourse inherent to it, together with discursive practices and disciplines that shape it as a part of this life.

Now just as ascesis in general has both as its goal and as its gift a share in the divine nature; so too then, the Spirit grants theology in the particular case of discourse as the formal teaching of the church, a share in the divine discourse incarnate in (the corporate body of) Jesus Christ. The Spirit gives the Logos to human discourse through perfected discursive habits formed, in part, by the discipline found in the mutual deference of Christian council. Thereby the Spirit "adds" Christian discourse to Christ's discourse just as the Spirit "adds" Christian bodies to Christ's body. In both cases, following Radner, one has the training of church structures in virtue.

Theology reforms and restructures human discursive habits. Just as ascesis in general is concerned with disciplining over-all human habits, so too theology—the ascesis of discourse—up-roots poor discursive habits and ingrains healthy discursive habits in their place. Council is the formal, corporate form in which this re-habituation takes place. Creed, as formal theology, enables human discourse to become habituated to the incarnate discourse of God. Theology is therefore ascesis because formal theology, as conciliar creed or statement, is a form of corporate Christian ascesis.

Council is ascesis. This makes sense in terms indigenous to Christianity because council gives (the body of) human discourse a share in the incarnate discourse of God. Burrus argues that just as narrative itself may be seen as an ascetic form of discourse, so too conciliar texts and their *acta* are also ascetic. Ephraim Radner contributes to a picture where the specific insight of conciliar *acta* as ascetic texts broaden out and apply to the doctrinal statements of councils in general and Nicea in particular. Theology is ascesis, therefore, because council is an ascetic act, and when setting forth a creedal statement council is the formal, discursive, articulation of Christian theology.

CONCLUSION

An Ascesis of Theology

THIS BOOK has so far chiefly claimed that the nature and logic of Christian teaching and, concomitantly, theological reflection upon that teaching are fundamentally ascetic. The project demands one final step to complete its argument, to point out that Christian theology, to be recognized as such, must be pursued within its proper, broader context of ascesis as a particular ascetic discipline among others that cannot be effectively practiced outside of the general practices of which it constitutes merely an example. First, this conclusion briefly revisits the definition of the term ascesis. It then provides a recapitulation and summary of the argument of the body of the work. Next, it discusses the meaning and significance of the unfolding of Christian teaching into life and discourse. Finally, the conclusion answers a possible objection and closes with the reassertion that ascesis, and therefore theology, is a divine gift.

Ascesis Revisited

THIS SECTION reviews the preliminary definition of Christian ascesis given in the introduction as a review of the body of the work. Ascesis is 1) those traditionary disciplines of self-denial that 2) Christians recognize as divine gifts in themselves. In light of chapter four, whatever effort may be put forth on the part of the Christian ascetic practitioner, the disciplines themselves, and the ability to will them, are gifts granted the Christian in the freedom of the Spirit.

Christian ascesis 3) always includes (but sometimes transcends) bodily practices. There is no Christian asceticism without somatic self-denial—mortification of the flesh. Nevertheless, as discussed especially in chapter five, some ascetic practices verge on the incorporeal, such as contemplative prayer. Contemplative prayer transcends the physical but is still an ascetic practice insofar as it takes its proper place within the context of a general regimen of somatic ascesis. Christian ascesis is 4) performed as an imitation of Jesus Christ. Chapters three and seven demonstrate how ascesis allows for the active imaging of God. Jesus Christ, as the incarnate image of God, restores the fallen human *imago Dei* and provides, through the pattern he establishes, the means for this restoration on the part of the individual Christian.

Such ascetic practices 5) open out the ascetic to receive the gift of communion with and contemplation of the triune God. Chapter One describes ascesis as the foundational practice of Christian discipleship and the means to *theosis*. In terms of human discourse, *theoria*, or contemplative prayer, is the goal of all ascetic practice. Finally, Christian ascesis 6) renders the ascetically disciplined Christian body an intelligible contribution to discourse about God. Following recent asceticism scholarship, as perused in the introduction, and translating it into an indigenous Christian context, ascesis takes the fallen and therefore unintelligible human body and renews it as a sign of God and God's kingdom to those who can read it.

Because ascesis forms the body as a sign, it maintains, even while collapsing, the distinction between "practice" and "discourse." Ascesis collapses this distinction because discourse is itself a practice in need of discipline (theology), and (ascetic) practice itself is a means of making an intelligible assertion. Ascesis maintains the distinction between practice and discourse, however, because of the demand on the part of Christian discipleship for discourse about Christian practice or reality always to be in service to the life of discipleship in general.

Theology does not escape this maintenance and collapse of the distinction between discourse and practice. In fact, it is the emanating source of its force. Theology is a practice that entails embodiment and may be construed broadly enough to include (ascetic) non-verbal expression. On the other hand, theology as discourse is necessarily subordinate to ascesis as its context and definition. For the Christian religion, discourse without practice is worthless. Nevertheless, practice that is not itself discursive is unintelligible and therefore evil or false. Speaking in terms of dogmatics, theology is the emanating force behind this necessary and paradoxical maintenance-in-collapse of the distinction between discourse and practice precisely because the divine Logos (discourse) demands expression chiefly as incarnation (practice).

In the practice of ascesis the ascetic practitioner renders the physical intelligible and the intelligible physical. It is therefore analogous to the incarnation. It is incarnational. It is a share in the incarnation of God. Ascesis renders the body intelligible as a sign-act of the story of the transcendent. Ascesis also renders a body to that which would otherwise remain incorporeal, that is, the purely intelligible, for it enacts the claim that the meaning of the Christian "myth" is only to be found in its actual embodiment.[1]

Recapitulation

THE MAJOR claims of the two parts of this book converge to assert the thesis that theology is ascesis. Part one asserts that ascesis is the active means by which Christianity is taught, by which it is appropriated. Ascesis teaches Christianity. So, insofar as "theology" names Christian teaching, then theology is ascesis. Part two asserts that theology, understood as dogmatics, is an ascesis of Christian discourse. So, insofar as dogmatics names ascetic reflective discipline, theology is ascesis.

The four chapters of part one converge to portray a picture of ascesis as that which teaches Christianity. Ascesis teaches 1) ecstatic person-hood and thus the Christian vision of God as triune. Ascesis teaches 2) *imago Dei* as a performance through re-aligning broken human *mimesis*. Ascesis teaches 3) kenotic *mimesis* through witness within and as the Christian body. Ascesis teaches 4) salvation by grace alone. In terms of what is traditionally called Christian "doctrine," Christian ascesis teaches these central tenets of Christian faith because ascesis unfolds them into, within and as the Christian body. In this sense, ascesis *teaches* Christianity concretely as subjective appropriation. From an indigenous Christian perspective, this subjective appropriation is possible because it places the ascetic in direct ontological contact with, or participation in, reality itself. Briefly, ascesis *teaches* (Christian) *reality*. So, together with other central indigenous Christian practices,[2] ascesis *teaches* Christianity.

The four chapters of part two flesh out a vision of theology as an ascetic discipline for the somatic human practice of discourse. In this case, theology is ascesis as self-denial found in submission on the part of the corporate Christian body and the individual theologian 1) to the goal of *theoria* and the apophatic demand for analogical discourse,

---

[1] This "meaning" is the *res* of Augustine's semiology.

[2] Other central indigenous Christian practices that teach Christianity would be, for example, liturgy, fellowship and mission.

2) to the practice of dialogue within and as a part of the Christian life, 3) to the disciplinary strictures of scriptural exegesis, and 4) to council and the ongoing unfolding of the rule of faith within the Christian community. This entails submission on the part of councils to previous councils, etc. Such conciliar formation is one of the key ways in which Christian teaching is unfolded as a corporate ascesis. In this sense, theology is ascetic as a discursive practice of self-denial. Theology, then, forms a part of the many ascetic practices that places the Christian in ontological contact with (Christian) reality.

The dogmatic claims found in the four chapters of each of the two parts of this book follow the shape of a dogmatic theology in an attempt to describe how the over-all thesis of each section is fitting to the realities that Christianity claims to teach. Chapters five through eight correspond to and, in terms of discourse, provide a microcosm of the dogmatic picture painted concerning ascesis in general found in chapters one through four. The dogmatic claims move from the doctrine of the Trinity, through the doctrine of the creation of human being in the image of God, to the incarnation of the Son of God and culminate in the economy of salvation by gift alone. Together, each part coheres as its own four-part dogmatics in miniature.

So, the first part asserts that ascesis makes sense in terms of Christian dogmatics because God is ecstatically personal, because human being is made to imitate that ecstasy, because God underwent extreme kenotic ecstasy for the sake of human being in the incarnation and the cross, and finally because atonement requires that the Spirit make human beings one with the body of the crucified. In the second half, theology itself is read as a disciplinary practice within the life of the church because God is self-giving discourse, because human being is made to imitate God's self-giving discourse, because the divine discourse provides the measure of fidelity in the shape of the life of Christ, and finally because in order for human discourse to be taken up into the divine discourse the Holy Spirit adds human discourse to the body of the crucified Christ.

Again, the dogmatic claims in the second part provide a microcosm, in terms of discourse of the dogmatic picture painted concerning ascesis in general in the first part. The use of Denys' (chapter five) apophatic "reversal" of analogy in contemplation—*theoria*—is the discursive counterpart to *theosis* in general (chapter 1). Human being and, therefore, human discourse are made one with the triune God, because the interior life of the Trinity is the native environment of both personhood and predication.

Talking things through (dialogue) as a means of fleshing out reality in discourse (chapter six) is the discursive counterpart to the mimetic generation of culture as an essential part of the *imago Dei* (chapter two). Human being and human discourse share in the creative *mimesis* of the divine life. Because human discourse may be taken up into the divine discourse, the mode of human knowledge of God is the same as God's own self-knowledge—but at an infinite, created and analogical remove.

The ascetical interpretation of scripture according to the rule of faith (chapter seven) is the discursive counterpart to Christian witness to Christ in martyrdom and the "white" martyrdom of ascesis (chapter three). Human being and human discourse perform a *mimesis* of God through participation in the work of the Son of God made human—Jesus Christ. The life of Christ as an existential measure of fidelity to God together with the rule of faith as a discursive account of the narrative of Christ's life both discipline Christian life and its concomitant discourse, respectively.

Finally, the submission to council on the part of both local churches and individual theologians to the corporate body of Christ is the discursive counterpart to the "active passivity" of the Christian ascetic life in general. Human being and human discourse perform salvation as pure divine gift through these active disciplines of reception. Council, as a gift to the corporate body of Christ, is an analogical participant in ascesis in general as the Spirit's gift of a body, both corporeal and corporate, to the Logos of God. This section has summarized the internal logic of the argument of the body of this work.

Unfolding Christian Teaching

IN THE INTRODUCTION certain postcritical possibilities emerged with respect to theology as an indigenous Christian practice. For example: if transcendent realities actually open out through traditionary disciplines, then contact with these transcendent realities should dictate the direction that Christian teaching unfolds. This means that theology ought to entail contemplation of the transcendent realities to which any given religion, especially Christianity, promises contact. This section sketches how one might address these important issues in light of this project's main argument.

Unfolding Christian life and discourse

AT THIS POINT it is important to emphasize that Christian teaching is itself the ascetic unfolding of Christian reality into the life of the Christian body. Ascesis is both the "how" and the "what" of Christian teaching. That is to say, ascesis is the means by which Christianity is taught and is also consistent with the nature of reality as encountered through the Christian religion. The introduction covered major categories of Christian ascetic practices such as prayer, fasting, alms-giving, repentance, and spiritual direction in terms of freedom from enslavement to falsehood, the development of virtue, and the disclosure of Christian reality to the practitioner. Without going into detail, the various Christian realities dogmatically discussed throughout the body of this text are "taught" by these ascetic practices. These practices open out the ascetic body to (Christian) reality. Likewise, the vision of Christian reality found in these "teachings" provides a world where ascesis serves as the proper means of knowledge and salvation.[3]

In light of this ascetic unfolding of Christian teaching into Christian life, the conclusion can now take up the specific set of issues set in motion in the introduction concerning the relationship between *scholarship* concerning Christian thought, the *unfolding* of Christian teaching within Christianity itself, and that practice that Christians call "theology." Is simple logical coherence all that is implicit in the indigenous unfolding of Christian thought? If not, what else is involved?

Any science (in the Aristotelian sense) requires a subject matter to which the scientist has access. Theology is an odd "science" because it must begin by asserting the absolute inadequacy of the knower to the "thing" known. This is the apophatic imperative of Christian theology. Nevertheless, Christian thought does not end there, but practices predication concerning God because of the assumption that the practice of theology—as gift of the Spirit—puts the Christian in contact with God. Ascesis, therefore, is the means by which the theologian, as scientist, gains access to his or her "subject matter:" God.

Furthermore, *discourse* about Christian teaching itself needs discipline. And, as established throughout the course of this project, the name of that discipline is (dogmatic) theology. "Ascetic traditions are

---

[3] More detail about how each discipline discussed in the introduction (along with many that could not be) corresponds to the appropriation of Christian teaching represents a direction that further research in this area might take in future.

forms of collective memory enacted in the body through *praxis* and enacted in language through discourse."[4] Ascetic traditions are not just enacted in the body, but in language and discourse. If ascesis unfolds Christian teaching into the life of the Christian body, then theology, as an ascetic practice, unfolds that same teaching into discourse. So, what ascesis opens out ontologically, theology extends epistemologically and discursively. This discursive extension corresponds to what has been called the "development of doctrine" in the Roman Catholic tradition since John Henry Newman's introduction of this term in the nineteenth century.[5]

To sum up, Christian "teaching" unfolds in its primary sense as the life of the Christian and the Christian community. In this sense, "unfolding" means "development" as a Christian body. In its secondary sense, the unfolding of Christian teaching indicates the knowledge of reality granted in and by this Christian life, and that usually in the form of (a) discourse. In this sense, "unfolding" means the "development" of more explicit knowledge. These two senses of the unfolding of Christian teaching correspond to the broader relationship of the ontological to the epistemological in the order of discourse. The

---

[4] Flood, 9.

[5] Scholarship on the work of John Henry Newman and the Roman Catholic theology of the development of doctrine is vast and beyond the scope of the conclusion of this project. Many recognize John Henry Newman's *Essay on the Development of Christian Doctrine* (1845), ed. J. M. Cameron (Harmondsworth, Eng.: Penguin Books, 1974) as the first treatise explicitly to describe this theological concept. This project has deliberately used the term "unfold" with respect to teaching or doctrine, rather than "development," in order to avoid two possible problems with the Roman Catholic term. First, the term "unfold" makes it clear that its primary sense is that of the life and practices of concrete Christian bodies. The "unfolding" of Christian teaching into discourse is a secondary and derivative sense of this first and primary meaning. The second reason is that Protestants in general, and Anglicans in particular, have been wary of the Roman Catholic use of the term "development of doctrine." Protestants have often perceived this as the name Roman Catholics give to their proclivity to introduce "innovations" in Christian teaching as "development of doctrine" (e.g., the immaculate conception of Mary and the infallibility of the Pope). This project has used the term "unfold" in place of "develop" in order to make it clear that what is intended is the organic and logical clarification of the content of Christian teaching, the initial manifestation and content of which remains unchanged. Nevertheless, the term "unfold" may be construed in such a way as to allow it to be compatible with the Roman Catholic use. In this way the use of the term "unfold" represents an attempt at an ecumenically neutral phrase.

first sense of the unfolding of Christian teaching, above, is ontological and primary. The second sense of this unfolding is epistemological in nature and thereby derivative of the primary sense.[6]

The Christian theologian

THE MUTUAL submission of discourse for the sake of the whole body implies that when *individual* Christian bodies take up the role of theologian, they do so under discipline. Theology, then, is not only an ascetical program for the corporate body and its discourse but also an ascetical practice given to the individual theologian. In the practice of theology, the Spirit disciplines the individual theologian's discourse for the sake of the whole so that, as a living and non-identical part of the whole, her discourse may be taken up into the divine discourse as a somatic activity within the corporate Christian body.

Needless to say, this construction of the nature of theology as discursively ascetic entails that the individual theologian cannot fully contribute to the body of discourse of the whole unless that theologian is already engaged in a general practice of somatic deference to the body corporate. More to the point, theology is merely a subpractice within the general Christian regimen of ascesis. Therefore, because theology is an ascetical practice within Christian ascesis in general, it is actually absurd to the indigenous logic of Christian faith to imagine an individual practicing theology outside of the regular regimen of Christian discipline or discipleship. It would be like someone fasting without praying or meditating without attending New Covenant worship, or like someone practicing the Christian Rosary in order to "calm his or her mind" instead of as a devotion to something transcendent. Such a practice would be similar to how many westerners practice "Yoga" not only without believing, but without even attempting to comprehend the ascetical goal of *moksha* that is the supposed *telos* of the yogic practitioner. These religious and philosophical practices cannot be separated from their goals and the realities that they inculcate into, and open out for, those who practice them.

---

6   In terms of the work of Michael Polyani, the first sense represents *tacit* participatory knowledge, the second represents *explicit* knowledge. See Michael Polanyi, *Personal Knowledge: Towards a Post-Critical Philosophy* (Chicago: Univ. of Chicago Press, 1958), and *The Tacit Dimension* (Garden City, NY: Doubleday, 1966).

This brief reflection on the nature of theology as a part of the regular ascetic practice of the individual theologian also makes sense of Evagrius Ponticus' maxim that "[i]f you are a theologian you truly pray. If you truly pray you are a theologian."[7] For on this model, theology is merely a means to an end, that end being chiefly prayer or *theoria*. But theology is not only a means; it is also a means that contains the end within it—true theology is itself an ascetic prayer for the sake of human discourse. Theology as rumination by an individual theologian upon the formal teachings of the Christian body *is an ascetic act*. For here theology is the practice of discursive deference of the *corporeal* Christian body (of discourse) to and for the sake of the whole, *corporate*, Christian body (of discourse).

Simple examples of daily acts of Christian discipleship demonstrate the claim that theology is a part of the over-all gift of rehabituation in the Spirit. Daily office, doxology, *lectio divina*, dialogue, and the like are signs and means of the Spirit's restoration of human discourse to and within divine discourse. These quotidian acts of discipline are the stuff of which theology is made. These simple habits of the particular theologian serve as a part of his or her general and regular regimen of ascesis. And so, both at the corporate level, through council, and at the corporeal level, through the theologian's own ascetic practice, the Spirit grants human discourse a share in the incarnate discourse of God—the body (and discourse) of Jesus Christ.

In this respect, this project is not unlike Hadot's in the field of philosophy. That is to say, in describing Christian theology as ascesis, this project implies more than a description of theology. In the act of providing this description, the text has also performed a normative claim.[8] The task of the theologian requires contact with the realities the theologian discusses and "unfolds" into discourse. Ascesis is the means of such contact within the context of the Christian religion.

---

[7] Evagrius Ponticus, *Chapters On Prayer* 60; For a recent critical edition, see *The Praktikos & Chapters on Prayer*, trans. John Eudes Bamberger, Cistercian Studies Series: Number Four (Kalamazoo, MI: Cistercian Publications, 1981).

[8] This is not unlike the way that Gadamer provides a kind of phenomenological account of interpretation but, in so doing, sets a kind of norm or standard for the relationship of *truth* to *method*. Hans Georg Gadamer, *Truth and Method* (New York: Crossroads, 1982).

This corresponds to Peter Brown's note on the emphasis of the need for "purity of heart" to "see God" in the early Christian centuries.[9]

Relationship of Christian theology to the secular academy

THE DISCURSIVE unfolding of Christian teaching must be done according to the internal logic of that teaching and according to intellectual and, today, even academic canons of rigor. One who does not practice Christianity may understand its teachings logically. Nevertheless in order that the on-going community of practicing Christians, i.e., the church or the Christian body, recognize and ratify such unfolding, it must occur within the practice of Christian discipline, or, ascesis and within the practice of theology as a discipline that itself opens out the Christian body to the realities that such practices (claim to) engage. Mere logical extension is not sufficient for the unfolding of Christian doctrine *qua* Christian because Christianity is not (an) ideology.

This phenomenon—the discursive unfolding of Christian teaching as requiring more than mere logical coherence—can be explained in two ways. One way is ethnographic in character, bracketing ontology. The other way may be voiced in a manner more indigenous to Christian thought, bringing ontology back in play. Ethnographically, one can simply say that the Christian community eventually comes to recognize only those unfoldings of the logic of Christian teaching that are formed within and informed by the indigenous and somatic practices that conform the members of the community to the shape of the tradition. This explanation is still entirely immanent and consistent with a "religious studies" approach.

On the other hand, one can explain this phenomenon in terms indigenous to Christianity by noting fallen reason's incapacity on its own to trace out logical connections in Christian teaching without error. The narrative of tradition must somatically shape the logical thought of the theologian through ascetic practice. Furthermore, the unfolding of Christian teaching necessitates the unfolding of Christian discourse concerning the transcendent realities that the practices of the Christian tradition open out. Only Christian practice opens up (Christian) reality. Understood as ascesis, the discipline of theology

---

[9]   Matthew 5.8. For more on the integration of the Beatitudes into the Christian ascetic tradition see Gregory Collins, "Simeon the New Theologian," especially pages 348-9. (see ch. 1, nt. 29)

unfolds Christian teaching within a somatic self-denial (corporeal and corporate) that opens out discourse to the gift of (Christian) reality.

The difference between these two approaches is whether or not a transcendent causality is allowed as (a part of) the *ratio* of the given account. Either way, the outcome is the same: no ascesis, no unfolding that is acceptable to the Christian community. And either way, theology is the ascesis of Christian discourse.[10] Furthermore, the individual who takes up a call to perform the role that Christians name theologian (for in one sense all Christians are theologians, insofar as discipleship itself entails intelligible discourse about God) can only fulfill such a calling, at least according to Christian criteria, by engaging in it as only an example and single part of an over-all life of Christian discipleship and asceticism.[11] So long as the Christian theologian also adopts the rigors of the secular academy, such an approach—though odd to those not Christian—is in no real conflict with the academy.

If theologians pursue the task of theology as an ascesis, then theology must be taken up with the assumption that it will lead, by means of (divine) gift, to actual and intelligible contact or communion[12] with the reality or realities theology teaches—namely, God and God's mighty acts. That is to say, the theologian must begin with the assumption that the practice of theology itself, within its native context of Christian ascesis in general, grants actual ontological contact with the realities in which Christianity puts its trust, namely, again, God and God's mighty acts. Such trust in transcendent causality—and even contact—means possible conflict with the structures of the modern secular academy. However, insofar as the secular academy in general and "religious studies" in particular are open to postcritical approaches, then, such an approach should pose no real problem to

---

[10] How this thesis concerning the nature of dogmatic theology might affect other branches of theology represents another direction research in this area might explore in future.

[11] This conception of the practice of Christian theology as a kind of scholarly and academic second order discursive reflection for the sake of the Christian community but with the possibility of speaking to and with the secular academy and in conformity to its canons of rigor, corresponds roughly with the Postliberal approach in recent theology.

[12] This conception of the practice of Christian theology as expecting and having as its goal contact with the transcendent in order to alter the structure of knowledge itself, corresponds roughly to the participatory view adopted by the recent "Radical Orthodox" approach to theology.

secular academics. Where this is not the case, however, the *Christian* theologian may be forced to face a choice.

The apparent separation of the practice of theology from the general Christian life may perhaps be the result of an unchristian anthropology of discourse. "Academic theology" sometimes seems to be approached as though discourse were an independent, "second order" activity "super-added" to human nature, instead of as an activity that is intrinsically somatic, essential to being human and therefore just as much in need of salvation as any other aspect of being human. The ascetic nature of Christian theology is then further obscured by the (sometimes false) "ascesis" that academia has enjoined upon "academic" theology.[13] Needless to say, an immanentist "scholarship" about Christian thought cannot of its own qualify as what the Christian community identifies as theology.

Christian theology presupposes *theosis* in general and its discursive counterpart *theoria* in particular. This presupposition of *theosis* means that Christian theology has as its goal contact with the realities it teaches and reflects upon. Such direct contact with the reality studied and taught dictates the manner in which it is unfolded—either into the life of the Christian body or as the "development of doctrine." So, Christian theology, to be recognized as such by the Christian body, must be pursued within its proper broader context of ascesis as a particular ascetic discipline among others. It cannot be effectively practiced outside of the general practices of which it constitutes merely an example. And this holds true at both the corporate level of the Christian body, in terms of the teaching of the various churches, and at the level of the corporeal Christian body, in terms of the practices of the one who desires to pursue the vocation of what the Christian body recognizes as a *theologian*.

---

[13] The rigor of the professional academy certainly entails behaviors of self-denial, sometimes even physical self-denial. Insofar as these are intended for the immanent end of the discernment of "truth" through an immanent chain of causality (at best), or for advancement on the part of the professional through a kind of honor system (at worst), the goals of these disciplines are immanent and therefore not ascetic in the truest sense of the word. These disciplines may confuse and sometimes conflict with the classic discipline of Christian theology when immanent methods eclipse transcendent goals.

Possible Objection

SOMEONE might object to the over-all approach of this project from the point of view of a hermeneutic of suspicion such as, for example, some forms of feminist theory and theology.[14] A classic enlightenment modernist line towards ascesis could be adopted, claiming that asceticism is in "its very nature authoritarian"[15] and therefore hierarchical in a negative sense. Feminist theologians may worry that if theology is construed as an ascetic action, then it will rule out the possibility of its use in denouncing false and abusive forms of power and power structures within society, e.g., misogyny.[16]

In light of recent scholarship about the nature of ascesis, this construal of the effects of asceticism on Christian theology is not tenable.[17] Ascesis is a means of renouncing one form of social order and social construction of the self for the sake of another. It renounces an imbalanced approach to reality and desire and appropriates a new, balanced retrieval of the "natural" condition of being human, making way for the possibility of eschatic transfiguration.

Under the anthropology of a classic Christian ascetical theology, misogyny may be described as an excessive desire, and the distorted social construction that both generates and is generated by this desire,

---

[14] Because of limitations of space, this section must be a mere sketch of the direction that this research could take with regards to such possible objections to approaching Christian theology as an ascetic discipline.

[15] Cameron, 149. (See Intro., nt. 22)

[16] See, for instance: Virginia Burrus, "Word and Flesh: The Bodies and Sexuality of Ascetic Women in Christian Antiquity," *Journal of Feminist Studies in Religion* 10 (Spring 1994): 27—51; Elizabeth Castelli, "Virginity and Its Meaning for Women's Sexuality in Early Christianity," *Journal of Feminist Studies in Religion* 2 (Spring 1986): 61—88; Elizabeth A. Clark, "Theory and Practice in Late Ancient Judaism: Jerome, Chrysostom, and Augustine," *Journal of Feminist Studies in Religion* 5 (Fall 1989): 25—46; Gail Corrington, "Anorexia, Asceticism, and Autonomy: Self-Control as Liberation and Transcendence," *Journal of Feminist Studies in Religion* 2 (Fall 1986): 51—61; Ellen Driscoll, "Hunger, Representation, and the Female Body: An Analysis of Intersecting Themes in Feminist Studies in Religion and the Psychology of Women," *Journal of Feminist Studies in Religion* 13 (Spring 1997): 91—104.

[17] Rosemary Radford Ruether, "Asceticism and Feminism: Strange Bedmates?" in *Sex and God: Some Varieties of Women's Religious Experience*, ed. Linda Hurcombe (New York: Routledge and Kegan Paul, 1987). Ruether argues that "to reduce asceticism to hostility to women, body, and nature fails to do justice to the complexity of the ascetic tradition in Christianity and in human culture generally" (229).

for the relationship between male and female human bodies, which exist physiologically and phenomenologically in a state of sexual dimorphism. Not denying this physiological and phenomenological feature of human existence, Christian asceticism realigns the human cultural construction of this desire for the sake of protological harmony between the sexes and for the possibility of eschatic transfiguration in the "neither male nor female" of Christian eschatological hope.

Theology understood under this vision of ascesis liberates discourse from such idolatry and ideology. Most of this recent burst of scholarship on asceticism claims ascesis as a positive cultural phenomenon.[18] It may even be a means of political resistance through the formation of alternative political bodies.[19] Traditional Christian ascesis can be a withdrawal from secular, immanent, "false" ascesis.

Traditional thought is ascetic because the "self" is doubted and critiqued before the tradition. Ascetic tradition has inherent methods of self-criticism in the forms of the very narratives that enjoin ascesis upon that given tradition's adherents. To throw off this system of self-criticism, modern thinkers doubt, or "critique," the ability of tradition to pass on the true and the good. In order to do so, modern thought has to ground itself on something stronger—the *cogito*, the undeniable concrete subject. So, instead of the ascetic *receiving* the "criticism," that is, the ascesis of the tradition, the modern subject critiques tradition, and in turn loses the capacity of self-criticism or self-awareness because it cannot afford such shaky footing.

Enlightenment rationality allows for the proliferation of highly individuated self-justifying ideologies and their corresponding personal representatives. But idiosyncrasy is not usually considered a virtue when truth is discerned in community.[20] That is why the ancient Christians would have called such ideologues "idiots." Ascesis is the true enemy of modernity in both its trust of and willingness to submit before tradition. In critiquing the "hubris" of tradition, mod-

---

[18]   Wimbush and Valantasis, xxv.

[19]   Valantasis, Richard, "Practices and Meanings of Asceticism in Contemporary Religious Life and Culture: A Panel Discussion," in *Asceticism*, eds. Vincent L. Wimbush and Richard Valantasis (New York: Oxford Univ. Press, 1995), 593.

[20]   Contemporary historians and ethicists (following Foucault and Nietzsche) assume what the tradition rejects and reject what the tradition embraces as somehow what is of the essence of being human: radical individual freedom of choice (Milhaven, 377; see Intro., nt. 9).

ern thinkers actually generate something worse, because modernity itself evolves into a kind of tradition in reverse. But unlike non-modern tradition, this "anti-tradition" of modernity does not possess any built-in mechanisms of self-critique or self-limitation. In this sense then the retrieval of ascesis is one more crucial step in the postcritical and "post-modern" retrieval of non-modern tradition and traditions.

The Gift of Theology

THIS CONCLUSION emphasizes practices and how they transform human community and action. Before closing, however, it is important to stress one last time that the point of Christian asceticism and ascetical theology is that Christian practice, and Christian intellectual thought construed as a practice, exist only to serve an ultimate goal which they may not of themselves put into practice. One may receive this goal only *as a gift*: the contemplation of God.

Recall from the introduction that Flood proposes that theologians ask the question,[21] can discipline itself be described as a (divine) gift? In describing the coherence of ascetic practice within the context of Christian teaching and the further coherence of the practice of Christian theology as itself ascetic, this book, at least in part, has responded to that question. In chapter four ascesis is described as (one of) the very means by which Christianity teaches salvation by sheer gift. This project has performed, therefore, a paradoxical statement within dogmatic theology by defining the field of dogmatic theology in terms of a foundation (the manifestation of God) and goal (participation in God) that necessarily lie beyond—granted only as a (divine) gift.

This project has been chiefly concerned with the nature of Christian teaching and concomitantly, theological reflection upon it. Theology, in both of these senses, is ascesis. The author hopes that those engaged in the indigenous practice of Christian theology will therefore set to the task of the ascesis of theology by practicing their discipline within its broader ascetic context and with the constant goal of contact with the triune God. After establishing such a goal and set of practices, all that Christian theologians may do is wait for that Reality who holds them accountable for their efforts to reward them with the gift for which they cannot labor—the fruit of the meaningful unfold-

---

[21] Flood, xi.

ing of Christian teaching into Christian life, thought and discourse. May they find themselves so blessed.

Bibliography

Abelard, Peter. *Exposition of the Epistle to the Romans* (An Excerpt from the Second Book). Trans. Gerald E. Moffatt. Ed. Eugene Rathbone Fairweather, *A Scholastic Miscellany: Anselm to Ockham*, 276–87. Philadelphia: Westminster Press, 1956.

Anatolios, Khaled. "The Immediately Triune God: A Patristic Response to Schleiermacher." *Pro Ecclesia* 10, no. 2 (2001): 159-178.

Arnold, Duane W. H., and Pamela Bright. *De Doctrina Christiana: A Classic of Western Culture*, Christianity and Judaism in Antiquity, Vol. 9. Notre Dame, IN: University of Notre Dame Press, 1995.

Ashley, Benedict M. *Theologies of the Body: Humanist and Christian*. St. Louis: Pope John Center, 1985.

Augustine. *De Doctrina Christiana*. Ed. and trans. R. P. H. Green. New York: Clarendon Press, 1995.

———. *On Christian Doctrine*. Trans. D. W. Robertson, Jr. Library of Liberal Arts. New York: Macmillan Publishing Company, 1958.

———. *The Trinity*. Ed. John E. Rotelle. Trans. Edmund Hill. New York: New York City Press, 1991.

Auerbach, Erich. *Mimesis: Dargestellte Wirklichkeit in der abenländischen Literatur*. Berne: Francke, 1946.

———. *Mimesis: The Representation of Reality in Western Literature*. Fiftieth Anniversary Edition. Princeton, NJ: Princeton University Press, 2003.

Ayres, Lewis. *Nicaea and its Legacy*. New York: Oxford University Press, 2004.

Baillie, John, John T. McNeill, and Henry P. Van Dusen, eds. *The Library of Christian Classics: Icthus Edition*. Vol. III, *Christology of the Later Fathers*, ed. Edward R. Hardy. Philadelphia: The Westminster Press, 1954.

———. *The Library of Christian Classics*. Vol. XII, *Western Asceticism*. Ed. Owen Chadwick. Philadelphia: The Westminster Press, 1953.

Barnett, John. "Mysticism and Liturgy in Denys the Areopagite." *Downside Review* 118 (Apr. 2000): 111–36.

Basil the Great. *Basil to Gregory. St. Basil: Letters and Selected Works*. Trans. Blomfield Jackson. Second Series, Vol. VIII, *Nicene and Post-Nicene Fathers of the Christian Church*. Eds. Philip Schaff and Henry Wace. Grand Rapids, MI: Wm. B. Eerdmans, 1983.

Beckwith, Sarah. "Passionate Regulation: Enclosure, Ascesis, and the Feminist Imaginary." *South Atlantic Quarterly* 93 (Fall 1994): 803–25.

Berthold, George C., ed. *Maximus the Confessor: Selected Writings*. Classics of Western Spirituality. Mahwah, NJ: Paulist Press, 1985.

Blacking, John. *The Anthropology of the Body*. New York: Academic Press, 1977.

Boyarin, Daniel. "Body Politic among the Brides of Christ: Paul and the Origins of Christian Sexual Renunciation." *Asceticism*. Eds. Vincent L. Wimbush and Richard Valantasis, 459–78. New York: Oxford University Press, 1995.

Brakke, David. *Athanasius and the Politics of Asceticism*. Oxford: Clarendon, 1995.

Brown, Peter. *The Body and Society: Men, Women, and Sexual Renunciation in Late Antiquity*. New York: Columbia University Press, 1988.

Bryant, Christopher. "The Nature of Spiritual Direction: Sacramental Confession." *The Study of Spirituality*, eds. Cheslyn Jones, Geoffrey Wainwright, and Edward Yarnold, 568–70. New York: Oxford University Press, 1986.

Burns, J. Padout, ed. *Theological Anthropology*. Philadelphia: Fortress Press, 1981.

Burrell, David B. "Creation, Metaphysics, and Ethics." *Faith and Philosophy* 18 (April 2001): 204–221.

———. *Freedom and Creation in Three Traditions*. Notre Dame, IN: Notre Dame University Press, 1993.

Burrus, Virginia. "Ascesis, Authority, and Text: The Acts of the Council of Saragossa." *Semeia* 58 (1992): 95–108.

———. *The Making of a Heretic: Gender, Authority, and the Priscillianist Controversy*. Berkeley: University of California Press, 1995.

———. "Word and Flesh: The Bodies and Sexuality of Ascetic Women in Christian Antiquity." *Journal of Feminist Studies in Religion* 10 (Spring 1994): 27–51.

Burton-Christie, Douglas. *The Word in the Desert: Scripture and the Quest for Holiness in Early Christian Monasticism*. New York: Oxford University Press, 1993.

Bushell, William C. "Psychophysiological and Comparative Analysis of Ascetic-Meditational Discipline: Towards a New Theory of Asceticism. " *Asceticism*. Eds. Vincent L. Wimbush and Richard Valantasis, 553–67. New York: Oxford University Press, 1995.

———. "Psychophysiological and Cross Cultural Dimensions of Ascetico-Meditational Practices: Special Reference to the Christian Hermits of Ethiopia and Application to Theory in Anthropology and Religious Studies (vols. I and II)." Ph.D. dissertation, Columbia University, 1994.

Cameron, Averil. "Ascetic Closure and the End of Antiquity." *Asceticism*. Eds.Vincent L. Wimbush and Richard Valantasis, 147–61. New York: Oxford University Press, 1995.

Carrithers, Michael, Steven Collins, Steven Lukes, eds. *The Category of the Person: Anthropology, Philosophy, History*. Cambridge, UK: Cambridge University Press, 1985.

Carruthers, Mary. *The Book of Memory: A Study of Memory in Medieval Culture*. Cambridge Studies in Medieval Literature, Vol. 10. Cambridge, U.K.: Cambridge University Press, 1992.

———. *The Craft of Thought: Meditation, Rhetoric, and the Making of Images*, 400-1200. Cambridge Studies in Medieval Literature, Vol. 34. Cambridge, U.K.: Cambridge University Press, 1998.

Castelli, Elizabeth A. "Asceticism—Audience and Resistance: Response to the Three Preceding Papers." *Asceticism*. Eds. Vincent L. Wimbush and Richard Valantasis, 178–87. New York: Oxford University Press, 1995.

——. "Virginity and Its Meaning for Women's Sexuality in Early Christianity." *Journal of Feminist Studies in Religion* 2 (Spring 1986): 61–88.

Cavanaugh, William. *Theopolitical Imagination: Discovering the Liturgy as a Political Act in an Age of Global Consumerism*. Edinburgh: T. & T. Clark, 2002.

——. *Torture and Eucharist: Theology, Politics, and the Body of Christ*. Malden, MA: Blackwell Publishers, 1998.

Charry, Ellen. *By The Renewing of Your Minds*. New York: Oxford University Press, 1997.

Chryssavgis, John. "A Spirituality of Imperfection: The Way of Tears in Saint John Climacus." *Cistercian Studies Quarterly* 37 (2002): 359–72.

Clark, Elizabeth A. "The Ascetic Impulse in Religious Life: A General Response." *Asceticism*. Eds. Vincent L. Wimbush and Richard Valantasis, 505–12. New York: Oxford University Press, 1995.

——. "Theory and Practice in Late Ancient Judaism: Jerome, Chrysostom, and Augustine." *Journal of Feminist Studies in Religion* 5 (Fall 1989): 25–46.

Clark, Gillian. "Women and Asceticism in Late Antiquity: The Refusal of Status and Gender." *Asceticism*. Eds. Vincent L. Wimbush and Richard Valantasis, 33–48. New York: Oxford University Press, 1995.

Clement of Alexandria. *Protreptikos pros Ellenas; Exhortation to the Heathen*. Trans. B. P. Pratten. *Ante-Nicene Fathers*, vol. II. Eds. Alexander Roberts and James Donaldson. Christian Literature Publishing Company, 1985. Reprinted, Peabody MA: Hendrickson Publishers, Inc. 1994.

Collins, Gregory. "Simeon the New Theologian: An Ascetical Theology for Middle-Byzantine Monks." *Asceticism*. Eds. Vincent L. Wimbush and Richard Valantasis, 343–56. New York: Oxford University Press, 1995.

Corrington, Gail. "Anorexia, Asceticism, and Autonomy: Self-Control as Liberation and Transcendence." *Journal of Feminist Studies in Religion* 2 (Fall 1986): 51–61.

Cross, F. L. and Livingstone, E. A. ed. *Oxford Dictionary of the Christian Church*. 3d ed. New York: Oxford Univ. Press, 1997.

Cyril of Jerusalem. *Catechesis*. Trans. Edwin Hamilton Gifford. Second Series, Vol. VII, *Nicene and Post-Nicene Fathers of the Christian Church*. Eds. Philip Schaff and Henry Wace. Grand Rapids, MI: Wm. B. Eerdmans, 1983.

Dawson, John David. *Christian Figural Reading and the Fashioning of Identity*. Berkeley: University of California Press, 2002.

Debray, Regis. *God: An Itinerary*. Trans. Jeffrey Mehlman. New York: Verson, 2004.

de Certeau, Michel. *La Fable Mystique*. XVIe-XVIIe Siècle. Paris: êditions Gallimard, 1982.

de Lubac, Henri. *Corpus Mysticum: L'Eucharistie et L'église au Moyen Âge*. Paris: Aubier, 1944.

——. *Exégèse Médiévale: Les quatre sens de l'écriture*. 2 parts in 4 vols. Paris: Aubier, 1959-1964.

Derrett, J. Duncan M. "Primitive Christianity as an Ascetic Movement." *Asceticism*. Eds. Vincent L. Wimbush and Richard Valantasis, 88–107. New York: Oxford University Press, 1995.

Derrida, Jacques. *De la Grammatologie*. Collection Critique. Paris: Minuit, 1967; *Of Grammatology*. Trans. Gayatri Chakravorty Spivak. Baltimore: John Hopkins University Press, 1976.

Delkeskamp-Hayes, Corinna. "Between Morality and Repentance: Recapturing 'Sin' for Bioethics." *Christian Bioethics* 11 (Aug. 2005): 93–132.

Dillon, John M. "Rejecting the Body, Refining the Body: Some Remarks on the Development of Platonist Asceticism." *Asceticism*. Eds. Vincent L. Wimbush and Richard Valantasis, 80–97. New York: Oxford University Press, 1995.

Driscoll, Ellen. "Hunger, Representation, and the Female Body: An Analysis of Intersecting Themes in Feminist Studies in Religion and the Psychology of Women." *Journal of Feminist Studies in Religion* 13 (Spring 1997): 91–104.

Eisenman, Tom L. *The Accountability Man*. Downers Grove, IL: InterVarsity Press, 2004.

Elm, Susanna. *"Virgins of God": The Making of Asceticism in Late Antiquity*. Oxford: Clarendon, 1994.

English, Edward D., ed. *Reading and Wisdom: The De doctrina christiana of Augustine in the Middle Ages*. Notre Dame Conferences in Medieval Studies, No. 6. Notre Dame, IN: University of Notre Dame Press, 1995.

Evagrius Ponticus. *The Praktikos & Chapters on Prayer*. Trans. John Eudes Bamberger. Cistercian Studies Series: Number Four. Kalamazoo, MI: Cistercian Publications, 1981.

Evans, G. R. *Old Arts and New Theology: The Beginnings of Theology as an Academic Discipline*. Oxford: Clarendon Press, 1980.

Evdokimov, Paul. *The Sacrament of Love*. Crestwood, NY: St. Vladimir's Seminary Press, 1985.

Flood, Gavin. *The Ascetic Self: Subjectivity, Memory, and Tradition*. New York: Cambridge University Press, 2004.

Florensky, Pavel. *La colonne et le fondement del la vérité: essai d'une théodicée orthodoxe en douze lettres*. Trans. Constantin Andronikof. Paris: L'Age d'homme, 1975.

———. *The Pillar and Ground of the Truth: An Essay in Orthodox Theodicy in Twelve Letters*. Trans. Boris Jakim. Princeton, NJ: Princeton University Press, 1997.

Foucault, Michel. *Histoire de la sexualité*. Vol. 2, *L'Usage des plaisirs*. Paris: Gallimard, 1984.

———. *Les mots et les choses—une archéologie des sciences humaines*. Paris: Gallimard, 1966.

Frei, Hans W. *The Eclipse of Biblical Narrative; a Study in Eighteenth and Nineteenth Century Hermeneutics*. New Haven: Yale University Press, 1974.

———. *The Identity of Jesus Christ: The Hermeneutical Bases of Dogmatic Theology*. Philadelphia: Fortress Press, 1975.

———. "Epilogue: George Lindbeck and the Nature of Doctrine." *Theology and Dialogue*, 275-282. Notre Dame, IN: University of Notre Dame Press, 1990.

Frei, Hans W., George Hunsinger, and William C. Placher. *Types of Christian Theology*. New Haven: Yale University Press, 1992.

———. *Theology and Narrative: Selected Essays*. New York: Oxford University Press, 1993.

Gadamer, Hans Georg. *Wahrheit und Methode*. Tubingen: J. C. B. Mohr, 1960; *Truth and Method*. New York: Crossroads, 1982.

Gasparro, Giulia Sfameni. "Asceticism and Anthropology: Enkrateia and 'Double Creation' in Early Christianity." *Asceticism*. Eds. Vincent L. Wimbush and Richard Valantasis. New York: Oxford University Press, 1995: 127–46.

Giddens, Anthony. *Modernity and Self-Identity: Self and Society in the Late Modern Age.* Stanford, CA: Stanford University Press, 1991.

Glucklich, Ariel. *Sacred Pain: Hurting the Body for the Sake of the Soul.* New York: Oxford University Press, 2003.

Godelier, Maurice and Michel Panoff. *La production du corps: approches anthropologiques et historiques.* Amsterdam : Archives contemporaines, 1998.

Gregory of Nazianzus. *Five Theological Orations. The Library of Christian Classics.* Vol. III. *The Christology of the Later Fathers,* ed. Edward Rochie Hardy. Philadelphia: The Westminster Press, 1954.

Grimwood, Tom. "The Body as a Lived Metaphor: Interpreting Catherine of Siena as an Ethical Agent." *Feminist Theology* 13 (Sept. 2004): 62–76.

Hadot, Pierre. *Exercices spirituels et philosophie antique.* 2nd edition. Paris, êtudes augustiniennes, 1981.

———. *La philosophie comme manière de vivre.* Paris: Albin Michel, 2001.

———. *Philosophy as a Way of Life.* Trans. Michael Chase. Malden, MA: Blackwell, 1995.

———. *Qu'est-ce que la philosophie antique?* Paris: Gallimard, 1995.

———. *What is Ancient Philosophy?* Trans. Michael Chase. Cambridge: Belknap Press, 2002.

Hadot, Pierre and Arnold Ira Davidson. *Philosophy as a Way of Life: Spiritual Exercises from Socrates to Foucault.* Oxford, UK: Cambridge: Blackwell, 1995.

Harpham, Geoffrey Galt. "Asceticism and the Compensations of Art." *Asceticism.* Eds. Vincent L. Wimbush and Richard Valantasis, 357–368. New York: Oxford University Press, 1995.

———. *The Ascetical Imperative in Culture and Criticism.* Chicago: University of Chicago Press, 1987.

Harre, Rome. *Social Being: A Theory for Social Psychology.* Totowa, NJ: Rowman and Littlefield, 1980.

Hart, David. "A Gift Exceeding Every Debt: An Eastern Orthodox Appreciation of Anselm's *Cur Deus Homo.*" *Pro Ecclesia* 7 (Summer 1998): 333–49.

Harton, F. P. *The Elements of the Spiritual Life: A Study in Ascetical Theology.* London: SPCK, 1933; Reprint, 1960.

Harvey, Susan Ashbrook. "Embodiment in Time and Eternity: A Syriac Perspective." *St. Vladimir's Seminary Quarterly* 43 (1993): 106-30.

———. "The Sense of a Stylite: Perspectives on Simeon the Elder." *Vigiliae Christianae* 42 (1988): 376-94.

———. "The Stylite's Liturgy: Ritual and Religious Identity in Late Antiquity." *Journal of Early Christian Studies* 6:3 (Fall 1998): 523-39.

Hauerwas, Stanley. *A Community of Character: Toward a Constructive Christian Social Ethic.* Notre Dame, IN: University of Notre Dame, 1981.

Heil, Günter, and Adolf Martin Ritter, eds. *Corpus Dionysiacum,* Vol. 2. Berlin: Walter de Gruyter, 1991.

Higgins, John Thomas. "Toward the Good: Levinas, Platonism and Philosophy as Practice." Ph.D. dissertation, University of Virginia, 2004.

Hooker, Richard. *Of the Laws of Ecclesiastical Polity.* Ed. Georges Edelen. *The Folger Library Edition of The Works of Richard Hooker,* ed. W. Speed Hill. Vol. 1. Cambridge, MA: The Belknap Press of Harvard University Press, 1977.

Hurcombe, Linda, ed. *Sex and God: Some Varieties of Women's Religious Experience.* New York: Routledge and Kegan Paul, 1987.

Ignatius of Loyola. *Spiritual Exercises. Ignatius of Loyola: The Spiritual Exercises and Selected Works,* ed. and trans. George E. Ganss. Classics of Western Spirituality. Mahwah, NJ: Paulist Press, 1991.

Irenaeus. *Adversus Haereses; Against Heresies.* Trans. M. Dods. *Ante-Nicene Fathers,* vol. I. eds. Alexander Roberts and James Donaldson. Christian Literature Publishing Company, 1985. Reprinted, Peabody MA: Hendrickson Publishers, Inc. 1994.

Isaac, Ephraim. "The Significance of Food in Hebraic-African Thought and the Role of Fasting in the Ethiopian Church." *Asceticism.* Eds. Vincent L. Wimbush and Richard Valantasis, 329–342. New York: Oxford University Press, 1995.

Johnston, William. *Mystical Theology: The Science of Love.* London: HarperCollins, 1995.

Kadel, Andrew. *Matrology.* New York: Continuum, 1995.

Kelly, J. N. D. *Early Christian Creeds.* 3rd edition. New York: D. McKay Co., 1972.

Lee, Theresa Man Ling. "Feminism, Postmodernism, and the Politics of Representation." *Women and Politics* 22 (2001): 35–58.

Lewis, C. S. *The Discarded Image: An Introduction to Medieval and Renaissance Literature.* London: Cambridge University Press, 1964.

Lindbeck, George A. *The Nature of Doctrine: Religion and Theology in a Postliberal Age.* Louisville, KY: Westminster John Knox Press, 1984.

Lindbeck, George A., and James Joseph Buckley, eds. *The Church in a Postliberal Age.* Radical Traditions. London: SCM, 2002.

Lindbeck, George A., and Bruce Marshall. *Theology and Dialogue: Essays in Conversation with George Lindbeck.* Notre Dame, IN: University of Notre Dame Press, 1990.

Lossky, Vladimir. *The Mystical Theology of the Eastern Church.* London: James Clarke & Co., Ltd., 1957.

Louth, Andrew. *The Origins of the Christian Mystical Tradition: From Plato to Denys.* Oxford: Clarendon Press, 1981.

———. "The Place of Deification in Modern Orthodox Theology." Paper delivered at *Partakers of the Divine Nature* lectures at Drew University, Madison, NJ, 21 May 2004.

Luckman, Harriet A., and Linda Kulzer, eds. *Purity of Heart in Early Ascetic and Monastic Literature: Essays in Honor of Juana Raasch, O. S. B.* Collegeville, MN: The Liturgical Press, 1999.

Luibheid, Colm. *Pseudo-Dionysius: The Complete Works.* Classics of Western Spirituality. New York: Paulist Press, 1987.

Malina, Bruce J. "Pain, Power, and Personhood: Ascetic Behavior in the Ancient Mediterranean." *Asceticism.* Eds. Vincent L. Wimbush and Richard Valantasis, 162–77. New York: Oxford University Press, 1995.

Malone, Edward. *The Monk and the Martyr.* Washington, DC: Catholic University Press, 1950.

Marshall, Bruce. *Trinity and Truth.* Cambridge Studies in Christian Doctrine. New York: Cambridge University Press, 2000.

Martin, Thomas F. "'An Abundant Supply of Discourse': Augustine and the Rhetoric of Monasticism." *Downside Review* 116 (Jan. 1998): 7–25.

McGinn, Bernard. "Asceticism and Mysticism in Late Antiquity and the Early Middle Ages," *Asceticism.* Eds. Vincent L. Wimbush and Richard Valantasis, 58–74. New York: Oxford University Press, 1995.

———. *The Presence of God: A History of Western Christian Mysticism.* Four Volumes. New York: Crossroads, 1991–2005.

Milbank, John. *Theology and Social Theory: Beyond Secular Reason.* Invitation Series. Cambridge, MA: Blackwell, 1991.

———. *The Word Made Strange: Theology, Language, Culture.* Cambridge, MA: Blackwell, 1997.

———. *Being Reconciled: Ontology and Pardon.* Radical Orthodoxy Series. New York: Routledge, 2003.

Milbank, John, and Catherine Pickstock. *Truth in Aquinas.* Radical Orthodoxy Series. New York: Routledge, 2001.

Milbank, John, Catherine Pickstock, and Graham Ward, eds. *Radical Orthodoxy: A New Theology.* New York: Routledge, 1999.

Milhaven, J. Giles. "Asceticism and the Moral Good: A Tale of Two Pleasures." *Asceticism.* Eds. Vincent L. Wimbush and Richard Valantasis, 375–394. New York: Oxford University Press, 1995.

Miller, Patricia Cox. "Desert Asceticism and 'The Body from Nowhere.'" *Journal of Early Christian Studies* 2 (Summer 1994): 137-53.

———. "Dreaming the Body: An Aesthetics of Asceticism." *Asceticism.* Eds. Vincent L. Wimbush and Richard Valantasis, 281–300. New York: Oxford University Press, 1995.

Minge, J. P., ed. *Acta Concilii Caesaraugustani.* Patrologia Latina 84 (1850): 315–18.

Mitchell, Stephen A. *Relational Concepts in Psychoanalysis: An Integration.* Cambridge, MA: Harvard University Press, 1988.

Moltmann, Jurgen. *The Crucified God.* Translated by R. A. Wilson and John Bowden. New York: Harper and Row, 1974.

Newman, John Henry. *Essay on the Development of Christian Doctrine* (1845). Ed. J. M. Cameron. Harmondsworth, Eng.: Penguin Books, 1974.

Nietzsche, Friedrich. *On the Genealogy of Morals.* Trans. Walter Kaufmann and R. J. Hollingdale. New York: Random House, 1967.

Norris, Frederick W., ed. *Faith Gives Fullness to Reasoning: The Five Theological Orations of Gregory Nazianzen.* Trans. Lionel Wickham and Frederick Williams. Supplements to *Vigiliae Christianae*, Vol. 13. New York: E.J. Brill, 1991.

O'Laughlin, Thomas. "Martyrs." *Encyclopedia of Monasticism*, ed. William M. Johnston. Chicago: Fizroy Dearborn, 2000.

Olivelle, Patrick. "Deconstruction of the Body in Indian Asceticism." *Asceticism.* Eds. Vincent L. Wimbush and Richard Valantasis, 188–210. New York: Oxford University Press, 1995.

Origen. *Contra Celsum; Against Celsum.* Trans. Frederick Crombie. *Ante-Nicene Fathers*, vol. IV. Eds. Alexander Roberts and James Donaldson. Christian Literature Publishing Company, 1985. Reprinted, Peabody MA: Hendrickson Publishers, Inc. 1994.

————. *De principiis; On First Principles*. Trans. G. W. Butterworth. Gloucester, MA: Peter Smith, 1973.

Pannenberg, Wolfhart. *Jesus- God and Man*. *2nd Edition*. Translated by Lewis L. Wilkins and Duane A. Priebe. Philadelphia: The Westminster Press, 1982.

Parsons, Susan Frank, ed. *The Cambridge Companion to Feminist Theology*. Cambridge Companions to Religion. Cambridge, UK: Cambridge University Press, 2002.

Pelikan, Jaroslav. *Credo: Historical and Theological Guide to Creeds and Confessions of Faith in the Christian Tradition*. New Haven: Yale University Press, 2003.

Pelikan, Jaroslav and Valerie R. Hotchkiss, eds. *Creeds and Confessions of Faith in the Christian Tradition*. New Haven: Yale University Press, 2003.

Perl, Eric. *Methexis: Creation, Incarnation, Deification in St. Maximus Confessor*. Ph.D. dissertation, Yale University, 1991.

Peters, E. Francis. *Greek Philosophical Terms: A Historical Lexicon*. New York: New York University Press, 1967.

Pickstock, Catherine. *After Writing: On the Liturgical Consummation of Philosophy*. Malden, MA: Blackwell, 1998.

————. "Music: Soul, City and Cosmos After Augustine." *Radical Orthodoxy: A New Theology*, eds. Milbank, John, Catherine Pickstock, and Graham Ward, 243–77. New York: Routledge, 1999.

Pinsent, John. "Ascetic Moods in Greek and Latin Literature." *Asceticism*. Eds. Vincent L. Wimbush and Richard Valantasis, 211–19. New York: Oxford University Press, 1995.

Plato. *Georgias*. Trans. Donald J. Zeyl. *Plato: Complete Works*, ed. John M. Cooper. Indianapolis, IN: Hackett Publishing, 1997.

————. *Meno*. Trans. G. M. A. Grube. Plato: Complete Works, ed. John M. Cooper. Indianapolis, IN: Hackett Publishing, 1997.

Polanyi, Michael. *Personal Knowledge: Towards a Post-Critical Philosophy*. Chicago: University of Chicago Press, 1958.

————. *The Tacit Dimension*. Garden City, NY: Doubleday, 1966.

Pozdeevsky, Feodor. *Iz chtenii po pastyrskomy bogosloviiu: Asketika* (Lectures on Pastoral Theology: Asceticism). Delivered in Sergiev Posad, Russia, 1911.

Pseudo-Dionysius. *De Divinis Nominibus. Corpus Dionysiacum*, Vol. 1, ed. Suchla, Beate Regina. Berlin: Walter de Gruyter, 1990.

Raasch, Juana, Harriet Luckman, and Linda Kulzer, eds. *Purity of Heart in Early Ascetic and Monastic Literature: Essays in Honor of Juana Raasch, O.S.B.* Collegeville, MN: Liturgical Press, 1999

Rabbow, Paul. *Seelenführung: Methodik der Exerzitien in der Antike*. Munich: Kösel-Verlag, 1954.

Radner, Ephraim. *The End of the Church: A Pneumatology of Christian Division in the West*. Grand Rapids, MI: W.B. Eerdmans, 1998.

————. "To Desire Rightly: The Force of the Creed in its Canonical Context." In *Nicene Christianity: The Future for a New Ecumenism*, ed. Christopher R. Seitz, 213–28. Grand Rapids, MI: Brazos Press, 2001.

Radner, Ephraim, and George R. Sumner. *Reclaiming Faith : Essays on Orthodoxy in the Episcopal Church and the Baltimore Declaration*. Grand Rapids, MI: William B. Eerdmans, 1993.

Reno, R. R. "Theology in the Ruins of the Church." *Pro Ecclesia* 12 (2003): 15-36.

Rodriguez, Felix. "Concilio I de Zaragoza: Texto critico." *Primero Concilio Caesaraugustano:* MDC aniversario, 9–25 (Zaragoza, 1981).

Rogers, Eugene. *After the Spirit: A Constructive Pneumatology from Resources Outside the Modern West.* Grand Rapids, MI: William B. Eerdmans, 1995.

———. *Sexuality and the Christian Body.* Cambridge, MA: Blackwell, 1999.

———. *Theology and Sexuality: Classic and Contemporary Readings.* Blackwell Readings in Modern Theology. Cambridge, MA: Blackwell, 2002.

Rousseau, Philip. *Ascetics, Authority, and the Church in the Age of Jerome and Cassian.* Oxford: Oxford University Press, 1978.

Rorem, Paul. "Moses as the Paradigm for the Liturgical Spirituality of Pseudo-Dionysius." *Studia Patristica* 18 (1989): 275–79.

Rowland, Christopher, ed. *The Cambridge Companion to Liberation Theology.* Cambridge Companions to Religion. Cambridge, UK: Cambridge University Press, 1999.

Ruether, Rosemary Radford. "Asceticism and Feminism: Strange Bedmates?" *Sex and God: Some Varieties of Women's Religious Experience,* ed. Linda Hurcombe, 229–50. New York: Routledge and Kegan Paul, 1987.

Stalow, Michael L. "Shame and Sex in Late Antique Judaism." *Asceticism.* Eds. Vincent L. Wimbush and Richard Valantasis, 535–43. New York: Oxford University Press, 1995.

Scaramelli, Giovanni Battista. *Direttorio ascetico in cui s' insegna il modo di condurre l'Anime per vie ordinarie della grazia alla perfezione christiana, indirizzato ai direttori della Anime.* Naples, 1752.

———. *Il direttorio mistico indrizato a' direttori di quelle anime che Iddio conduce per la via della contemplazione.* Venice, 1754.

Scarry, Elaine. *The Body in Pain: The Making and Unmaking of the World.* New York: Oxford University Press, 1985.

Schilling, Chris. *The Body and Social Theory.* London: Safe Publications, 2003.

Silber, Ilana Frederich. *Virtuosity, Charisma and Social Order: A Comparative Sociological Study of Monasticism in Theravada Buddhism and Medieval Catholicism.* Cambridge Cultural Social Studies. New York: Cambridge University Press, 1995.

Starr, James. "Does 2 Peter 1:4 Speak of Deification?" Paper delivered at *Partakers of the Divine Nature* lectures at Drew University, Madison, NJ, 21 May 2004.

———. *Sharers in Divine Nature, 2 Peter 1:4 in Its Hellenistic Context.* Coniectanea Biblica. New Testament Series 33. Stockholm: Almquist and Wiksell International, 2000.

Stout, Jeffrey. "What is the Meaning of a Text?" *The New Literary History* 14 (Autumn 1982): 1-12.

Suchla, Beate Regina, ed. *Corpus Dionysiacum,* Vol. 1. Berlin: Walter de Gruyter, 1990.

Tanner, Kathryn. *God and Creation in Christian Theology: Tyranny or Empowerment?* New York: Blackwell, 1988.

———. *The Politics of God: Christian Theologies and Social Justice.* Minneapolis: Fortress Press, 1992.

———. *Theories of Culture: A New Agenda for Theology.* Guides to Theological Inquiry. Minneapolis: Fortress Press, 1997.

——. *Jesus, Humanity and the Trinity: A Brief Systematic Theology.* Minneapolis: Fortress Press, 2001.

Tanner, Norman P., ed. *Decrees of the Ecumenical Councils.* Vol. 1, *Nicaea I—Lateran V.* London and Washington, DC: Sheed & Ward and Georgetown University Press, 1990.

Tanquerey, Adolphe. *Abrégé de théologie ascétique et mystique.* Paris: Société de S. Jean l'Évangéliste, 1927.

Thomas Aquinas. *Romanos.* In *Super epistolas, Pauli lectura,* 8th rev. ed., ed. Raphael Cai, 1953.

——. *Summa Theologica.* Vol. 1. Trans. Fathers of the English Dominican Province. New York: Benziger Bros., 1948.

Tolkien, J. R. R. "On Fairy-Stories." *The Monsters and the Critics and Other Essays.* London: HarperCollins, 1997: 109–61.

Vaage, Leif E., and Vincent L. Wimbush, eds. *Asceticism and the New Testament.* New York: Routledge, 1999.

Valantasis, Richard. "A Theory of the Social Function of Asceticism." *Asceticism.* Eds. Vincent L. Wimbush and Richard Valantasis, 544–552. New York: Oxford University Press, 1995.

——. "Practices and Meanings of Asceticism in Contemporary Religious Life and Culture: A Panel Discussion." *Asceticism.* Eds. Vincent L. Wimbush and Richard Valantasis, 588–606. New York: Oxford University Press, 1995.

——. "Constructions of Power in Asceticism." *Journal of the American Academy of Religion* 63 (Winter 1995): 775-822.

Von Balthasar, Hans Urs. *Cordula oder der Ernstfall.* Einsiedeln: Johannes Verlag, 1966.

——. *The Glory of the Lord: A Theological Aesthetics.* Vol. 1, *Seeing the Form.* Trans. Erasmo Leiva-Merikakis,. Eds. Joseph Fessio and John Riches. San Francisco: Ignatius Press, 1982.

——. *Herrlichkeit.* Bd. 1, *Schau der Gestalt.* Einsiedeln: Johannes Verlag, 1988

——. *The Moment of Christian Witness.* Trans. Richard Beckley. San Francisco: Ignatius Press, 1994.

——. *Prayer.* Trans. Graham Harrison. San Francisco: Ignatius Press, 1986.

Wainwright, Geoffrey. *Doxology.* New York: Oxford University Press, 1980.

Ward, Graham. *Cities of God.* London: Routledge, 2000.

Ware, Kallistos. "The Way of the Ascetics: Negative or Affirmative." *Asceticism.* Eds. Vincent L. Wimbush and Richard Valantasis, 3–15. New York: Oxford University Press, 1995.

Wawrykow, Joseph P. *God's Grace and Human Action: 'Merit' in the Theology of Thomas Aquinas.* Notre Dame, IN: University of Notre Dame Press, 1995.

Wesche, Kenneth Paul. "Christological Doctrine and Liturgical Interpretation in Pseudo-Dionysius." *St. Vladimir's Theological Quarterly* 33 (1989): 53–73.

Wilken, Robert L. "Maximus the Confessor on the Affections in Historical Perspective." *Asceticism.* Eds. Vincent L. Wimbush and Richard Valantasis, 412–23. New York: Oxford University Press, 1995.

Williams, Rowan. *Anglican Identities.* Cambridge, MA: Cowley, 2003.

——. *The Wound of Knowledge.* Second Rev. Edition. Cambridge, MA: Cowley, 1990.

Wimbush, Vincent L. and Richard Valantasis, eds. *Asceticism.* New York: Oxford University Press, 1995.

Zizioulas, John D. *Being as Communion.* Crestwood, NY: St. Vladimir's Seminary Press, 2002.

Zumkeller, Adolar. *Augustine's Ideal of the Religious Life.* Trans. Edmund Colledge. New York: Fordham University Press, 1986.

———. *Das Mönchtum des heiligen Augustinus.* Würzburg: Augustinus-Verlag, 1968.

Index

• R •

• S •

• T •

• V •

• W •

• Z •